# Online
# **Public Relations**

# PR in Practice Series

## Published in association with the Chartered Institute of Public Relations
## Series Editor: Anne Gregory

Kogan Page has joined forces with the Chartered Institute of Public Relations to publish this unique series, which is designed specifically to meet the needs of the increasing numbers of people seeking to enter the public relations profession and the large band of existing PR professionals. Taking a practical, action-oriented approach, the books in the series concentrate on the day-to-day issues of public relations practice and management rather than academic history. They provide ideal primers for all those on CIPR, CAM and CIM courses or those taking NVQs in PR. For PR practitioners, they provide useful refreshers and ensure that their knowledge and skills are kept up to date.

**Professor Anne Gregory** is one of the UK's leading public relations academics. She is Pro Vice Chancellor of Leeds Metropolitan University and Director of the Centre for Public Relations Studies in the Business School. She is the UK's only full-time professor of public relations. Before becoming an academic, Anne spent 12 years in public relations practice and has experience at a senior level both in-house and in consultancy. She remains involved in consultancy work, having clients in both the public and private sectors, and is a non-executive director of South West Yorkshire Mental Health NHS Trust with special responsibility for financial and communication issues. Anne is Consultant Editor of the PR in Practice series and edited the book of the same name and wrote *Planning and Managing Public Relations Campaigns*, also in this series. She was President of the CIPR in 2004.

## Other titles in the series:

*Creativity in Public Relations* by Andy Green
*Effective Internal Communication* by Lyn Smith and Pamela Mounter
*Effective Media Relations* by Michael Bland, Alison Theaker and David Wragg
*Effective Writing Skills for Public Relations* by John Foster
*Managing Activism* by Denise Deegan
*Planning and Managing Public Relations Campaigns* by Anne Gregory
*Public Affairs in Practice* by Stuart Thompson and Steve John
*Public Relations: A practical guide to the basics* by Philip Henslowe
*Public Relations in Practice* edited by Anne Gregory
*Public Relations Strategy* by Sandra Oliver
*Risk Issues and Crisis Management in Public Relations* by Michael Regester and
    Judy Larkin
*Running a Public Relations Department* by Mike Beard

The above titles are available from all good bookshops. To obtain further information, please go to the CIPR website (www.cipr.co.uk/books) or contact the publishers at the address below:

Kogan Page Ltd
120 Pentonville Road
London N1 9JN
Tel: 020 7278 0433      Fax: 020 7837 6348
www.koganpage.com

PR IN PRACTICE SERIES

# Online
# Public Relations

### A practical guide to developing an
### online strategy in the world of social media

Second Edition

David Phillips and Philip Young

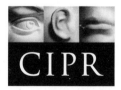

CIPR

KOGAN
PAGE

London and Philadelphia

First published in 2001 by Kogan Page Limited
Second edition 2009
Reprinted 2009

120 Pentonville Road
London N1 9JN
United Kingdom
www.koganpage.com

525 South 4th Street, #241
Philadelphia PA 19147
USA

ISBN    978 0 7494 4968 1

---

**British Library Cataloguing-in-Publication Data**

A CIP record for this book is available from the British Library.

**Library of Congress Cataloging-in-Publication Data**

Phillips, David, 1945 July 14–
   Online public relations : a practical guide to developing an online strategy in the world of social media / David Phillips, Philip Young. — 2nd ed.
      p. cm.
   Includes bibliographical references and index.
   ISBN 978-0-7494-4968-1
1. Public relations. 2. Social media. I. Young, Philip. II. Title.
HD59.P455 2009
659.20285'4678 — dc22

2008054391

---

Typeset by JS Typesetting Ltd, Porthcawl, Mid Glamorgan
Printed and bound in India by Replika Press Pvt Ltd

# Contents

Contents

# Foreword

Without doubt, a new age of communication has arrived. With it has arrived a revolution in public relations. This revolution not only involves the way we communicate, but the nature of communication itself.

In this book on e-public relations, the authors show how the internet and especially social media, are revolutionizing the role and work of the public relations professional. The book is not for those who wish to learn the mechanics of how to construct a social networking site or how to set up a virtual press office. It is about how to use this potent and energizing medium intelligently and effectively.

Much has been written on the internet as just another means of communication. Nothing could be further from the truth. It is a channel of communication, but it is much more than that. Its unique properties of reach, richness and personalization have transformed the mode and quality of mediated communication. Furthermore, the nature of internet publics, or communities, is quite different from those that have been traditionally the domain of the PR practitioner.

They provide an overview of the online communication environment and its potential. They then go on to explore how an organization can meaningfully engage with internet communities and exploit the communication potential that is inherent in the various 'tools' that are now available. Developing an online strategy that is realistic and robust is essential, as is monitoring, measuring and evaluating your presence and actions. Of vital interest are the topics of reputation and issues management on the internet.

The ability of groups to form quickly and mobilize action provides a great opportunity as well as being a potential threat for PR professionals who are the guardians of organizational reputation. They explore how reputations can be destroyed or enhanced depending on how relationships are managed and also provide similar advice on managing issues as they arise. Their warnings of the dangers that await those who engage with individuals and communities in a naïve, unprofessional and unethical way need to be heeded.

The potent effect of online communications is well demonstrated as the authors go on to show how the internet is changing the news agenda and news itself. The internet within an internal communications context is also discussed: its uses, abuses and how to harness its power effectively.

Rounded off with a chapter on Corporate Social Responsibility and a look into the future, this book provides a timely and authoritative overview of e-PR. It provides some clear pointers for organizing public relations professionally now and indicates a vision of the future. Any public relations professional wanting to conduct his or her business in the modern interconnected world will regard this book as a must.

*Professor Anne Gregory*
*Series Editor*

# Acknowledgements

## DAVID PHILLIPS

This book is possible because of three groups of people. First it was made possible by public relations professionals and thinkers like my co-author Philip Young and friends like Shel Holtz, Neville Hobson and Richard Bailey. They have provided a reality check as have the growing host of PR people who are interested in online relationships and PR. Some are people who share their research and thinking and can see forward beyond my attention span deficit. They include David Weinberger, Don Tapscott, Clay Shirky and William Dutton among many others who offer insights that can be synthesised for PR practice.

Then there is a huge group of people who make stuff available. They are the academics across so many disciplines who share their research, social science and technology practitioners who share their knowledge and skills and the folk out there who are passionate about the channels for communication they invent and offer to us all. Every hour of every day their contributions come via RSS feeds to inform PR. In all, something like 100 contributors.

Who could write a book like this without robust debate with Toni Muzi Falconi on his PR Conversations blog, fellow For Immediate Release pod-casters and futurologists and software magician Girish Lakshminarayana?

Finally there are the people who really make these things possible. Work colleagues and clients, supportive friends and understanding publishers have been wonderful, especially Margaret, my wife, an internet widow if ever there was one

# PHILIP YOUNG

Most of all I would like to thank David for inviting me to help with the second edition of *Online Public Relations*. I have learnt more about social media from him than anyone else and am grateful for the opportunity to make a contribution to this book. I would also like to thank my Delivering the New PR friends Chris Rushton, Tom Murphy, Neville Hobson, Stuart Bruce and Elizabeth Albrycht, my EuroBlog partners Ansgar Zerfass, Swaran Sandhu and Anne-Marie Cotton, and the blogger I think has done most to help PR students, Richard Bailey. All of them exemplify my belief that the more you put into social media the more you get out of it.

# Part 1

## Everybody's public relations

# 1

# The battleground

When writing a book like this, it is hard to avoid making the claim that 'the internet changes everything'. In some ways, nothing changes everything, but for public relations practice the unavoidable conclusion is that nothing will ever be the same again; the advent of an online world means almost every aspect of the discipline needs to be rethought.

Crucially, it is not just a case of devising, adopting and developing new tools and tactics, or restructuring to meet the ever-shrinking timescales for campaigns that are increasingly played out on a global stage. Far beyond this, what we might call 'the new PR' demands a dramatically different approach at the level of strategy. Indeed, it is the need to radically rethink strategy that provides the intellectual justification for using a term like 'the new PR' in the first place.

We will look in detail at strategy and management in Part 3. First we need to understand what the internet is, partly as a technological tool but more importantly as the enabling mechanism for a communications revolution that is driving significant changes in the dynamics of society. This section looks at the significance of the internet, providing the framework for an analysis of key terms such as *social media* and *aggregation*, and their role in an evolving PR practice.

# WHY EVERYTHING IS CHANGING

Almost all definitions of public relations agree that at some level it is a discipline concerned with an exchange of information. In practice, this usually involves the management of an organization trying to convey this information to external and internal audiences and, to varying degrees, trying also to receive information from a range of stakeholders.

Sometimes this is simple factual data, perhaps a council telling local residents that dustbins will now be emptied on a Tuesday; more often it is about persuasion, where public relations seeks to change perception or behaviours. Usually, such communications seek to enhance or consolidate reputation, which can be seen as the basis of *trust*. Indeed, some regard 'reputation management' as a useful explanation of the purpose of PR.

Reputation can be seen as an aggregation of lots of individual opinions, some derived from personal experience ('I bought one of those cars and it was always breaking down') but more often a synthesis of fragments of information derived from a wide range of sources, some more accurate than others ('I haven't been there myself but I have heard...').

We would argue that a more sophisticated definition of public relations goes beyond reputation to be concerned with the broader and more challenging realm of *relationship optimization*, in which reputation clearly plays a part but which demands an understanding of a much more complex set of factors.

The point is that at each level the core processes demand the exchange of information, and the outcomes are predicated on responses and reactions to this information. The challenge for the PR practitioner is to understand how this information is exchanged and then work out how to influence such exchanges in a way that benefits the client.

In the roughest and crudest terms, let's examine how information is exchanged in modern Western societies. To get us underway, let's pretend it is 1984, not for its Orwellian connotations (though they may help to inform our analysis!), but because that was when Grunig and Hunt wrote *Managing Public Relations*.[1]

# BUT THIS ISN'T 1984

In 1984, as for the previous hundred years, it was possible to split information into two areas, that of mass communications and micro-communications. Yes, there is a significant grey area in between the two, but for present purposes these categories are distinguished by a qualitative difference between that which is made available to large numbers of people and involves a decidedly asymmetrical relationship between provider and audience, and that which is fundamentally an exchange between individuals and may have a greater degree of symmetry.

Mass communications includes newspapers, magazines, television and radio, and for our purposes can include books and directories, perhaps located in libraries, and extend down to, say, organizational newsletters and business-to-business publications with a relatively limited circulation. The detail doesn't matter; the key point is that all such communications require capital and labour investment to produce what are, by and large, static texts. Clearly the content of such exchanges is influenced by audience expectation and reaction, but this can be a slow and inefficient process. And the texts are usually produced to an extended timescale, whether scheduled television news bulletins, the daily production of a newspaper or the monthly publication of a periodical.

Micro-communications are infinitely more flexible, in terms of timescale, reach and influence. The most obvious example is a conversation, perhaps between you and a friend: 'Where shall we go tonight?' 'I have heard there's a new Italian restaurant on the High Street.' Perhaps you go on to discuss a number of restaurants, perhaps you include information gleaned from newspapers and magazines, but also friends and colleagues – word of mouth and peer recommendation. Such exchanges can be replicated by groups and extended over time, and in 1984, augmented by the (fixed, quite expensive, landline) telephone and by slow and time-consuming letters. In the vast majority of cases telephone conversations involve two people, and are ephemeral – their contacts are overwhelmingly not recorded and not accessible to other people. Yes, letters can be duplicated and sent to a whole host of people, but each mailing is discrete; only the sender is likely to have an overview of responses. It is quite difficult even to think of circumstances in which the contents of these letters or telephone calls could have been made more widely available except by the laborious process of transposition to a mass medium.

Somewhere above the one-to-one or small group conversations, micro-communications can also include office meetings, and associations of hobbyists (railway enthusiasts or flower arrangers) that can develop communicative structures – perhaps photocopied newsletters, distributed by mail, for example.

We will look at all this in more detail later, but the essential points revolve around the vectors of communication – the direction of travel, from A to B (and back again?), and the ability for individuals or groups to collect together that information in a usable way. There are of course other significant dimensions, including reach and time, but the argument here is that in these cases the vector of communication remains the same; if we move on from Grunig's 1984, we can see a letter being superseded by a fax (in business at least), then by an e-mail, but remaining essentially the same type of one-to-one written communication. There is a significant change in that an e-mail flashes around the world in a second whereas a letter to Australia takes many days, but this does not alter the A to B vector.

Fast forward from 1984 and we see a changed world, where the exchanges are defined not only by time and reach but also by aggregation, a complex phenomenon that is intimately connected with the minute building blocks of PR, those atoms of information that coalesce in complex and ever-changing ways into reputation, which in itself shapes the core dynamics that underlie cognitive relationships.

# THE WRITABLE WEB

We have entered the world of search engines and the writable web. The difference is not in tools of communication – although they have advanced greatly to make the world a smaller place (and we must look carefully at the impact of those changes later in this book) – but in their *connectivity*. One of the essential factors that formed the mass communication model was simple economics – it was very expensive to launch a newspaper or TV station, and the capital investment necessarily precluded the vast majority of individuals from entering that market.

All that has changed. Today anyone with access to a computer, an internet connection and basic literacy can make his or her voice heard to a global audience, and in many different ways. Here is where traditional corporate culture and the internet clash. Once managers were gatekeepers of information, to some extent even the arbiters of company gossip. Management had a role and facility for control. Today managers must be facilitators of information dissemination. There is no defence mechanism behind which an organization can protect itself from the influence of the internet. No bulwark and no bunker protects the unprepared or ignorant. With the advent of interactive media, one in 10 employees, suppliers, customers, shareholders, local citizens, politicians and priests has the ability to comment and to act using the social networking site Facebook (which claimed over 6 million users in 2007). Add to that the 4 million bloggers the *Guardian* claimed to exist in the United Kingdom, and a range of other social media in common use.

Just as weblogs and other social media allow (or have the potential to allow) organizations an effective environment in which to create dialogues and communicate directly with publics and stakeholders (without the mediation of traditional gatekeepers), so they allow users, clients, opponents and competitors to communicate freely with each other, with the potential to create a discourse that is largely outside the control of the subject.

More importantly, it is becoming increasingly easy to track and search this information. Conversations are increasingly digital, and focused around a myriad of interlinked nodes of communication that are catalogued – *aggregated* – by search engines and connected people.

This has profound consequences. Until quite recently, organizations and businesses had the impression that they had control of what was said and believed about their activities. The marketing and PR departments, a few directors and salesmen were the mouthpieces of the company, and would see to it that only they would have the opportunity to interact with opinion-influencing third parties such as journalists, mass media and consumers. This exchange of information across the membrane that somehow divides an organization from its external publics was always porous – people gossiped and spoke to a select band of opinion formers from most parts of the organization. In reality there were always leaks – and the boundaries were never quite clear. But today the membrane is being punctured in ever more ways, as those within and without exploit, consciously or otherwise, the new communications channels that are becoming available to them. These vitally important concepts of transparency, porosity and internet agency are discussed in more detail here.

Organizations were able to claim control of how they represented themselves because only a limited number of players had access to the mass media. But in recent years, the mass media has been fragmenting at an astonishing rate. Thirty years ago, most people got their news and lifestyle information from a handful of television channels, radio stations, local and national newspapers and magazines. You could go to work in the morning relatively confident that your colleagues would have watched the same television programmes and read a similar newspaper over breakfast.

The media landscape has changed radically. But more importantly so has access. Now every stakeholder can and does provide knowledge and opinion into networked communication systems freely. Networks of people using the mobile phone text-messaging system SMS, e-mail and instant messaging are each bigger, by far, than for any channel of a decade ago.

In addition, anyone can create a website; they can have it hosted for free, they can add discussion lists and chat facilities, they can include campaigning banners, all at the click of a mouse – and they do. Remember, too, that we are not just talking about words. The same revolution is affecting sound and vision – often in even more spectacular ways.

This is blurring boundaries. Multi-media is a reality, but more importantly the boundaries and distinctions between audience and producer are vanishing. This is the age of *consumer-generated content*.

Just as weblogs (blogs) and other social media allow (or have the potential to allow) organizations an effective environment through which to create dialogues and communicate directly with publics and stakeholders (without the mediation of traditional gatekeepers), so they allow users, clients, opponents and competitors to communicate freely with each other, with the potential to create a discourse that is significantly beyond the control of the subject.

Organizations such as Apple, Wal-Mart, Dell, McDonald's and United Airlines are discovering that the internet is a great leveller, that individuals now have the power to enter critical debate at a mass level.[2] That in itself is a challenge to public relations practice. But the significant step forward is that the messages propagated by individual weblogs or social networks that articulate positions hostile (or favourable) to corporate positions are not discrete; their influence on reputation is not limited to visitors to those particular sites – the sites are merely prominent nodes on wider networks of interlinked, networked and aggregated conversations that correspond to a tangible, measurable reputation.

---

### IN BRIEF

- Nothing will ever be the same again; the advent of an online world means that almost every aspect of the PR discipline needs to be rethought.
- Internet-mediated PR demands a dramatically different approach at the level of strategy.
- The exchange of information and its outcomes are predicated on responses and reactions.
- Mass communications require capital and labour investment to produce static texts. Mass communication exchanges are influenced by audience expectation and reaction in a slow and inefficient process.
- Micro-communications are infinitely more flexible, in terms of time-scale, reach and influence.
- These exchanges are defined by time and reach and, additionally, aggregation.
- We have entered the world of search engines and the writable web.
- The difference is not in tools of communication, but in their connectivity.
- Once managers were, to a degree, gatekeepers of information, to some extent even the arbiters of company gossip. Management had a role and facility for control.
- Today managers must be facilitators of information dissemination.
- There is no defence mechanism behind which an organization can protect itself from the influence of the internet.
- There are more ways for information to be exchanged between the organization and its publics. Organizations are becoming more porous.

---

## Notes

1. Grunig, James E and Hunt, Todd (1984) *Managing Public Relations*, Harcourt Brace
2. Clark, A (2006) Companies wake up to blogs' barking, *The Guardian*, 19 September, http://business.guardian.co.uk/story/0,,1875644,00.html (accessed 20 October 2008)

# 2

# The geography of social media: a quick guide to key terms

This chapter provides a quick look at some common channels for communication available in 2008. It is not comprehensive (and how could it be with new types of communication becoming available so fast?), but briefly introduces the most significant.

Communication today is an adventure playground for people with an interest in the subject. There are so many ways people can communicate. They can use PCs, laptops, mobile phones and devices, gaming machines and interactive screens. They have access at home, on the go and at work. At the same time people have a vast array of channels for communication and will often use a number of them concurrently. In writing this chapter the author was using iGoogle, Twirl (to monitor Twitter), search engines, instant messenger, Facebook (to send messages between authors), MusicFM and Skype. The mobile phone was on and the work was being saved to a USB stick, which itself included the word processing software using portable applications (Open Office, Skype, Firefox, a media player, Audacity, Google talk and FileZilla, etc) that meant any computer could be used for editing and interactivity from podcasting to instant messaging to file sharing and

– well – writing a book, with the wisdom of millions of people available online.

Although this not a 'how to' book or a manual for technicians, it is important that public relations practitioners who are looking to understand the opportunities and challenges offered by the era of social media have an awareness and understanding of key terms. Some readers will be confident they have the knowledge to skip though this section, but many others will understand how the authors felt, when writing this book, when we realized that we were mentioning channels for communication that were new to us! Even those who feel at home in cyberspace – and how dated that term feels today – may find it is worth slowing down and considering the implications of this fast-changing and unruly new world.

So here goes…

On the day this was written, Neville Hobson mentioned in the For Immediate Release (www.forimmediaterelease.biz) PR podcast that he had received a 'tweet' from David Phillips. However hard he might try, David will never become a bird.

So what do we mean? Podcast? Tweet? Here is a very quick tour of some of the channels for communication, which include blogs, chat, e-mail, games, instant messaging, message boards, monitoring and evaluation, social media releases, online conferencing, podcasting, RSS, online surveys, Usenet (Google Groups), video-sharing, virtual environments, virtual communities, VoIP, websites, widgets, wikis. Yes, it is a long list and might give pause to PR practitioners who would imagine that they are communications specialists.

Each channel in this list is different and can be used by people in a variety of ways. To begin with they can be accessed on a PC with or without broadband connection. They are available on laptops using WiFi (wireless internet connection). Alternatively, the device (communication platform) could be a mobile phone, and the list goes on.

These channels have uses as varied as personal letters, diaries, books, newspapers and magazines are in print. They reflect different interests, cultures and languages. There are techniques relevant to each that are, in their own way, comparable to the traditional PR that engages with in-house publications, the press, events and the panoply of communications techniques in common use at the turn of the century.

What is important to note is that although these channels were significant at the time of writing, some will wither and fade, others will evolve beyond our expectations, and yet others will emerge of which we know nothing in 2008. We offer help for practitioners on how to keep up to date later in the book.

# WHAT IS A BLOG?

A weblog, usually shortened to blog, is a type of website. It allows the owner (the blogger) to write web pages (posts) and make them available in reverse chronological order. Most blogs are public, but many companies have internal blogs for staff to read, create, write and add content to.

There are millions of blogs (4 million in the United Kingdom alone) created by people who have mastered almost no technology to make public almost anything they wish. Most blogs allow readers to make comments about the owner/author's posts.

> By 2005, according to the research company Hitwise, one in 200 UK web visits were to blogs.
>
> Technorati is a specialist blog search engine. In 2007 it was tracking over 70 million weblogs, and about 120,000 new ones were created worldwide each day. That's about 1.4 blogs created every second of every day.

Blogs are mostly edited online through a web browser (Chrome, Internet Explorer, Firefox or Opera) but many bloggers use a 'blog editor' that allows content to be written and edited offline before uploading.

Because blogs are web pages, it is possible to embed pictures, video, voice files, diagrams and much more into blog posts.

Although there are some blogs with huge readership figures, most tend to have a small following (often accessed by readers when their RSS feeder shows there is new content). The power of blogs comes from the network effect. When experts' blogs make a point that has value to a wider audience, the word spreads ('word of mouse') and the subject can be very widely blogged about.

Lots of people say they have never read a blog. This is extremely unlikely if they use search engines or read online news. What has happened is that people do not recognize a blog from other forms of website.

> When Clodagh Hartley, *The Sun*'s Home Affairs Correspondent, wrote an article headlined 'Just 2 in 3 Brit babies are white' in August 2008, one could be forgiven for believing this was just another news story. In fact it was a blog post and within eight hours had 36 comments added to it from members of the public.

Our tip: read more than one post on a blog before jumping to any conclusions.

# WHAT IS CHAT?

Online chat is any form of synchronous conferencing, but mostly relates to those technologies that allow two or more people to exchange text messages in real time. ICQ (Internet Relay Chat) and a number of other technologies were commonly used as stand-alone services in the early days of the internet and were among the forerunners of today's social media: from real-time online chat over instant messaging and online forums to fully immersive graphical social environments.

A number of companies embed chat agents into their websites as an alternative to telephone support systems, and they have been used by PR practitioners to provide a means for journalists to 'talk' to account managers.

Today, chat can also come in the form of voice messaging from providers like Meebome (www.meebome.com) and video chat such as Eyeball Chat (www.eyeballchat.com). The online telephony provider Skype (www.skype.com) offers a chat facility, while the online version of *Sugar* magazine, http://www.sugarscape.com, offers readers a range of online chat facilities. Chat is now offered as web widgets in open and closed environments such as wikis, blogs and intranets as well as public websites.

> BUPA International has an online chat service that aims to provide its members with 24-hour access to a customer adviser from wherever they are in the world. Called Webchat, it provides a live and secure online chat-room environment, which members can access by logging onto the Members' World Homepage. Members will then be connected to an adviser for a two-way online conversation.

Our tip: think of chat as an alternative to other one-to-one and many-to-many communications environments.

# WHAT IS DELICIOUS?

Social bookmarks allow you record web pages of interest through online lists that can be sorted, indexed, shared with small groups of colleagues or made available to the wider public. The most popular of these sites is Delicious (http://delicious/). These are very useful services for practitioners.

One of the ways a website can be developed is for its main pages to be indexed on Delicious. News pages as well as product and service pages in websites would benefit from a capability to allow readers to quickly insert the page into their own Delicious collections.

Beside each story in the online version of the *Daily Telegraph*, there is a facility for readers to bookmark and share the story using a range of social bookmarks, including Delicious, Digg, Facebook, Fark, Google, Newsvine, NowPublic, Reddit and StumbleUpon. It follows that a story provided by a practitioner and published in the *Telegraph* has an extended online presence created by readers. Is this another way of measuring the effectiveness of PR, measuring the extent to which it is bookmarked in social media?

Our tip: use this type of site to provide resources for publics (such as journalists) relevant to a subject or launch, or to provide deep background briefing.

# WHAT IS E-MAIL?

It may come as something of a surprise to most that e-mail dates back to the early 1960s. The inventors were Tom Van Vleck and Noel Morrison at the Massachusetts Institute of Technology (MIT).

Electronic mail is a store-and-forward method of composing, sending, storing and receiving messages over electronic communication systems. The term 'e-mail' applies both to the internet e-mail system based on the Simple Mail Transfer Protocol (SMTP) and to web-based e-mail. This is a classic case of convergence, with SMTP working in collaboration with Hypertext Transfer Protocol (HTTP – the web). Of course, e-mail is also available on mobile devices such as mobile phones.

While spam (sending unsolicited e-mails to one of more recipients) has given e-mail a bad name, there are still a number of effective e-mail distribution techniques (indeed, most press releases were still issued by means of e-mail as this book goes to press).

E-mail marketing does have a significant role for many activities and should not be dismissed lightly. In the United Kingdom it is illegal to spam, but it is legal to issue e-mails to lists of people who have provided permission prior to mailing. Many companies use the consumer as the e-mail distributor by the simple invitation, 'e-mail this to a friend'.

Spam levels crept up again in July 2007, accounting for 91.52 per cent of all e-mail, according to messages scanned by SoftScan, the internet security company (http://www.softscan.co.uk).

E-mail has been at the centre of a host of PR disasters, and 'leaked' e-mails (internet porosity – see Chapter 4) have brought the careers of many a politician to an end. Common examples are forwarding to an inappropriate recipient, content at the bottom of a list of exchanges that is inappropriate, and poor use of language. PR departments should review e-mail policies, implement regular internal training, and have the crisis management capability in place to deal with e-mail being used badly.

Our tip: be wary of using e-mail for marketing unless your permission list of e-mail addresses is highly targeted and no older than six weeks.

## WHAT IS FLICKR?

There are a lot of photo-sharing websites and web services that allow people to upload photographs, tag them with keywords, and invite friends to view and download them. Many, like www.flickr.com, provide a facility to use photos stored on their sites to embed into web pages, blogs, wikis and other sites. The range of services available is extensive and can be used commercially. There are some wonderfully named services like http://www.pixagogo.com/.

Our tip: use online photos to offer a lot of richness that can be added to your presentations and sites.

## WHAT ARE GAMES?

Computer games are almost as old as computers. From the early Pacman, played alone on a mainframe terminal, to today's massively multi-player online role-playing game (MMORPG), the genre has become both a huge industry (using PCs, hand-held gaming devices like the Wii, or Sony's Play Station and Microsoft's XBox) with games produced by huge studios and individual developers. Games have a range of commercial applications too, and now they are internet-enabled they are a significant communication channel for the PR industry.

There are also a host of management games. An example of the use of online games is the Royal Marsden Hospital's The Adventures of Captain Chemo, which has been turned into an interactive computer game to help cancer patients worldwide.

Most games today have superb graphics and many have interactive elements, often available as 'plug-in' widgets.

In 2007, the Chinese-developed Fantasy Westward Journey reached 1.5 million peak concurrent users (PCUs) and Blizzard, a leading provider of MMORPGs, announced that the user base for its World of Warcraft game had reached 9 million players worldwide. In 2007, the average age of players was climbing and a historic divide between the sexes was shown to have closed.

Many games machines are now able to act in many ways like a laptop with a broadband and WiFi connection. Sending messages to other gamers and holding voice conversations was beginning to take hold in 2008, opening up yet another channel for communication on a different platform.

# WHAT IS INSTANT MESSAGING?

Instant messaging (IM) is a form of real-time communication between two or more people based on typed text. It is probably the oldest social medium (dating back to the 1970s), originally used across multi-user operating systems to facilitate communication with other users logged in to the same mainframe computer, a local network or across the internet. According to Nielson Online, Britons were found to have spent the most amount of time overall on MSN Messenger 2007.

IM used to be text based but some modern manifestations allow forms of multi-media. IM is also used as a platform to exchange files (word-processed documents, photographs, URLs, video, etc).

Many publicly available providers have high numbers of users. Examples include: AIM, 53 million active users; Jabber, between 40 and 50 million; MSN, 27.2 million active; Yahoo! Messenger, 22 million users; and Skype, as part of their VoIP service, 9 million. ICQ and Aim (owned by AOL) claimed that 2 billion IM messages were sent and received by their services every day. The Annual Instant Messaging Trends Study showed that 58 per cent of people use IM at and for work.

Gartner analyst David Smith forecasts that 95 per cent of employees will use instant messaging (IM) as their *de facto* tool for voice, video and text chat by 2013.

Our tip: ask around the office to find out how much IM is used, and to assess how useful it could be as a channel for internal and external communication.

# WHAT ARE MESSAGE BOARDS?

Wikipedia, the online encyclopaedia, describes an internet forum as a web application for holding discussions and posting user-generated content. Internet forums are also commonly referred to as web forums, message boards, discussion boards, (electronic) discussion groups, discussion forums or bulletin boards. The terms 'forum' and 'board' may refer to the entire community or to a specific sub-forum dealing with a distinct topic. Messages within these sub-forums are then displayed either in chronological order or as threaded discussions.

Examples are Google's Groups (a successor to Usenet) and Yahoo Groups. There are many other examples and they are very useful in developing sequential contributions to a theme or topic online. Groups can be small, but many are very large with a lot of contributors.

Groups dedicated to specific topics (consumer-generated technical help is a classic application) have been in common use for decades and do need moderators. Their popularity in the 1980s and 1990s inspired a lot of the early thinking that informs much contemporary social media theory.

---

The BBC uses message boards for many of its programmes. In 2007 its series about family trees attracted 180,000 comments.

---

Our tip: consider embedding forums in wikis where there is a need to add additional interactivity.

# WHAT IS A MICRO-BLOG?

Micro-blogging is a form of blogging with very limited space for text (140–200 characters usually). These small comments are made available for people to follow and monitor on their PCs or mobiles. The first such service was Twitter, which was launched in July 2006 (http://www.twitter.com), and its main competitors are FriendFeed, Jaiku and Pownce. There are a number of copycat services and embedded examples in popular social networking websites Facebook and MySpace that have a micro-blogging feature, such as 'status update.'

There are a lot of useful applications for these services. Because people can follow them easily and they take very little time, some services are popular; these include the BBC news and, for some, the Press Gazette.

Each entry is called a 'tweet', and applications for keeping executives informed are certainly an option in PR.

In July 2008 many people in Austin, Texas, saw at first hand what Twitter can do with a few dedicated people and a great idea.

It was the inaugural Austin Blood Drive Tweetup, timed for 3 July, just before an Independence Day weekend when accidents tend to happen and the need for blood is high. It was launched using a variety of online tools: particularly with the Tweetup announcement post on co-organizer Michelle Greer's blog, but also with other blog posts, lots of tweets (Twitter messages, even including some from Australia), e-mails and a Facebook page.

The push started on 29 June, a Sunday – a mere three days for people to find out about it, get some time off from work and participate.

One hundred people signed up online for a donation timeslot to come in and give blood; the Blood Center normally averages around 40 a day. The professionals who run the Blood Center said they'd never seen so many first-time donors.

On 18 July 2007, TwitDir.com identified 340,000 public Twitter accounts. On average 2,000 new Twitter accounts were created every day.

# WHAT IS THE MOBILE INTERNET?

Abbreviated internet protocols make the mobile internet very versatile. The development of the W3C (World Wide Web Consortium) Mobile Web Initiative brought internet protocol to mobile phones, the convergence of SMS, web and e-mail from mobile phones, PDAs and other portable gadgets to the web. This opened the door to mobile internet online. Access does not require a desktop computer and, as more people have mobile devices than computers, this is an important development for PR practice.

Mobile web access is evolving and overcoming interoperability and usability problems that are due to the small physical size of the screens, the incompatibility of many mobile devices with computer operating systems and the format of much of the information available on the internet. Micro-formats and evolving mini-blog applications (like Twitter) offer interesting applications for communicators.

Sir Martin Sorrell, CEO of the marketing group WPP, suggests that mobile phones, along with internet television and computer games, are set to secure a 15 per cent share of all spending on advertising by 2010. Alongside the advertising, there will be big demand for content.

Mobile connectivity is also offering capability to allow laptops and other PCs access to the internet where there is no WiFi or other connectivity.

Of all the evolving developments for the internet in the near future, mobile is the one that should be watched most. As this chapter was being edited, an application of Bluetooth technology to broadcast localized messages to mobile phones (over 200 metres) was used by a PR consultancy to attract people to a street exhibition.

Our tip: use mobile for quick comments and briefing. The best application we know about is a corporate affairs director who gets Twitter (see above) briefs on his mobile while in meetings.

## WHAT IS A NEW MEDIA RELEASE?

Electronic press kits have been used for a long time and an evolution of this is the new media release, an electronic form of press release. The first such releases conformed to the now defunct XPRL (eXtensible Public Relations Language) language, but they are increasingly being developed using Web 2.0 tools based on a template developed by Shift Communications in the United States in 2006.

Still using e-mail and press release distribution methods, the new media release is enhanced with RSS and other social media capabilities (for example an add to the Delicious tool – see above) to assist with distribution of news stories both to the traditional media and to the online community media. Stories are presented in a way designed to help journalists, bloggers or indeed machines quickly to identify key parts of the story and related content for rapid editing and publishing.

Releases typically provide access (hyperlinks) to rich resources like photographs, written, videoed and recorded voice content, background briefing, comments and blog posts/searches.

Our tip: use social media press releases as well as the traditional outlets.

## WHAT IS ONLINE CONFERENCING?

Once, there was a need for significant infrastructure to create a secure environment where groups of people in many locations could join a conversation. To include real-time video was expensive, and adding transfer of digital information and drawings at the same time was almost impossible. Today, such facilities are available free or at low cost, so this rich medium is a communication channel for everyone – child, adult, communications specialist and even for remote baby-sitting. Although often not delivered as two-way communications, 'webinars' can be regarded as another example of online conferencing.

Facilities are provided by Skype (http://www.skype.com), Convenos (http://www.convenos.com) and GoToMeeting (http://www.gotomeeting. com), among others. This is a small selection, but all offer a range of both open and closed conferencing tools.

Our tip: add conferencing in your wiki to facilitate client meetings and save time and cost.

## WHAT ARE ONLINE SURVEYS?

All manner of surveys and polling are available online. Many offer real-time results and most have the ability to handle both open and closed questions as well as comments. They can be web based, as widgets, or in e-mail format, and many have considerable analysis features and presentation graphics as standard. There are many commercial online survey companies that are also available to practitioners.

> Breakout: Sainsbury's Home Insurance commissioned a poll for a marketing promotion in which YouGov research revealed that 5.6 million homes were damaged by children or pets during the previous year's summer holidays.

Vendors include: Confirmit, InstantSurvey, Keypoint, Merlinplus, Net-MR, Snap, SphinxSurvey, Survey Monkey, SurveyWriter.com, The Survey System and WebSurveyor.

Our tip: this is a symmetrical form of communication that can be used for almost instant opinion polling and evaluation, a great tool for planning and management.

## WHAT IS PAY PER CLICK?

Many websites, and notably search engines, carry small advertisements with embedded URLs. When a person clicks on these advertisements, the organization that put them there is charged. This is the fastest growing form of advertising worldwide; it is not difficult to master and is another tool for online communication.

Unlike traditional advertising, this form of communication is user activated.

PPC advertisements can be placed in a wide range of online properties (search engines being the most common, but social networks are also popular). They can be geographically targeted to highly selected publics by location, age and interest, and very powerful evaluation tools are available to monitor effectiveness and outcomes.

Our tip: don't be put off because this is 'advertising'; it has a lot of PR applications.

# WHAT IS A PODCAST?

A podcast is an audio file (typically an MP3 file) embedded into a web page (typically a blog), with 'show notes' and the means by which listeners can comment on or respond to content in the show. These radio-like audio programmes can be listened to on a PC or laptop, iPod or mobile phone and, according to podcaster Eric Schwartzman, have these specific PR benefits:

- They allow listeners to time-shift and place-shift media consumption.
- There is 100 per cent efficiency, since episodes are only downloaded by listeners on an opt-in basis.
- They are easily accessible to a global audience that is not defined by geographic boundaries.
- They provide access to an educated, influential audience with a high disposable income.
- Electronic programming can be leveraged without an outside news media filter.
- They form the most cost-effective electronic media distribution channel available.

Podcasting is also one of the fastest growing technologies of all time. The number of podcast feeds managed by FeedBurner was growing by 15 per cent per month in 2007. The number of subscribers, though, is growing even faster, at a rate of 20 per cent per month. According to FeedBurner, podcast sites exceeded the total number of radio stations in the entire world, by 2007. In their book *How to Do Everything with Podcasting*, Shel Holtz and Neville Hobson offer all that a practitioner needs to know about the genre, including very practical advice on how to produce podcasts.[1]

Podcasts are offered by all manner of organizations, from giants such as the BBC and IBM to the British Council, not forgetting a considerable number of private individuals. Some are made available on company websites and intranets. Some purists argue that a true podcast is an audio file that is delivered by RSS, which means that new content is automatically downloaded to the listener/subscriber's computer as it is created.

Our tip: this is a useful medium for internal as well as external communication. Experiment first.

# WHAT IS RSS?

By embedding some code into a web page, search engines are able to identify new content. In some instances (blogs for example) when a post is added, the software will tell specialist services that new content has been added (called a 'ping'). RSS readers are programs that collect this information and submit it to users who have stated that they want to follow new developments from these sites. Besides blogs and podcasts, many sites – including most newspaper, magazine, radio and TV websites and some search engines – provide RSS feeds, which means that practitioners can use RSS in a similar way to a news feed or clipping service.

Pages displaying the symbol shown in Figure 2.1 provide RSS feeds.

**Figure 2.1** *Symbol to show a page provides RSS feeds*

There are a variety of services available including:

- For Windows: Newz Crawler, FeedDemon, Awasu;
- Mac OS: Newsfire, NetNewsWire;
- Web based services: Bloglines, FeedZilla, NewsGator, Google Reader.

There are also some very good experts whose knowledge is helpful to practitioners:

- Robin Good, http://www.masternewmedia.org;
- Wikipedia, http://en.wikipedia.org/wiki/RSS;
- RSS Specification, http://www.rss-specifications.com.

Our tip: use RSS to spread the word about your work pages on your websites and other web-based communications; use it to monitor both traditional and social media developments.

## WHAT ARE SEARCH ENGINES?

Search engines are the most widely used of all websites, because their job is to locate information. The most commonly used search engine is Google (www.google.com), which served almost 3.8 billion searches in April 2007, according to data from Nielsen//NetRatings (www.netratings.com). But search engines come in many flavours, some with very specific uses. For the most part, search engines go out and look for web pages and content in web pages, by looking for and following hyperlinks (which are the navigation elements – codes sometimes called URLs – in web pages) that they read and then list (this is known as indexing). When someone enters a word or combination of words into the search engine, it produces a list of pages containing those words, and includes links to those pages. Google incorporates a number of different types of search, such as for words, news, images, blogs, videos, discussions and much more. There are other search engines that are directories, which are subject-specific lists of websites. Yahoo! (www.yahoo.com) is a directory and a search engine. There are specialist search engines too. Technorati (www.technorati.com) is a specialist for blogs, podcasts and video.

RBA (Rhodes–Blakeman Associates) was set up in 1989 by Karen Blakeman and provides a range of interesting publications, not least her blog (http://www.rba.co.uk/wordpress/), which provides really good insights into the world of search.

There are many specialist services that practitioners may want to use for their search and monitoring activities. A good place to start looking is www.searchenginewatch.com.

Most PR practitioners will use a search engine most days, and understanding a little of how they work will sharpen research skills. More importantly, developing an appreciation of search engines helps to shed light on some very important principles of online PR. Google is a lot of people's first port of call when they want to find out about an organization, an event or a product. As we know, even quite specific searches can throw up hundreds, thousands even millions of results – but research shows that most users only look at the first page or 10 results, and a high proportion only click on the first link on the first page. If your organization's website is at the forefront of your communications strategy, it must be visible to searchers – and it must be more visible (come higher on the list) than your rivals, competitors and detractors. In addition, when most people search for your organization your work in search engine optimization should ensure that they are not presented with old, outdated or trivial links.

There are many techniques for trying to second-guess how different search engines will rank your site. It is no longer guesswork. There are procedures that provide excellent and reputation-enhancing solutions.

One of the most important techniques, one that is at the heart of the algorithms that power Google, is a form of peer recognition; Google counts the number of other websites that link to yours, on the reasonable assumption that if lots of people link to it, it must have some added value. The interconnected, aggregated network of sites and comments is creating reputation so, in a way, Google ranks on reputation – but this is internet reputation. Google doesn't say: 'ABC Limited was founded in 1857 and is a blue chip firm and a household name'; Google says: 'lots of people are talking about ABC, so it goes to the top of our list'. The problem is that the reality might be that lots of people are saying bad things about ABC and the site they are saying it on, and linking to, is www.ihateabc.com! This reputation is spread by virtual word of mouth, at high speed and without geographical limits.

Our tip: optimize search for reputation management. Why not create your own subject/website search engine for your website blog or wiki using this Google tool: http://google.com/coop/cse/? (See the section on search engine optimization below.)

## WHAT IS SEARCH ENGINE OPTIMIZATION (SEO)?

Search engine optimization is the method by which websites can gain enhanced positions in the organic listings (on the top left-hand side of the page) in major search engines such as Google, Yahoo! and MSN. It is important because of the way the web is used:

- The web is the primary source for work-related information and an aid to purchasing.
- 93 per cent of web users use the web every day, spending an average of 4.8 hours per week online (2007).
- Most web page access is through search, favourites and e-mails.
- A majority of people use search engines instead of a list of favourites to remember the names of websites.
- 82 per cent of people using the web use B2B websites, and most access B2B web sites in the first instance using search.
- 62 per cent of people use the web to review products and suppliers.

If people find the page easily using search it enhances reputation. When people are frustrated when trying to find a web page using search they are dismissive of organizations.

When people are searching for information on the web, they input the words most obvious to them into search engines. Many searches are specific, and when building web pages there are opportunities to reflect this specific interest, using keywords that can be indexed and stored by search engines. This information is provided in the source code (HTML) of the page (which you can see by clicking on 'view/page source' in Firefox and 'view/source' in Internet Explorer). For example: the CIPR has various clues to help search engines store the right information about the site, including:

- an accurate description: <meta name="description" content="The CIPR is the professional body for the UK public relations industry, providing PR training and events, PR news and research." />;
- clues about the content of the page: <meta name="keywords" content="public relations, PR, PR professional body, public relations training, PR education, PR jobs, PR news, PR research, PR awards, PR conferences, PR advertising, PR sponsorship, cipr member information, PR careers" />;
- the title of the page: <title>Chartered Institute of Public Relations, CIPR, the professional body of the PR industry</title>.

Each page on a web site is different and describes the site and the page for the search engine to help people who use search engines to arrive on the right page on the basis of the search terms they have used.

There is always something of a trade-off between having a high-ranking word among search engines and being specific to the precise need, and therefore to the specific words used by people to find information on a site. Of course, targeted traffic is of equal importance to achieving a high ranking.

Search engines develop fast and constantly monitor attempts to trick them. If a search engine believes your site has been artificially manipulated to attract more traffic, especially unrelated traffic, then it is likely your website rank will go down significantly and it is possible that your site could banned from the search engine for life.

SEO is a PR issue. The basics of good SEO is not rocket science; the best SEO will rank your site highly but is much harder, so use an expert.

## WHAT ARE SOCIAL NETWORKING SERVICE SITES?

MySpace.com, Bebo.com and Facebook.com are the three most recognized social media services. They are micro-websites that allow people to exchange interactive, user-submitted content among a network of friends through personal profiles, blogs and comment discussion lists. They are very quick to set up, and don't require the writing skills or pose the challenges of content creation of a website or blog; it is easy to add photos, music and videos. They are very popular with a wide range of audiences. The UK marketing magazine *Brand Republic* reported that 10 per cent of the UK population accessed Facebook in 2007.

In 2006, MySpace was the world's sixth most popular English-language website. Facebook, a near rival, was said to be generating advertising revenue of over $1.5 million per week in 2006. The speed at which Facebook has grown in the United Kingdom (in May 2007, it gained 527,000 new users) gives a graphic example of just how quickly the social media landscape can change.

Music was the first sector to recognize the potential of social networks, with many bands building a fan base through MySpace. Facebook is built around networks of special interest groups, originally based on the university or college the member attended, but now including thousands and thousands of niche groups. In addition, users can add a range of applications to incorporate other forms of rich interactive content.

---

Figures from Nielsen/NetRatings suggest that Facebook received 6.5 million unique visitors in August 2007, compared with 6.4 million for MySpace. Both sites are now visited by one in five UK surfers.

---

There are many other such sites and it is possible for the practitioner to create networks for client activities both in-house and for wider audiences. Ragan Communications, a PR services provider, and Melcrum, the research and training business, both offer social networking sites exclusively for PR practitioners.

PR is just waking up to the potential of social networking but – more than almost any other part of this book – few would predict with any confidence quite how MySpace and Facebook will develop.

# WHAT IS VIDEO-SHARING?

Video-sharing hit the big time when Google paid $1.6 billion for YouTube in 2006. It grew from there. comScore reported that 27.4 million British internet users viewed 3.5 billion videos online in March 2008, with almost half seen on YouTube. There are many such sites that allow people to upload video, edit content, add tags, create groups and share videos to a wide or narrow audience. It is possible to have your own video-sharing facility inside a firewall and in closed groups, wikis or on websites. Ideal for newscasts, lectures, conferences and embedded in presentations, online video is an important channel for communication. Production cost and expertise does not always have to be 'top drawer' because typical screen size is small.

> BBC Radio Berkshire's website was inundated with hundreds of pictures and videos from the public after floods swept the area in July 2007. Broadcast journalist Oliver Williams used Google Maps to create an interactive map, plotting pictures and YouTube videos being sent in by the public to the locations around the county that they referred to. Over 100,000 newspapers, blogs and other websites highlighted this BBC web 'mashup'.

There is a lot to be considered when it comes to video. BBC iPlayer, which accounted for between 3 and 5 per cent of internet traffic by mid-2008, is obviously a popular channel (the first episode of *The Apprentice* was watched 100,000 times via iPlayer). User-generated content can be broadcast live using services like Seesmic (http://seesmic.com), which adds to the range of video options available.

Our tip: use online video to support relationship building with key audiences – they will like it and share interesting content. Be very careful with copyright material. Check first.

# WHAT ARE VIRTUAL WORLDS?

Second Life was the first of many online virtual worlds to catch the interest of the mainstream media. Virtual worlds come in many forms, often including software on a PC that allows the participant to enter a graphical representation of an online world.

People create a virtual image of themselves (called an avatar) and can explore a virtual world, meet other 'residents', chat, and participate in individual and group activities. They are able to create virtual properties, trade with one another, exchange information and lectures, or enjoy a wide range of social activities.

To be able to get best advantage from these online properties you will need a reasonably fast computer with a good quality graphics capability and a good (5mg plus) broadband internet connection.

A lot of virtual worlds are used in commerce, including simulation software (for example, to learn to fly an aeroplane), but development of online versions is only just becoming a reality for public relations activities. There are software services for practitioners to develop 3D virtual reality programs for creating room interiors, including kitchen, bathroom, bedroom, study, retail store and office space designs. Some programs are used in architecture and for 'visualizing' a wide range of locations, with the ability to 'fly round' buildings and locations.

Sony has used virtual worlds to promote its technologies, and Sony Home is a 3D interactive virtual world.

Our tip: keep a close eye on these developments, because they offer rich content and will develop into a very significant part of online PR.

## WHAT IS VOIP?

The protocols that allow people to speak to each other using computers languished in the background for a long time before a group of programmers in Estonia came up with Skype. They were lucky. They brought their product to market as broadband became common. Now it is possible to make calls between Skype users free, and to make calls to ordinary telephones as well from the same computer or equipment.

In 2007, there were 30 million users of VoIP services in Europe, with 1million VoIP BT users in the United Kingdom.

VoIP has many other uses. It can be embedded into blogs, wikis, games and websites as web widgets; it can be used for conferences and broadcast and can include a wide range of facilities for voice and video communication. Many organizations now use VoIP instead of the more common telephone and PABX systems.

## WHAT ARE WEBSITES?

The first website was put up in 1991. Most websites have a 'home page' or common root URL from which other web pages cascade in a hierarchy. Sites can comprise one or many web pages, images, videos and other digital assets. Most sites are kept as a file on a computer (called a web server). Some sites are maintained on several servers for security and to ensure that there is no interruption of service.

A web page is a document, typically written in HTML (Hypertext Markup Language), that is almost always accessible via internet protocols known as HTTP (Hypertext Transfer Protocol).

> The first web project proposal was written and circulated for comment in March 1989, with the first web page published in 1991 by an Englishman, Sir Timothy John Berners-Lee. In 1993, CERN announced that the world wide web would be free to anyone. By 2007, there were over 8 billion web pages. There were more than 100 million websites on the internet in November 2006. This included 3.5 million new sites created in the preceding month. Collectively, these millions of sites comprise the 'world wide web'.

There are many uses for websites. Most are used to aid business transactions for government, commercial and not-for-profit organizations, and personal websites. The most common personal websites are social networking service sites such as social networks, blogs and wikis, but the basic technology is used in many applications in addition to traditional websites.

Websites are most commonly accessed by people using computers, mobile phones and local area networks by means of a 'web browser' such as Internet Explorer, Firefox or Google's Chrome. However, a lot of platforms for communication will render web pages in other formats, including Internet Protocol Television (IPTV), the common television standard across Europe.

There is a significant industry that supports the web. Vendors range from organizations that transmit content, host and provide security of service to designers of applications and websites and pages.

The evolution of the internet and its technologies is such that almost anyone can create a website and it can be available worldwide by a hosting service for free.

There is a wide range of software systems that can be embedded into websites, such as JavaScript and many others that are available to generate dynamic web systems and dynamic sites. Sites may also include content from one or more databases or provide access by using technologies based on XML (eXtensible Markup Language), such as RSS (see above).

Plug-ins (often called web widgets) are available to increase the richness of user experience and are rendered by the web browser. Technologies include Adobe Flash, Shockwave and small bits of code written in

JavaScript. Dynamic HTML (DHTML, a collection of technologies used together to create interactive and animated websites) also provides for user interactivity and real-time updating within web pages (ie, pages don't have to be loaded or reloaded to effect any changes). The most commonly used plug-ins include the ability to add video (eg a YouTube video) to a website (such as a blog). At the time of going to press, Google had 8,000 of these plug-ins for use in its service, which are also available for any HTML-coded web page such as a blog.

---

Much of the coding in hypertext mark-up language (HTML) is not visible to most people and is not used by the public. Having a simple idea of what lies behind a web page is useful for practitioners.

To understand what goes on behind a web page (the HTML code) is easy. In Internet Explorer, click on 'View' and then 'Source'. It is important to know what is going on there so that you can add things to your blog or wiki or website. The best way of doing that is to edit a blog by using its HTML capability. Creating a blog is simple and free, and you may just use it for experimenting so that you can understand how websites work. Your challenge, should you wish to undertake it, is to create a blog and embed a YouTube video in it. A simple tip to help your understanding is to find someone young enough to have done it, because most have.

---

To discover the indexed pages of a website, the service by Yahoo! is valuable (https://siteexplorer.search.yahoo.com). It also shows who is linking to the website (which media publications, blogs, directories and other sites are linking in).

Our tip: it is worth going to one of the many evening courses in website design for beginners.

## WHAT ARE WIDGETS?

If there was a 'year of the web widget' it was 2007. Typically using Adobe Flash or JavaScript programming languages, widgets (called gadgets by Google) are small pieces of code that can be inserted into a blog, wiki, social media site, web page or other HTML-based property. They have a capability to bring together different information and combine it ('mashup') to present added richness.

Embedding a YouTube video into MySpace is common among teens, and the YouTube code is a widget. There are some very sophisticated widgets and some that are very relevant to PR practice, such as those that can embed news coverage in a website or wiki driven by RSS to ensure immediate updating of news. The authors use a widget to present slideshows and video (Jumpcut and Eyespot are used with and without voice and music), and videos embedded in a wiki.

> Showing how web widgets can be used to spread rich content, the publisher Forbes launched eight separate widgets in July 2007. Covering topics ranging from 'technology' to 'lifestyle', Forbes.com encouraged users to embed the widgets in their blogs, social media pages and home pages, thereby spreading its content across the web.

Our tip: look up 'web widgets' online and use all the creativity you can muster to use this vast array of communications devices.

## WHAT IS A WIKI?

A wiki is a form of website. Wikis are mostly used inside organizations to allow a group of people to create, reference and edit web pages to form an evolving body of knowledge for the group. Wikis can be open to view by just a few people, or made publicly available. Editing rights can be given to everyone or to a few, and these decisions are made by the owner or 'wiki master'.

Wikis have become popular for PR people because if you want to know more about any channel for online communication it will almost certainly be described in some detail by a number of experts in Wikipedia.com.

Wikipedia is a wiki – a wonderful example of how social media works. Imagine, 10 or 15 years ago, you were talking with a group of friends and it suddenly occurred to you that each of you was an expert in something the others knew little or nothing about; Jill was a film buff who knew a great deal about French cinema, Susan had read a lot about rhinoceroses, and Peter collected Commonwealth stamps. You say: 'Hey everyone, together we could begin to write an authoritative encyclopaedia that would be used every day by people all over the world. Let's go home and start typing!' Jill, Susan, Peter and the others would melt away and leave you to your ravings. But that is pretty much what happened with Wikipedia, which was launched in 2001.

Simply by tapping into people's enjoyment of creating content, Wikipedia has grown rapidly into one of the largest reference websites. There are more than 75,000 active contributors working on some 5,300,000 articles in more than 100 languages. As of 2008, there are 2,037,274 articles in English; every day hundreds of thousands of visitors from around the world make tens of thousands of edits and create thousands of new articles to enhance the knowledge held by the Wikipedia encyclopaedia; these statistics were, of course, taken from Wikipedia's own 'About' page (on 6 October 2007).

The same processes can be used to bring together and develop knowledge and expertise in any size of organization. Examples of commercial applications include Dresdner Kleinwort bank, which has set up a proprietary wiki system that has 5,000 pages and over 2,500 users worldwide. Students studying for their PR degrees at Bournemouth University created over 800 pages of content for their year-long 'Online PR' module in 2006 (this remains available and is continuously updated to this day).

Wikis can be plain, like Wikipedia, or can be colourful, dynamic, rich and interactive. Contributors can add or edit pages at any time with text, and can embed videos, pictures, diagrams, voice files and polls. VoIP telephony can be embedded to allow people to interact by voice or video conference direct from a page or sidebar. Documents (including Word, PDFs, spreadsheets, etc) can be uploaded and accessed from inside a wiki. Wikis can include their own blogs and discussion lists, indeed almost anything that can be added to a website – and without having to learn HTML.

Wikis can be hosted in-house on an organization's own system or by one of the many online services, including PBWiki. Some very useful wiki hosts are free, and others offer services at a low cost. Modern wikis are edited online through a web browser (Internet Explorer, Firefox, Chrome or Opera).The editing process can use a specific wiki language but some of the most popular services use an interface that looks like an ordinary word processing package.

Our tip: although wikis are getting more user friendly all the time, they are a little harder for the beginner to master than, say, a weblog. If you are going to use wikis, it is worth appointing someone as wiki master who can tidy up the stuff that people can't quite manage. Wikis are easy to use but take time to master (for a useful list of available wikis, visit http://www.wikimatrix.org/).

We have dealt with some of the more popular channels here. Many of them are available for practitioners to build themselves so as to provide comparable services for their own publics. Most are 'mashable': that is to say, they can be embedded into each other (often using 'widgets'). This makes the new media fun – the limitations are no closer than the extent of our imaginations.

Having earlier examined the commercial significance of the internet for organizations, we have now glanced at the new channels for communication that are important for the practice of online PR today.

## Note

1. Holtz, S and Hobson, N (2007) *How to Do Everything with Podcasting*, McGraw-Hill Osborne Media

# Part 2

---

# A shift in culture, communication and value

# 3

# Transparency

At the turn of the century, no PR department would send a copy of a press release to a competitor at the same time they sent it to the press. Today a very large proportion of organizations do. This is part of the new transparency and PR people are involved.

In fact, they don't sent press releases to competitors, but they do load them onto the website where competitors can download them. In addition, these newsrooms are published for others to access, such as the list of newsrooms in the 'PR Books' wiki maintained by the Leeds Met academic and blogger Richard Bailey at http://prbooks.pbwiki.com. Transparency, however inadvertent, is alive and well in online PR.

A lot has been said about the shift in transparency in recent years. Organizations are invited to become more transparent, and for PR this shift is also part of a new imperative as the internet mediates more organizational communication.

---

In a just a week during August 2008, not the high spot for big news in the United Kingdom, there were over 20 different stories calling on organizations to increase transparency. Among the more telling ones:

- The UK Government's Business Secretary urged energy companies to address the 'lack of transparency' in their accounts or face the possibility of having to open their books to reveal the profits of their supply and generation arms. (Reported in *Financial Director*.)

- The greater independence being granted to the USB's three divisions suggests that changes will be aimed at improving flexibility and transparency. (Reported in the *Financial Times*.)
- Commenting on the continuing rise of online retail sales, Stuart Tofts remarked: 'What really interested me this month, though, was a comment made by Mike Petevinos, Head of Consulting for Retail at Capgemini UK. He explained growth is rapid, even within the current gloomy economic climate. One reason he gave was "the increased choice, price transparency and convenience that online has to offer".'
- The BBC reported the AA saying that a $2 fall in the price of a barrel of oil should be reflected in a 1p fall at the pumps. This would be the equivalent of prices dropping by 14p from the peak to the latest low. But the motoring organization said that a lack of transparency in pricing meant that it was very difficult to tell whether motorists were getting a fair deal.

Transparency is in the news and across a range of sectors.

Transparency has to be considered in a wide context. It is one of the core elements that drive online public relations, the others being internet agency, internet porosity, richness in content and reach. These five basic elements of online public relations are mediated by three other components: the platforms or devices we use to access the internet, the many and growing channels for communication, and the context in which all these elements come together for people to enjoy.

Practitioners are at the heart of organizational transparency, and knowing its many faces is very useful in online PR.

Transparency, as used in the humanities, implies openness, communication and accountability. The term is a metaphorical extension of the meaning used in the physical sciences: a 'transparent' object is one that can be seen through.

Examples of transparency are typified when government meetings are open to the press and the public, when budgets and financial statements may be reviewed by anyone, when laws, rules and decisions are open to discussion. Then decisions are seen as transparent and there is less opportunity for the authorities to abuse the system in their own interest. Transparency is, in this sense, a building block of democracy. The extent to which political PR practice is comfortable with the nature of transparency has a number of advantages. It provides a framework for good practice.

## CASE STUDY: GOVERNMENTS ARE BEING LOBBIED TO INCREASE TRANSPARENCY

Poland's finance minister vowed greater transparency in the public finances of European Union members as he unveiled long-promised draft legislation designed to streamline government spending in 2008.

The United Kingdom's Information Commissioner, Richard Thomas, said the government needed to strengthen data-sharing rules, as well as taking steps to clarify and simplify the legislation over the loss of government-held personal data by one of its contractors. But he said businesses also had to take responsibility around data sharing, because there was a 'lack of transparency and accountability' in the way many firms dealt with personal information.

Stephen Hockman, commenting in *The Guardian* on 19 August 2008, noted the understandable reluctance of developing countries to sign up to carbon commitments unless the developed world is prepared to make an equitable contribution, and called for more radical options. Those options must be realized at state, regional and international levels, and they will require political, economic and legal solutions. In this mix, international legal instruments are crucial. The existing tools lack the necessary jurisdiction, clout and transparency.

In economics, a market is transparent if much is known by many: what products and/or services are available, at what price and where. Transparency is the bastion against cartels and price fixing, a guarantor of product efficacy and at the core of competition.

Transparency in communication is evident when the media are transparent, such as when there are many, often competing, sources of information; when much is known about the method of information delivery; and when the funding of media production is publicly available.

In each case, the internet is now a major component in delivering the advantages of transparency and nowhere more so than for organizations and managers with roles as guardians of reputation.

## RADICAL TRANSPARENCY

Radical transparency is a management method whereby nearly all decision making is carried out publicly. All draft documents, all arguments for and against a proposal, are freely available; the decisions about the decision-making process itself, and all final decisions are made publicly and remain publicly archived.

The case for transparency, according to Frank Buytendijk, Vice President of Corporate Strategy at Hyperion, is compelling:[1]

With perfect corporate transparency, everyone within a company has access to relevant information. Management accurately represents the drivers of the business. Annual budgeting is replaced with a system of continuous planning supported by a collaborative process. Every manager knows exactly how his or her decisions affect other aspects of the company. There is visibility into how external changes impact internal matters. And the organization is able to predict precisely how the market will respond to various activities.

For most organizations, radical transparency offers a number of disadvantages, including competitive disclosure for companies, and risks to state secrets for some government departments. It can expose corporate intellectual property (IP) that may provide a unique competitive advantage, and in many organizations the conflict between radical transparency and loss of competitive advantage is an important concern.

---

Martine Courant-Rife, a professor at Lansing Community College, Michigan, attorney and blogger, wrote that 'what's becoming an all too common assertion of IP rights by estate holders is demonstrated by the case of a teacher (Dale Herbert) who's been conducting educational funded use of Flat Stanley and who may have to end his efforts which have reached across the globe' (http://www.flatstanleyproject.com/).

From the George Lucas Educational Foundation Article:

> Today, the project has become a veritable global phenomenon, and because of it, thousands of children from more than forty countries have exchanged pictures, stories, and goodwill, turning a half-inch-thin storybook character into a cultural icon. Flat Stanley look-alikes have even been photographed with Clint Eastwood on Oscar night, soared aboard a space shuttle, and visited heads of state around the globe. But now, as the project enters its thirteenth year, Hubert might be forced to pull the plug on the popular project.

Citing legal challenges from the estate of Jeff Brown, the late author of the original *Flat Stanley* book, Hebert posted a message on the project home page that reads: 'Sadly, the Flat Stanley Project may be forced to end.' Letters of support illustrating the project's – and the character's – far reach have since poured in.

There is a lesson here for PR practice, which is the fine line between a client's intellectual property and its use by the online community. At what point does transparency become an infringement of intellectual property or a commercial opportunity?

---

The extent to which transparency can be used as a tool for commercial advantage is shown by organizations as diverse as Procter & Gamble and Wikipedia.

In 2003 the website Ethicalcorp.com commented on the move by Procter & Gamble towards transparency. The article was supportive.

If you're worried about phosphonates in your detergent, want to know what's in your Fairy Liquid, or what chelators do for your wash, visit www.scienceinthebox.com. This website is a vivid demonstration of a move towards transparency by a company that has traditionally been one of the most secretive – the household products, beauty and foods group Procter & Gamble.

The company itself admits its past difficulty in talking to people. Chris Start, vice president of the Fabric Care division, jokes: 'Research & Development didn't even talk to Marketing – the first they knew of new products was then they bought them in the shops.'

Mr Start was speaking at an international event in Geneva designed to demonstrate how things have changed as well as how P&G views sustainable development.

The Science in the Box website combines both aims. First, by providing access to the EU Safety Data Sheets for each product, it allows consumers, NGOs and anybody else who is interested to find out what is in P&G products. So far this covers detergents, but coverage will be extended to other cleaning products and possibly others beyond the Fabric Care division. Other sections cover the impacts and safety aspects of particular chemical ingredients.

The strategic decision to embrace transparency as a corporate approach to communication is now helping one of the biggest companies in the world to gain competitive advantage. P&G is one of many examples of companies looking at how they can benefit from added transparency.

# CONTROLLED TRANSPARENCY

Controlled transparency is the controlled posting and release of information to the internet. It can occur through e-mail, web-based and other device channel outlets. It may be institutional, overt, covert and unintentional.

# INSTITUTIONAL TRANSPARENCY

Institutional transparency is where information about an organization is made available by a wide range of authorities. Many managers find it extraordinary that so much is made available online without the organization's say so. It may be the information about a company on the government's list held by Companies House and made available online, a register of members of a trade association, a list of suppliers made available through a trade journal portal or the registration details of an organization's website published by the registrars. There are hundreds, if not thousands of such places where information about an organization, its people, brands, services and products are declared online. It takes the form of information that is required by law, or the rules that are part of the infrastructure for a licence to operate. It's not just for companies. This form of transparency applies equally to voluntary organizations like charities and even to individuals.

# OVERT TRANSPARENCY

Overt transparency is where an organization seeks to make information available. This can be to markets, consumers, employees and many other organizations and constituencies. Often this form of transparency is on a website, offered in e-mails or provided to social media participants. For example, many organizations publish pages about corporate social responsibility on corporate websites or have listings in Wikipedia, with trade associations and so forth. Other forms of overt transparency are when an organization (or individual) makes information available to distribution technologies such as RSS.

# COVERT TRANSPARENCY

Covert transparency is where organizations 'push' or manipulate information. Push content includes online advertising and similar marketing promotion. It can be attempts by the organization to get an advantage, for example in making websites more prominent in search engine listings (called search engine optimization – SEO), or information delivered to social media.

Astroturfing (the practice of falsely creating the impression of independent, popular support by means of an orchestrated and disguised marketing exercise) is the antithesis of transparency.

# UNINTENTIONAL TRANSPARENCY

A classic case of unintentional transparency is the listing of a company website in Google. It is where information is available or made available through the offices of the organization and is 'harvested': that is, collected from websites and used to offer information to other internet users. This harvesting of information can be simply a person taking information from a page on the organization's website and transcribing it; it can be the same thing but done by a computer; in more recent years it may be use of information from just part of a web page that could be no more than a line of two, an image, video, sound file or hyperlink to other pages (such as a news story in a newspaper's website). Web widgets often contribute to transparency as well as contributing to internet agency (see Chapter 5).

Transparency happens because, as part of the licence to operate (both as a legal requirement and as part of building trust with constituents), information is available online. Some is required by regulatory bodies, and some comprises references in online directories, association membership data or rules of trade bodies. It happens when people are named in association with organizations (and that can be as simple as the name of the organization or website being listed, or because of e-mail addresses published online) and through social media. All organizations are to a greater or lesser degree transparent. So too are people. The amount of information made available about us all is quite considerable and is growing all the time.

---

### IN BRIEF

- Internet transparency is already affecting PR practice.
- It is a significant driver in modern management.
- It implies openness, communication and accountability.
- Transparency is a building block of democracy.
- It is a bastion against cartels and price fixing, a guarantor of product efficacy, and at the core of competition.
- It provides a framework for good practice.
- The media is transparent when, for example, there are many, often competing, sources of information; when much is known about the method of information delivery; and the funding of media production is publicly available.
- With perfect corporate transparency, everyone within a company has access to relevant information.
- Radical transparency offers a number of disadvantages, including competitive disclosure for companies and risk to state secrets for some government departments.
- Controlled transparency is the controlled posting and release of information to the internet.
- Institutional transparency is where information about an organization is made available by a wide range of authorities.
- Overt transparency is where an organization seeks to make information available.
- Covert transparency is where organizations 'push' or manipulate information.
- Unintentional transparency is the listing of a company website in Google. It is where information is available or made available through the offices of the organization and is 'harvested'.

---

## Note

1. Buytendijk, F (2008) Corporate transparency is a great thing...
or is it? http://blogs.oracle.com/frankbuytendijk/2008/02/corporate_
transparency_is_a_gr.html (accessed 20 October 2008)

# 4

# How organizations become porous

Throughout history, information has 'leaked' out of organizations, perhaps in the form of gossip at social gatherings or conversations between, for example, representatives of companies and customers or suppliers.

Today, the same thing happens but on a much grander scale. The same gossip is available in e-mails, instant messaging and web-mail discussion, SMS messages on a mobile phone and social media interactions at work and at home. In addition, the pub gossip of yesteryear can also find its way online. Porosity can be interpreted as a form of inadvertent transparency.

> Four songs from U2's upcoming album were leaked on to the internet after front-man Bono played them too loudly on his stereo at his villa in the south of France. A U2 fanatic from the Netherlands who was holidaying in the village of Eze, on the French Riviera, heard the new tracks being blared from Bono's window and decided to record them on his mobile phone. The fan boasted about his find on the forum of U2 fan site Interference.com, and members there advised him to publish the clips on YouTube, which he did and thus scooped the launch.
>
> Incidental porosity even affects top bands.

(Source: *Sydney Morning Herald*, 18 August 2008, http://www.smh.com.au/news/athome/bonos-boob-secret-songs-taped-for-you-too/2008/08/18/1218911539035.html.)

Many organizations have sophisticated processes for monitoring e-mail, instant messaging and other online transactions to help reduce the incidence of harmful porosity. But this is only one (not very effective) form of control. There is a need for employee policies to be in place to make clear what is acceptable for use of e-mail, instant messaging, blogs, social media and other forms of electronic communication. Unfortunately these policies are not generally established and, even when they are implemented, are frequently not well articulated. Such advice and guidance is essential and is part of effective internal PR programmes.

Jo Moore served as a British political advisor and press officer to the Transport, Local Government and Regions Secretary Stephen Byers. On 11 September 2001, after both World Trade Center towers and the Pentagon had been hit in terrorist attacks, Moore sent an e-mail to the press office of her department that read: 'It's now a very good day to get out anything we want to bury. Councillors' expenses?'

The Department did indeed announce on the following day two minor changes to the system of councillors' allowances. Nearly a month later, the e-mail was leaked to the press where it provoked a succession of stories deriding the cynical nature of spin.

In November the department appointed a new Director of Communications, Martin Sixsmith. It was hoped he would improve relations and avoid another leak scandal. However, on 13 February 2002 the row flared up again when a leak to the press alleged that Moore had made further attempts to 'bury' unfavourable railway statistics on the day of a major event. It was backed up by a copy of an e-mail from Martin Sixsmith saying: 'Princess Margaret is being buried [on Friday]. I will absolutely not allow anything else to be.' Both Moore and Sixsmith said the e-mail was a fabrication, but on Thursday 14 February it emerged that Sixsmith had indeed sent an e-mail in such terms (although the wording was not accurately reported).

On Friday 15 February Jo Moore resigned from her position. The degree of media attention focused on her, and the ongoing conflict with the Civil Service, had left her unable to do her job. Sixsmith also left the department, albeit in complicated and controversial circumstances.

Within three months, Stephen Byers had also resigned from Government after more leaked e-mails.

The history of internet porosity, in this case using e-mails leaked to the press, is well established in many cases over the years.

Porosity is not always a bad thing and is seldom committed with evil intent. Often it is incidental, as when in a long exchange between several people a single e-mail contains something that would have been better not said. It can be accidental, as when a firewall is not as robust as it should be. It can be intentional, often arising from frustration when corporate restrictions make communication too difficult and employees seek ways to enjoy unfettered (often business-related) external communication. Occasionally porosity is malicious.

---

While the Canon EOS 50D DSLR camera was designed and built under the tightest security Canon had ever created, it seems that even one of the leading camera manufacturers in the world is still prone to the odd blip and mistake. Details of the camera were leaked to the rest of the world in August 2008 after someone at the group added a page to the website and forgot to secure access!

---

A motivated, informed and alert workforce is the best and probably the only defence against unintentional porosity.

But porosity is not always bad. As with transparency, there are benefits. The authentic voice of organizations that flows through the corporate shell has tremendous impact outside and may be part of a managed process of making organizations more competitive.

---

Apple Inc is well known for managing leaks (managed porosity) about its products ahead of a launch. This leak, blogged two weeks before the launch of iTunes 8, is a classic:

> Apple has a more definite release date in mind for its new iPods and iTunes 8, Digg founder Kevin Rose says in the latest episode of This Week in Tech. Coloring in details left out of his controversial blog entry, Rose alleges early on in the episode that the new devices and their companion jukebox software should be unveiled on September 9th, or just two weeks from now (Source: http://www.electronista.com).

---

As organizations become transparent and begin to interact with external online communities (for example by selling goods and services online) they have to create systems to deal with interactions such as taking money, responding to orders and shipping goods. This means that the internet is changing the organization to meet the demands of the internet. Processes are corporate intangible assets, and so internet interaction is changing the value of the organization by releasing transactional information (a confirming e-mail for a purchase is an example).

Part of this process in a modern communication mix is the use of social media that, to be the 'authentic' voice of an organization, will release more information in a more informal way than would be expected in the traditional rigid and controlled marketing style of information provision. Conversational in tone, this form of transparency discloses more than in earlier times.

---

Lewis Green, writing for the MarketingProfs Daily Fix blog (http://www.mpdailyfix.com), examined the question 'Why outsourcing a blog might be smart'. He put forward some reasons for outsourcing:

1.  If the company doesn't have a communications or a marketing department, maybe you should.
2.  If the company doesn't have an executive spokesperson with the time, maybe you should.
3.  If the company's Legal and/or HR departments need to approve outgoing comments, maybe you should, but only if those departments get out of the way. Otherwise, don't do a blog.

And reasons against:

Or maybe not. And here are the arguments, as I understand them, against outsourcing the company blog. The point of blogging is:

1.  Having an authentic voice.
2.  Giving customers a personal connection to the company.
3.  Ghostwriters do neither.

And a pragmatic view:

Well, pardon me, but who do you think writes executive speeches, letters from the CEO, and all those personal words to shareholders one finds in the Annual Report, and website content, and most of the pithy executive quotes found in newspapers?

Where does the 'authentic voice porosity stop and managed transparency begin?

---

To create a rich experience for people online, organizations respond by means of e-mails, blogs, podcasts and online telephony, and other forms of direct and indirect interactions. Such interactions are a combination of technical and procedural responses, and also include people involved in conversations with external constituencies.

The competitive advantage of this rich exchange is a powerful incentive, but now the organization is being changed by people and technologies that are of the internet. In responding to online conversations, there is give and take and the online interaction begins to change the organization. A retailer with 10 per cent of sales online is a radically different organization to one with only a chain of shops.

As the interactions become more common, consumers (and others) invite the organization to change, sometimes suggest how and, if thwarted, vote with their fingers. Here we see the internet changing the organization, forcing it to be ever more transparent and porous; it is acting as an agent of change.

---

**IN BRIEF**

- Organizations have always been porous, with information 'leaking out'.
- Organizations use a range of technologies to prevent information escaping.
- Guidance to employees is important.
- Porosity can be incidental, accidental, intentional or malicious.
- Porosity is not always bad.
- It can contribute to the 'authentic voice' of the organization.
- It can provide competitive advantage.

# 5

# The internet as an agent

The internet allows people and computers to change content. First articulated by Alison Clark and Roy Lipski for the CIPR/PRCA Internet Commission in 1999, the concept of internet agency posits that a message (and, in this context, a message can be words, pictures, video, voice or even a computer program) can be changed by people and technologies, and in this process acts as an agent.

Internet agency offers a unique concept of transparency. There are so many examples that it is difficult to imagine where to start. Typical examples are where technologies provide a different context.

---

### EXAMPLES OF INTERNET AGENCY

Google added a new layer to Google Earth that shows Google News related to the area shown on the screen. Two different pieces of information, news and maps, combine to create a new insight. For example, adding content on Google maps was used in 2008 to show the location of British National Party members after the membership list was revealed online. It was pretty obscure to protect the actual locations.

---

http://www.avoision.com created a unique music video that trawls through the lyrics of songs and brings them to life with images taken from the photograph-sharing social media website Flickr to create a new music/picture combination. Images are frequently altered online. Using a search engine that looks for images online, it will produce a list of changed and defaced examples (http://tineye.com). The juxtaposition of results can change the impression of an organisation or person and can, for example, present Gordon Brown as Prime Minister in the context of Downing Street and as an estate agent in the top ten returns (Figure 5.1).

Symbian's research VP, David Wood, is reported as saying: 'In web 2.0, the network itself has intelligence, rather than just being a bit-pipe for pre-cooked information.'

---

### Number10.gov.uk
Number10.gov.uk logo The official site of the Prime Minister's Office. BETA. Home · News Communicate · Meet the PM · History and Tour · Number 10 TV ...
www.number10.gov.uk/output/Page1.asp - 20k - Cached - Similar pages - Note this

### Number10.gov.uk
**Gordon Brown** opens school in Port Glasgow. The Prime Minister travelled to the **Gordon Brown** has predicted honours awards for British medalists in ...
www.number10.gov.uk/ - 27k - Cached - Similar pages - Note this
More results from www.number10.gov.uk »

### **Gordon Brown** - Wikipedia, the free encyclopedia
**Gordon Brown** was born in Govan, Glasgow, Scotland. [10] His father John Ebenezer Brown, was a minister of the Church of Scotland. He was a strong influence ...
en.wikipedia.org/wiki/**Gordon_Brown** - 302k - Cached - Similar pages - Note this

See results for: gordon brown *estate agents*

### **Gordon Brown** Associates - Chester-le-street **estate agents**. Low ...
Chester-le-Street Low Fell Sunderland **Estate Agents**, Property Sales, Find a Property to Buy or Sell in Chester-le-Street. Chester-le-street **Estate Agent** ...
www.**gordon-brown**.co.uk/

**Figure 5.1**   *Results for Gordon Brown*

---

For example, a lot of websites are designed with a landing page. It is like the front cover of a newspaper, magazine or book, or the front door of an office, factory or shop. From it there is an assumption that people can navigate to the content that they need. But many websites have hundreds (some have thousands) of pages and it would take a long time to navigate to the one single page the user seeks. For many the solution is to provide 'flow', allowing people to follow the 'flow' hyperlinks to a particular page, but in many cases people search beyond this context and, using a range of tools, go straight to the page they want.[1]

To go straight to a page and miss the 'Home page' is easy. This means the public can go to any page that is their 'landing page' (Figure 5.2).

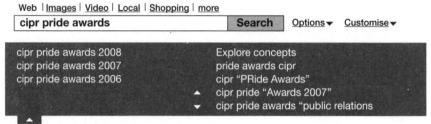

**Figure 5.2**   *Any page can be the 'landing page'*

An example is when a visitor is directed to a page or post by search engines and hyperlinks from other websites, blogs, wikis and other media. In these circumstances the origination and direction can be from a context that is created by either another author or a search engine listing. Internet agency creates these contexts.

'Agency' is the process of transformation of a message as it is passed from one person to another online, or as an online computer program adds to the original data, providing a new context and understanding (including text sounds and visual images). Agency is of itself neither benign nor malicious.

Internet agency, where a message or story is changed as it progresses through cyberspace, is commonplace. It is quite common to see blog posts that re-interpret content of other authors, which is human internet agency.

Technology-driven internet agency is both powerful and one of the fastest-growing areas of internet development. Being able to identify information in real time and mix and match it with other information from one or many other sources to create new information or new insights (called 'mashups') is a very powerful capability. For example, it may be that information about an organization's stock market listing is allied to information about the number of web page views, blog posts and press releases. Only the press release information comes from the company but all of these components can be presented as insights into the activities of the company on a single web page, created by the user's web browser and in real time. Add to this a capability to include calculations in the background and new and powerful insights are possible.

There are thousands of 'web widgets' available to organizations and the public alike. They frequently 'scrape' information, the rich content made available through corporate transparency, from websites and present it in a new and different format. Commonly called 'mashups', these online, real-time software applications are used in many ways and will become a significant part of communications in the very near future.

---

*The LondonPaper* (a free newspaper) has launched a website service (TheLondonKnowledge) which mashes up Google Maps with up-to-date listings data to provide a service to show in real time what is on and where. People can find cinemas, nightclubs, theatres, restaurants, pubs and bars, and the nearest tube and rail stations; links also allow bookings and other services.

Two online services, Hulu and Omnisio, offer users an ability to extract sections of clips people find on the web (eg YouTube, Google Video or Blip.tv). They can then take those clips and stitch them together to form new, embeddable compilations. The process from start to finish is easy enough: just copy and paste the URLs of the videos you want, and drag a few sliders to indicate where each should begin and end.

---

Google maps, for example are made available in web pages, blog posts and even e-mail using Google's web gadget.

There is a significant issue here for the public relations practitioner. Information out of context can and will be interpreted in new ways; the well-crafted content can be juxtaposed with content that changes the sense of what is intended. This means that there is a need to be able to manage such events as part of online practice.

---

**IN BRIEF**

- The internet acts as an agent.
- Messages can be changed by people and machines.
- Agency is used by people to navigate to information they seek.
- Agency can add to content.
- Agency is used to mix and match information online.
- Widgets are becoming common as internet agents.
- Agency can and does change PR messages.

---

## Note

1. Hoffman, D L and Novak, T (1996) Marketing in hypermedia computer-mediated environments: conceptual foundations, *Journal of Marketing*, **60**, pp 50–68

# 6

# Richness and reach

## RICHNESS

Richness of information is the process by which transparency is exercised. It is delivered because of the internet's reach.

The economics of information and the economics of physical things differ fundamentally from each other and we discuss this in the next chapter. But what is important is that organizations and third parties provide a lot of information online. As we will see, the pages on an organization's website are dwarfed by all the other pages that give an impression of the organization online. This richness is provided by both the organization and a host of other human and machine actors (agents).

Examples like Amazon and eBay gain a lot of their richness not from content they provide but from content offered freely and interactively by site visitors and customers. These companies have added richness because they incorporate social media as part of their selling proposition. Recommendations and other trust signals such as votes, star systems and histories about effective transactions are offered by the wider community and are delivered from a single central computer and not a chain of shops, stores and auction houses. These sites offer richness and reach, and use internet transparency agency and purposeful porosity to massive commercial advantage.

The internet thereby offers a breadth and depth of richness that is available to more than a billion people worldwide. In addition, the quality of richness and reach can be identified and evaluated in a wide variety of ways. The richness of information will be monitored by communication experts using analysis of websites, monitoring Usenet, blogs and tags about the organization, its issues and brands, and people in online community portals from YouTube to Digg and beyond.

In public relations there is a need be involved in two areas of richness development. This first, needless to say, is in the creation of rich content. Words, pictures, videos, diagrams, voice and music all add to the richness available to the public and internet technologies. This is very different from advertising, which does not have much by way of 'richness' as it seeks to gain reach through media like newspapers and posters.

The second area is the engagement of people who will add to richness in their own online communities and thereby add both richness and reach in a symbiotic process. This is achieved in a number of ways. It may be through their creation of and participation in forums, discussion lists, blogs, chat or wikis among the many channels that are available. In addition it can be through the development of online resources that make content transparently available, using technologies like search engine optimization, RSS, mashups and tagging.

# REACH

Reach is achieved in many ways. Of course there is the business of making web presence evident to people seeking information. Techniques like hyperlink exchange, search engine optimization, affiliate programs and online and offline advertising are common (and frequently essential) in practice.

In addition there is the engagement of the online community that brings people close to the organization by way of visiting the organization's website, premises or commercial and other products, brands and information partners. Reach is often developed by being part of existing or developing conversations among the many communities that develop online.

Richness and reach are important elements in developing competitive corporate transparency.

## IN BRIEF

- Richness and reach offer transparent information to online communities.
- Richness is provided by organizations and many other online actors.
- Along with online contributions, many organizations gain competitive advantage from the combination of user-generated richness and reach.
- PR practitioners create rich content and engage others to add richness in a symbiotic process.
- Richness and reach are used to promote competitive corporate transparency.

# 7

# New models of information exchange

The more we look at the many aspects of internet-mediated public relations, the more it seems that someone has sneaked into the place where they keep the management, public relations and marketing rulebooks and scribbled on most of the pages.

In their traditional role, public and stakeholder relations created understanding of the culture or context for a company or organization. People 'understood where they were'. This relationship, largely crafted by companies and other organizations (politicians, churches, civil service, charities and non-governmental organizations, etc), created an environment that allowed a company (or organization) to effectively promote its products and services. This created context and public knowledge and (sometimes) an empathy with the public. Within this context, advertising and marketing promoted products and services to achieve sales. The chain of supply, production, distribution and payment process took over and distributed the product or service (Figure 7.1). It was simple.

This process is now changed – someone has scribbled in the book! The public relations contribution is now increasingly subsumed into an internet-driven context. This conquest is both overt and hidden.

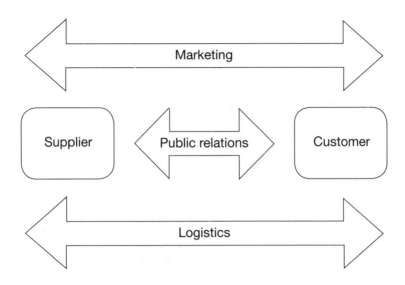

**Figure 7.1** *The chain of supply, production, distribution and payment process* © *David Phillips (1999)* The Traditional Information Value Chain.

The overt presence (promotion and interaction between an organization and its constituency) is now largely transparent. This is because of the influence of websites, online news distribution, web marketing, and relationships with market makers, auctions and marketing groups in business-to-consumer and business-to-business environments. The subliminal influence of the internet, as the means by which an organization is evident in the human (and machine) context, is not difficult to uncover.

The presence of information and messages about organizations is spread by and through many devices, platforms that transmit and receive information like PCs, laptops, mobile phones, iPhones and MP3 players, USB sticks, CDs and DVDs, games machines and, among many more, even satellite navigation devices. Distribution is effected by web crawlers and search engines and directories, with re-distribution of news and press releases, newsgroup conversations, chat, personal and corporate websites and much more. Even tracking a new message in cyberspace is daunting. Tracking all the messages, new and old, is probably already too difficult. The internet is thereby 'in charge' of creating the context in which an organization is evident to a broad constituency (see Figure 7.2).

A simple example helps explain this phenomenon. In 2007, somewhere in the visible part of the internet, there were 300,000 web pages that reference the Chartered Institute of Public Relations and they were generally available to the public. This is an institute asset of 300,000 impressions on the web. The Institute had just over 3,000 web pages available on its website

A message is made electronic

It goes into a network

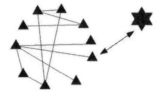

All networks are connected

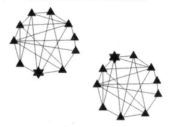

Control over the message is lost

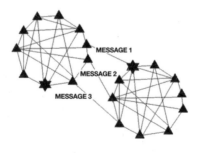

Always!

**Figure 7.2** *How information moves through the internet*

*Source:* Alison Clark, CIPR/PRCA Internet Commission, 2000

and held in search engine caches, and there were 13,000 web pages that referenced the Institute's URLs. All of this information was available using devices like PCs, laptops and mobile phones (in May 2008 over 16 million people accessed the mobile internet by using their mobile phone or mobile device in the United Kingdom).

---

The new generation of microchips now marketed by companies including Intel, Nvidia, Samsung and Texas Instruments allow internet connectivity into just about every kind of electronic device. The use of networks such as telephone cables, cellular radio, WiFi and WiMax, online all the time and everywhere is becoming the rule. The wider range of platforms includes televisions, in-car entertainment systems, hand-held devices, Bluetooth devices, MP3 players, headsets, electronic hoardings and much, much more. In 2008, Intel announced a range of new developments in this area, extending internet penetration into an even wider range of platforms.

Sony's Reader and iRex's Iliad both offer very useable, handy, portable, internet-connected e-books that can accommodate novels and other books, certainly, but also newspapers, work notes, jottings and so on.

---

The vast majority of pages online were not under the direct control of the Institute. Most had not been created by it. The Institute was probably not aware of the majority of the pages that reference it. In fact, most content available to the public about the Chartered Institute of Public Relations was created by third parties of whom the Institute is probably not aware.

The context in which the Institute is evident online has been provided by those people and organizations that reference it. The vast majority are in no way influenced by the Institute and there is no means by which the Institute can influence them all. The internet is in charge of creating the context in which the Institute is evident online.

This applies to almost every organization in the internet-developed world. Such change is of the internet. There is more. This change is also affecting the 'traditional' context more than most understand.

Because a large part of the physical world is now dependent on information delivered across the internet via websites, e-mail, blogs, wikis and internet-enabled electronic data interchange (EDI), and through a range of devices, the once separate relationship between traditional and internet-driven relationships has gone. For example, reporters and news providers have become heavily dependent on the internet, which leads one to ask how much 'traditional' newspaper readers are reading internet-driven news by proxy.[1] Traditional banks, recruitment agencies, estate agents, lawyers (the list is too long to enumerate) and more now depend on the internet for information to give them the franchise and authority to operate. The context by which an organization is known is only as good as its ability to use the internet and to be part of the internet culture.

New employment dependencies are becoming apparent, such as the printing, publishing and distribution of books and CDs benefiting from the online success of Amazon or Barnes and Noble and their competitors. Indeed, the ability of many organizations to employ people is due to its ability to optimize its operations using the internet.

Progressively, overtly and subliminally, internet technologies have taken charge throughout the supply/demand chain, or more appropriately the value chain, but more significantly throughout the 'value network'. Now, whole populations are completely reliant on the workings in cyberspace – whether they know it or not.

The context in which an organization can thrive is rapidly moving from its ability to create traditional relationships with publics (public relations) to its ability to do this in the online world (and mostly via third parties that are beyond its control). (See Figure 7.3.)

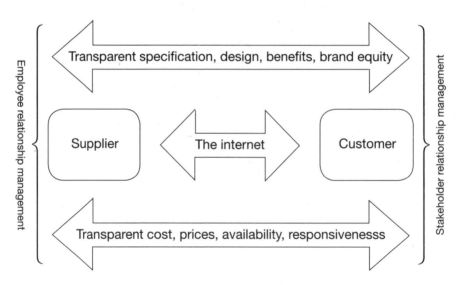

**Figure 7.3**   *The changed context of online relationships*
© *David Phillips (1999)* The New Information Value Network

The value network, extending upstream to suppliers and downstream to customers, also includes the value added by third parties to the transaction as well as other tertiary contributors in a network of networks. They will to an ever greater extent attenuate processes, as information flows transparently through the whole of the transaction network.[2] In such a networked structure the supplier can be at once customer, partner, social commentator and commercial foe.

This is starkly shown in the nature of Google advertising. Google Adwords is a form of advertising that presents advertisements in web pages. It is easy to deploy and anyone can do so. It is also effective. Many individuals, companies and advertising agencies (and a lot of PR agencies) use the service. At the same time, Google Adwords is a customer, supplier and competitor to the advertising industry. In addition, because Adwords is presented to the public in context (appropriate advertisements are presented in the right context when people use the web), it is also a commentator on the relevance of a product or service advertised in the context of the web page content.

As increasing information volume combines with accessibility, traditional information intermediaries are threatened. At the same time a growing number of information partners come into focus, offering a combination of value added content, enhanced communication facilities, wider reach and rich relationships for information consumers.

In his book *Here Comes EveryBody*, Clay Shirkey shows the difference between the traditional broadcast means of communication and the phenomenon of networked communication.[3] Where, for example, newspapers once distributed news to a mass readership, today there is an alternative form of news distribution. It is the network of interlinked people passing on information in their network of friends and acquaintances, whose members also have networks of additional friends and acquaintances. The news passes through this network, sometimes fast and unadulterated, and sometimes both slowly and often much changed. The network adds its own values to the news, and in doing so contributes to alternatives in public understanding. This process often has greater reach than traditional broadcast news distribution, and all too often is faster. This network process, of which more in Chapter 8, will not replace broadcast news distribution; they are systems that work side by side. Sometimes they complement each other and sometimes they present different perspectives.

The practitioner with 'messages' to present to a public is now confronted with this changed communications environment.

In 2008 *The Guardian* newspaper had a circulation of about 347,000, including about 44,000 copies sold outside the United Kingdom. The *Guardian* website had a daily web audience of about 771,000. Only 37 per cent of guardian.co.uk web users were in the United Kingdom. The print and online experiences are fundamentally different: on the web, most readers tend to focus on a particular section rather than browsing the full news range. The news section gets most impressions per month (almost 21 million, or 39 per cent of the total), followed by football with 7.2 million, education with 4.2 million, sport with 3.3 million, and arts and media with about 2.2 million each.

The *Guardian* had 300 million web page impressions online, which is a considerable online asset built up since 1996. Of those impressions, and from a standing start four years earlier, by 2008 over 5 per cent were in blog posts and other social media that added content to and about the *Guardian* and its stories. Most of them were written by the general public (the *Guardian*'s own blogging journalists provide only a fraction of these comments). It is reasonable to posit that, worldwide, there is more daily third-party comment online about *Guardian* stories than is represented in its total print circulation. Print and online broadcast communication sit side by side with network communication, adding to the total online asset of the newspaper.

This changed environment would suggest there is a new aspect to public relations. The practitioner, it seems, now needs to consider the organization's internet strategy. This is a discipline beyond the organization's web presence, social media presence and local presence, and is a discipline in its own right.

There is another phenomenon. The internet has added to the range of communication interactions available to people. We all understand communication between two people as one-to-one communication. This may be a chat with a mate in the pub or online instant messaging and e-mail. Great orators, newspaper editors and web masters can address and publish to mass audiences, which we understand as one-to-many communication. More difficult is a process of communication when many speak to many. But with the internet this is possible. It can be achieved by using e-mail and the writable web, notably wikis, where (in theory at least) anyone can initiate, write, read, change and comment on any content. The internet facilitates many-to-many communication. However, it goes further. There is growing use of many-to-one communication. RSS feeds, by which immediate alerts wing through cyberspace as soon as the author publishes an article, and the microblogging service Twitter are two examples. In the case of the latter, developments such as a service called 'Alert Thingy' (http://alertthingy.com/1) continually feed information written by friends on Twitter, Facebook, their blogs, FriendFeed and other social media directly to the individual. Many can and do communicate to one. Many-to-one communication is a reality and is popular.

Information and knowledge has been accumulating since the beginning of time, and those who posses this knowledge have an access to power and riches. This meant that knowledge was jealously guarded, fought over and often destroyed because of its power. Today, because of the nature and original intent of the internet, knowledge is very difficult to destroy. The internet presence of organizations exposes their information globally. It is packaged and passed, stored ('cached') and accumulated on thousands of computers and accessible in a myriad of ways. It cannot be destroyed.

---

One of the authors begins teaching his undergraduate courses with the maxim that: 'Everything you do and say online is there forever and can be retrieved moments and decades later to haunt the originator into old age.' He then invites the audience to recall those oh-so-intimate 'conversations' on instant messenger with partners. He relieves the instant 'group blush' by saying that it's a mistake that most make.

Among 50 students in one class in 2006, over 30 changed their Facebook profile in the following 24 hours.

---

The nature of information is therefore significant in management of online relationships and reputation.

Computer-stored information is accessed through over a billion websites, tens of billions of web pages, e-mails and other access technologies, and via a myriad of devices. This combination has given immense power to the communicators because it allows us, as Evans and Wurster show, to separate things, such as the head office, and information, such as the corporate intranet or wiki, and make the information available to all.[4]

---

### IN BRIEF

- PR, historically, provided the link between supplier and customer.
- The overt presence (promotion and interaction between an organization and its constituency) is now largely transparent across organizations and publics.
- The internet is 'in charge' of creating the context in which an organization is evident to a broad constituency.
- The context in which an organization is seen online is mostly not under the control of the organization.
- The once separate relationship between traditional and internet-driven relationships has gone.
- The value network, extending upstream to suppliers and downstream to customers, also includes the value added by third parties to the transaction, as well other tertiary contributors in a network of networks.
- Today, there are alternative forms of news distribution.
- The practitioner with 'messages' to present to a public is now confronted with this changed communications environment.

> • The practitioner now needs to consider the organization's internet strategy. This is a discipline beyond the organization's web presence, social media presence and local presence, and is a discipline in its own right.

## Notes

1. Netmedia 2000 (http://www.net-media.co.uk/survey/) and City University's Department of Journalism National survey of print and broadcast journalists. The survey was funded by Grant Butler Coomber using the Mediadisk journalists' database
2. Forrester Research (2000) eMarketplaces boost B2B trade, January 2000
3. Shirkey, C (2008) *Here Comes Everybody*, Penguin Press
4. Evans P and Wurster, W S (1999) *Blown to Bits*, Harvard Business School Press

# 8

# Information and things

One might take, as an example, a high street store as being a thing. It is a building. For the building to be of consequence, people need information. They need information to manage and run it; they need information about its purpose and location and the products sold behind its doors. Without, for example, the person who has the knowledge to open the front door to allow the store to be used, the building has little value – staff and shoppers can't get in. Such information can be kept anywhere on a computer and be available from the internet. But information about how to unlock doors can be used for many shops as well as houses and cars and so on. Most of it is not unique to any one single store. Information about the nature of keys, codes for security systems and microprocessors that set and unset alarms is not unique to any individual building. By extension, information (how to get in) can be separated from things (merchandise in the store). The value of the information (how to get in) is very high and is different from the value of the things needed by shoppers (the building and merchandise).

Information can be valuable in its own right. One cannot access products in a store without having the information needed to open the building. This makes such information valuable. It also tells us that a thing loses value when it is not associated with relevant information.

In his paper, 'The eEconomy: it's later than you think', Richard Melnicoff says:[1]

What eCommerce has allowed firms to do is to bring intangible assets to the fore – to tease out the value they add, and even to make a business of them, pure and simple. By making inter-firm collaboration easy and inexpensive, eCommerce allows intangible assets to be leveraged across a much larger buyer base. Time and space constraints no longer apply, so they no longer have to be co-located with the tangible means of production.

In other words the expert who provides internet-enabled information about keys can operate independently of the shop and make information available to householders and car manufacturers as well, opening up new markets for the related information and knowledge. In the communication field, we see newspapers publishing their news online often well ahead of the print version in order to leverage value from its publication on the website, citations in blogs, inclusion in television programmes (on- and offline) and so on. The newspaper (a thing) is now separate from the news (intangible asset).

Both as commodities and assets, intangibles such as brand equity and information are like a traditional inventory. In the same way that a company may benefit from the wealth that can be generated from a physical inventory, a corporate information inventory can be managed to access wealth.

Public relations benefits from this new environment when it provides the means by which people access information assets and can use them to benefit from both knowledge and things.

---

By deploying corporate inventory, a wide range of organizations are already providing information to the public to allow them to use this knowledge in designing bespoke products, services and even environments:

- Aston Martin is by no means the only example of a car manufacturer offering a bespoke service, but its website offers this opportunity for potential buyers (and wannabe owners). Its site offers the 'configurator': 'The Aston Martin Car Configurator lets you select and design your Aston Martin just the way you want it. You can then view your perfect car in 3D.'
- ICI Paints asks visitors: 'Want to see how a proposed colour scheme will work? Like to try out some colour alternatives and print them out for comparison? With MousePainter you can do all this at the touch of a button.'

These are capabilities made available by providing information about physical inventory in combination with corporate intellectual property and public creativity, using the internet. Such a capability offers a new form of relationship with a range of publics and is a communication tool

---

with wider PR capabilities for the creative practitioner. It is not completely wacky to imagine an organization offering journalists (among others) capability to create their own press releases online.

Information inventory that can be turned faster, that is used more frequently, can add to wealth. When it is used to access a high-value asset by a consumer or supplier, the value of this new form of inventory is also increased.

There is one big difference. When one sells ownership of inventory (a thing) it belongs to the customer. Ownership of information when shared, for financial gain or not, does not deplete the store of the corporate information inventory, or necessarily its worth. It remains and can (mostly) be used again. Many people buy holidays online. They use websites for selecting destinations, comparing prices and gleaning more information. This is done many times and is equivalent to browsing through brochures, spending time with travel agents and booking the holiday. In the 'real economy' there is a lot of cost associated with this transaction. Such costs include the brochures, travel agents, shop facilities and so forth needed for each customer. Online, there is one website that can be used many times for the same, comparatively low, cost at any time by thousands of customers sequentially or at the same time.

The same applies to an online press release – one posted on a corporate website or online distribution service versus many e-mails. Using social media press releases there is an even greater advantage when the information is made available to other interested parties such as bloggers.

Now here is the rub. Most press releases are still issued to newspapers and magazines. Their content, once published, takes on the authority of a third-party endorsement from the publication. Distribution can be enhanced through further distribution via social media such as blogs and social networks. But if the content was worthy in the first instance, is there a need for the intermediate step of publication in a newspaper or magazine? Would it not be distributed by the online community anyway? The answer is that for a number of organizations the online network effect is powerful. But this effect is only really relevant as part of a conversation. If it's interesting it will go a long way, and if it's spin it will probably die quickly. Some marketers have discovered this the hard way when trying to incentivize networks to spread the word. A good story is probably a better tool than any other incentive.

Many companies use the exposure of information in websites and through other internet-enabled devices to lever up added value. This transparency has a range of benefits. By making information available to all – that is, by exposing corporate information inventory – the company can share its information assets with most of its stakeholders. In this way the cost of moving information inventory is reduced. Instead of having to tell each public or each stakeholder group about information in turn, the company can provide information to all stakeholders in one go. Indeed, as we will argue later, there is an imperative for organizations to be more transparent.

The publication of CSR activities on corporate websites is a classic example. To be able to inform the wide range of publics likely to have an interest in ethical purchasing practices, environmental policies, charitable giving, employment practice and the like would be impossible without the internet. Today all these stakeholders can find this information at the click of a mouse and, better still, can share the information with others of a like mind by sending/posting an e-mail to a social media link like Delicious (http://delicious) in seconds.

The cost of storing information in one place (the website or database that feeds the website) is relatively low compared with having to store the information at a number of locations. The cost of maintaining web-stored information is also low. It needs to be maintained once, and not at each and every location for each stakeholder group. Furthermore, the cost of distribution is very low. It can be held in just one location to be available to all stakeholders.

## CASE STUDY: TO PRINT OF NOT TO PRINT

The cost of designing, writing and printing a brochure or catalogue is an expense that most organizations regard as a necessary evil. For some organizations, the use of PDFs has been a boon.

The essence of the argument is that if people need a printed document, it can be made available online; instead of the organization paying for the cost of printing, it is the user who pays for the process. Even in places where brochures are a necessity, the technology can be used to cut cost. Being able to print only the number of copies needed at the time means that long and often wasteful print runs can be avoided. There are a number of cases where the trade-off between information and things is used in this way.

Richard Stephenson, chairman and chief executive of online publishing specialist Yudu, argues that travel companies should continue their print runs but try to convert customers to the digital edition little by little.

> We're not 'print is dead' merchants. I would not ditch my print edition, but, if you can move a percentage of hard copy, say 20 per cent to 30 per cent, online, you can save money. Give people the option to take the digital edition, and if 30 per cent do and are happy with it, you are sending out fewer brochures. It is a bold move to ditch a glossy, beautiful brochure.

First Choice head of e-commerce Alun Williams is an advocate for that approach, and the tour-operating giant sees print and digital as supportive of each other.

> We know people are coming to our site with a (print) brochure because they are typing in their brochure code, so we see it as a marketing mechanism driving people to the retail network.

Williams adds that it is not a 'huge leap of faith' to think tour operators could slowly reduce print volumes as most people now begin their holiday research online.

According to Stephenson, producing a digital edition need not be expensive, but the cost depends on volumes and what you want to do within the brochure. He has witnessed travel companies substantially increase clicks through to the booking pages of their websites by using e-brochures.

---

This is one of the benefits of corporate wikis that have the benefit of collaboration. Here is an example. Once, the PR department kept a filing cabinet full of past press releases. If someone asked for an old press release, or worse asked about something covered in many press releases over a period of years, the process of finding, copying and posting it was long-winded and costly. Now, searching for it on the intranet and sending it by e-mail is easy, quick and cheap. Even more helpful is that anyone in the organization can do it. In addition, for well-run organizations, the information can be collected and collated by the person making the enquiry. The cost of running the press release archive has plummeted and most of the work can now be done by the person looking for the information as opposed to the practitioner.

Thus information about what stock is available inside a store can be shared with the customer, buyer, supplier and security chief. In the past, each would have needed a system and access to such information individually. Today each of the stakeholders can access the same information from a website. The cost of storing, maintaining and distributing information inventory is massively reduced and the availability empowers many more people.

In 2006 one of the authors was faced with having to keep a register of attendance for 60 undergraduates at lectures and seminars. A boring, bureaucratic activity that cut into precious teaching time.

Because the course was run primarily from a wiki, it was relatively easy to put one register on a page and get the students to enter their attendance at each lecture and seminar. The information was transparently available to all the students, providing a built-in check, and because the wiki page was available to the bureaucrats, the reporting process was eliminated and more time, in a much better atmosphere, was available for learning.

In sharing information, its wider use turns it into a commodity. Such information has value in its volume but also has costs associated with garnering, storage, processing and transfer. For example, in the past an old brochure was discarded with but a single copy held in the archive. Today every web page has potentially been bookmarked by lots of visitors. When building a new website, this entire inventory has to continue to be made available or the legacy value and relationships with stakeholders (not to mention the search engine optimization opportunity) will disappear.

In addition, some organizations can separate price and value of assets to grow markets and gain commercial advantage. In 2006, PR Newswire disconnected the relationship between the product and its price by using eBay to sell its services. It invited people to look at the value of its service instead. The consequence of its action is that the 'marketing' inside PR Newswire is now dependent on relationships and not the value chain.

Auctioning off your service may have been an interesting idea as a promotion but now the genie is out of the bottle. News release distribution costs are no longer what they seem – they are negotiable.

If information is valuable, losing it can be harmful. At what point ownership of information's value changes hands (and its value as copyright changes or passes into the value network) is a matter for wide debate. The extent to which any data, information or knowledge is vulnerable to inadvertent, accidental, careless or malicious distribution in an internet-enabled society, irrespective of the rule of law, is not in doubt. In principle there is no protection (once online, content cannot be destroyed and can be accessed moments and decades later) and the law of copyright is both inadequate and largely irrelevant to the new paradigm.

In 2008, a computer program (by a company called MediaDash – and part owned by one of the authors) captured 86 per cent of all the articles archived by Factiva using a combination of search engines. Many of the articles were behind firewalls and were defended by password-protected gateways by both Factiva and the publishers. No passwords or robot blocks were violated by this program. The developers found that all these articles were available to the general public using search engines from the list at http://www.searchenginecolossus.com.

Rothschild suggests in *Bionomics: Economy as Ecosystem* that the digital path between things and consumers is a river and, like all rivers, tends toward a straight line.[2] The digital rip-tide flows round historic information gatekeepers. They are no more than pebbles on a storm-tossed beach, temporary and exposed to the full force of the elements.

Data and information are very accessible from many sources. Information, being data relevant to its users' context, is now historically cheap and becoming more so, a trend that will continue. Managing, protecting, deploying and exposing information as content on computers and across the internet is critical to corporate relationships, reputation and profitability. In the internet era, this content is very vulnerable, and security breaches are costly for corporate reputation.

For the practitioner, this is a consideration to be included in all issues and crisis management planning and practice.

---

In 2008, nine out of 10 doctors in the United Kingdom had no confidence in the government's ability to safeguard patient data online according to a poll by *BMA News* magazine. Over 90 per cent of respondents said they were not confident patient data on the proposed NHS centralized database would be secure. The magazine said the profession's scepticism:

> appears to flow from scandals such as security breaches in the Medical Training Application System, the junior doctors' online job application service, and the HM Revenue and Customs loss of computer discs containing the details of 25 m child benefit claimants.

Online and data security is a reputation issue.

---

## IN BRIEF

- Information and things can be separated.
- Information can be valuable in its own right.
- The traditional supply chain is disrupted, with the internet acting as intermediary.
- Information is spread by many devices that are platforms for many channels of communication.
- Communications models include one-to-one, one-to-many, many-to-many.
- The internet has enabled organizations to act as customer, supplier and competitor at the same time.
- Intangible asset management allows practitioners to tease out the value they add, and even to make a business of it.
- The newspaper (a thing) is now separate from the news (intangible asset).
- Both as a commodity and an asset, intangibles such as brand equity and information are like a traditional inventory.

- Public relations benefits from this new environment when it provides the means by which people access information assets and can use them to benefit from both knowledge and things.
- Online, one website can be used many times for the same cost at any time by thousands of customers sequentially or at the same time, and at a lower price than creating brochures and print collateral.
- To be able to inform the wide range of CSR publics likely to have an interest would be impossible without the internet.
- The cost of running the press release archive has plummeted when it is available, and searchable, online.
- Managing, protecting, deploying and exposing information as content on computers and across the internet is critical to corporate relationships, reputation and profitability. In the internet era, this content is very vulnerable, and security breaches are costly for corporate reputation.

## Notes

1. Melnicoff, R M (1999) The eEconomy: it's later than you think, *Outlook*, **21**, pp 33–43 (Anderson Consulting)
2. Rothschild, R M (1995) *Bionomics: Economy as Ecosystem*, Henry Holt

# 9

# Knowledge

For some organizations, inherent knowledge is viewed as a considerable asset because of its capacity to change something or somebody.[1]

Microsoft proposes that people gain knowledge from their experiences and their peers' expertise, as well as from analysis of business data such as sales and financial reports.[2] As the internet becomes more pervasive we see wider evidence of exchanges of experience, ideas, insights, values and judgements, and widespread collaboration within organizational intranets and beyond into the internet. The use of this phenomenon, using what is called 'open source collaboration', by organizations such as BMW, Goldcorp and Procter & Gamble is transforming their business model and reducing development time and time to market, as described by Tapscott and Williams in their book *Wikinomics*.[3]

The use of e-mail, newsgroups and discussion lists, wikis, chat, blogs and other channels is now widespread in business.

'Today,' reports Microsoft, 'an individual's contribution to a firm is in the creation of new knowledge through collaboration with others and in synthesizing existing information and data.'

For some, and for Microsoft (with not a little self-interest), the exchange of knowledge is seen as being wholly desirable. Once, the differentiation between information and its application in the form of knowledge was the distinguishing feature for many organizations. It provided the foundation for more than a few companies to declare that 'our most valuable asset is our people'. No more. Knowledge is just as easily transferred across the internet as information. The half-life of knowledge is becoming shorter. Its potency expires almost as soon as it is conceived. But with wider engagement, knowledge can be turned into new forms of asset.

Google Maps Mania is a popular blog that lists news and examples of websites integrated with Google Maps. It reports a multitude of services, ranging from mapping popular fish species to finding and rating local nightclubs, to sharing information about GPS bike trails. The bloggers are not employed by Google but they do use something called an API (application programming interface) and the products/services they provide, called 'mashups', which seem to be everywhere.

Nearly 12,000 applications (not a few devised for PR campaigns) used the Facebook API Platform between May and December 2007; according to Adonomics those applications were used over 36 million times in a 24-hour period in December that year.

By engaging with everybody, organizations find many enthusiasts to enrich their products at virtually no cost, adding to the total fund of knowledge available to the organization. The most valuable asset for them is no longer just employees but an engaged public that includes employees.

Expertise in the form of knowledgeable people is becoming a commodity. It is not unreasonable to say that, unless an organization is extremely fortunate, every knowledgeable expert inside the company has many published counterparts across the internet. This means that, potentially, everything and every person dependent on information and its application (as even elemental units of resource are) becomes vulnerable in the internet era, when standardized forms of communication create the transparent means for both information and knowledge exchange and application throughout all areas of enterprise.[4] Collaboration with other experts in the creation of new knowledge and insights changes this threat into an opportunity. The value of the internal experts lies in their ability to collaborate, and collaboration requires communication expertise available from an informed practitioner such as the PR person. We dealt with some aspects of this earlier when discussing transparency and the porous nature of modern organizations.

Trinity Mirror started 'reverse publishing' free newspapers filled with stories gleaned from its 'hyper-local citizen journalism websites' in the North East of England. The *Teesside Gazette* established a series of experimental citizen journalism sites, based around local postcodes, in December 2006. In 2007, the paper rolled out a further five, bringing the total number of sites to 20.

The success of the pilot project has led the *Gazette* to publish, and distribute free to homes, six ad-supported print newspapers that contain a mixture of *Gazette* editorial and citizen journalism from its leading local websites.

Add information and knowledge to computing capacity obeying More's Law, use technology to enrich content interactivity and drama with growing bandwidth, and the exposure of information and knowledge becomes exciting for the information and knowledge consumer as well as the provider.[5]

Protecting knowledge, keeping it safe, is a major issue for many companies.[6] But as we saw when discussing transparency in Chapter 3, knowing where to draw the line is important. Comparing competitors in the same sector reveals how different organizations offer up more or less information to appeal to internet audiences. Protecting information can detract from corporate appeal; it can show an apparent lack of expertise or understanding, or evoke a sensation of secrecy. Organizations compete on the exposure of their expertise as well as their ability to protect vital information and access.

This means that there is a strategic public relations role in developing corporate transparency policies for organizations. Does the practitioner help the organization develop policies to lever up the values of open communication, or is the PR role one of maintaining the walled garden round intellectual properties? These are big issues for corporate and public affairs managers.

The Round Earth Project is investigating how virtual reality technology can be used to help teach concepts that are counterintuitive to a learner's currently held mental model.[7] Virtual reality (machine-generated environments) can be used to provide an alternative cognitive starting point that does not carry the baggage of past experiences. It can be used across the internet and opens up the possibility of changing long-held ideas and beliefs. At its best, it is an aid to education and a marketing tool in its infancy; at its worst, a dictator's dream machine!

In Chapter 19 we discuss the immersive nature of the internet from evolutionary and psychological standpoints; in discussing the (near and distant) future development of the internet and society, we see a role for virtual reality technology.

Betchtel, the UK Government's Department of Transport, Microsoft, BP, Royal Bank of Scotland and the auction house Christie's all have one form of communication in common. The medical profession also is using computer-generated images for surgery and, like all these organizations, uses virtual environments for imagery and communication. Yet none of them uses Second Life.

Some of these manifestations are 'walk-in' 3D representations and others are PC based, but they have in common an ability to create an almost believable virtual space.

And lying behind these developments are the computer programs that now write new computer programs, and the supercomputer centres around the world that are linking up over the internet to create a new generation of enormously powerful machines.[8]

Is all this irrelevant for PR applications? No – such developments are already helping the PR industry. In ongoing research from 2006, one of the authors of this book began experimenting with a form of computerized text analysis of news stories. The program was found to be capable of re-interpreting news. It is one of the algorithms used in summarization of extensive news archives by the media analysis company Echo Research. The work continues to project forward, with some degree of certainty, future news trends. There is much work to be done in this field but it is not beyond the realm of possibility that such programs will be used in PR for planning and managing news both from mainstream media and social media in the foreseeable future.

Part of the program was designed such that the content would re-programme the software on the fly. Today its application is in use to identify key and emerging topics in the news by Echo Research, and it holds promise for further, even more helpful applications. The prospect of being able to identify the news agenda several days or even weeks ahead with some degree of confidence would seem like nirvana in some realms of PR practice.

In this chapter we have looked at how much the world has changed because of the internet and how that change is already fundamentally affecting organizations. This is no future dream. It is today's reality for many organizations and is a very strong indicator of the extent and rate of change facing the PR industry as well as corporate management. For many practitioners it calls for a radical re-think of their role and work. In corporate relations this chapter may well form the basis for a further researched presentation to the board.

---

**IN BRIEF**

- People gain knowledge from their experiences and their peers' expertise.
- As the internet becomes more pervasive we see wider evidence of exchanges of experience, ideas, insights, values and judgements, and widespread collaboration within organizational intranets and beyond into the internet.
- The use of e-mail, newsgroups and discussion lists, wikis, chat, blogs and other channels is now widespread in business.
- Once, the differentiation between information and its application in the form of knowledge was the distinguishing feature for many organizations.
- It provided the foundation for more than a few companies to declare that 'our most valuable asset is our people'. No more.
- Every knowledgeable expert inside the company has many published counterparts across the internet.
- The value of internal experts lies in their ability to collaborate. Many organizations make intellectual properties freely available to allow third parties to extend the value of IP.
- Collaboration requires communication expertise available from an informed practitioner such as the PR person.
- Protecting knowledge, keeping it safe, is a major issue for many companies.
- Protecting information can detract from corporate appeal; it can show an apparent lack of expertise or understanding or evoke a sensation of secrecy. Organizations compete on the exposure of their expertise as well as their ability to protect vital information and access.
- There is a strategic public relations role in developing corporate transparency policies for organizations.
- Acquisition of information tends to overcome obstacles that raise transparency issues.
- Virtual environments are being deployed as communications channels in many ways.
- Computer programs that are self programming, so-called artificial intelligence, are already being used in the public relations industry.

## Notes

1.  'Knowledge is information that changes something or somebody – either by becoming grounds for actions, or by making an individual (or an institution) capable of different or more effective action' (Drucker, P F, *The New Realities*, 1989, Harper & Row)
2.  Practicing knowledge management: turning experience and information into results – the Microsoft knowledge management strategy – White Paper, http://www.infoperpus.8m.com/artikel/00006.htm (accessed 24 October 2008)

### How Knowledge Grows

Knowledge has its roots in three primary areas, all of which must be considered when developing a knowledge management solution. People gain knowledge from their experiences and their peers' expertise, as well as from the analysis of business data such as sales and financial reports. Through the synthesis of these three elements, new knowledge is created and opportunities are shaped. Effective knowledge management strategies manage and foster all of these sources of new knowledge.

**Business data** is generally characterized as a set of discrete facts about events and the world. Most organizations capture significant amounts of data in highly structured databases, such as ERP and MRP line-of-business systems. In addition, most firms subscribe to external data sources that provide demographic information, competitive statistics and other market information. The core value-building activity around business data is the ability to analyse, synthesize and then transform the data into information and knowledge.

**Information** is the outcome of capturing and providing context to experiences and ideas. Information, or explicit experiences, is typically stored in semi-structured content such as documents, e-mail, voice mail and multimedia. The core value-building activity around information is managing the content in a way that makes it easy to find, reuse and learn from experiences so that mistakes are not repeated and work isn't duplicated.

**Knowledge** is composed of the tacit experiences, ideas, insights, values and judgments of individuals. It is dynamic and can only be accessed through direct collaboration and communication with experts who have the knowledge. Knowledge management systems must provide the cultural incentives for sharing the personal experiences that have historically constituted an individual's value to a firm. Today, an individual's contribution to a firm is in the creation of new knowledge through collaboration with others and in synthesizing existing information and data.

3. Tapscott, D and Williams A D (2006) *Wikinomics*, Atlantic Books
4. The standards for the internet are provided by the World Wide Web Consortium (http://www.w3.com)
5. Gordon More, when chairman of Intel, observed that it is possible to double the number of transistor circuits etched onto a computer chip every 18 months, a phenomenon that has held good for 50 years and is being extended well beyond his vision to 2010

   Forward Concepts believes that the growing number of resources on the web that take advantage of, or indeed require, broadband access, combined with growing public awareness and falling connection prices, have improved the long-term potential for broadband deployment in North America. Its report provides calibration on the broadband access markets of tomorrow by examining the applications that are driving the business (http://www.forwardconcepts.com)
6. For information on security, see PriceWaterhouseCoopers' white paper, http://www.pwcglobal.com/extweb
7. At the Electronic Visualization Laboratory, University of Illinois at Chicago (http://www.evl.uic.edu, accessed July 2008)
8. Reported by the BBC, June 2000 (http://news.bbc.co.uk/hi/english/sci/tech/newsid_806000/806410.stm)

# 10

# Commercial implications of the internet

The internet is affecting corporate success and economies, and will be even more powerful in changing them. The commercial implications are immense and of the near future. In announcing the Seoul Declaration on the Future of the Internet Economy, OECD Secretary-General Angel Gurría said: '[the] infrastructure has become critical to our economies and societies.'[1]

As for the international community, so too for national economies and those who have a powerful role to play. This includes the public relations community and extends across all those disciplines affected by the Declaration, including business, civil society and technical expertise involved in promoting competition, and empowering and protecting consumers.

When Vinton G Cerf, Vice-President and Chief Internet Evangelist for Google and one of the two inventors of the internet, gave the Information Technologists' Lecture at City University London in April 2008, his last slide showed what he called the inter-planetary internet. It showed that the evolution of the internet has only just started. Cerf also pointed out to the US Senate Committee on the Judiciary in June 2006 that the internet has become a platform for innovation.

These are clear messages for public relations practice. Involvement by PR is critical to the future success of economic and social development through facilitating these opportunities and for application for the profession. For PR practitioners, this offers exciting new frontiers in management, communication and, even more significantly, relationships.

The biggest single economic contribution the internet makes is at a very human level. It allows individuals with common interests and values to come together to exchange ideas and information. Among these many interactions new products and services emerge, from dog-walking circles to enterprises as big as Google. In addition, traditional businesses lever up value through their online presence. It is PR's business to optimize these opportunities.

The internet has transformed global economies and continues to do so. Its impact on micro- and macro-economics is huge. An IMRG Capgemini E-Retail report noted that online UK retail sales amounted to £26.5 billion in the first six months of 2008, up 38 per cent from the same period in the previous year, and projected online retail sales would be between 30 and 50 per cent by 2011.[2]

This is a problem for many PR practitioners. They too use the internet in many ways and need to be aware, from an expert communications practitioner point of view, of how much these changes affect the nature of communication.

The internet is a considerable contributor in saving cost, stimulating economic growth and raising productivity.

---

There are many studies of the economic impact of the internet. For example, the Connected Nation study in the United States in 2008 provides a simple demonstration:

> In the USA a seven percentage point increase in broadband adoption could annually result in: $92 billion through 2.4 million jobs created or saved; $662 million saved in reduced healthcare costs; $6.4 billion saving from unnecessary driving; $18 million in carbon credits; $35.2 billion from three hours saved from accessing broadband at home and $134 billion per year in total direct economic impact of accelerating broadband across the United States.

BT estimated in 2004 that the use of ICT-enabled teleworkers allows the company to save over £60 million per year. According to the OECD:

> Canada, Ireland, the United Kingdom and Switzerland have the largest share of businesses purchasing via the internet, with about half of all businesses doing so. New Zealand, the United Kingdom and Denmark have the largest share selling goods or services via the Internet (over one-third of all businesses) (Source: OECD, ICT database and Eurostat, Community Survey on ICT usage in enterprises, April 2007).

While researching this book, its authors noted a progressive increase in online comments about brands in social media. Until the autumn of 2007, the number of posts for typical organizations was not huge but progressively building. Then, between October and November, the number of posts for a cross-section of organizations, showed a remarkable change. Use of these media showed progressive growth rising to near exponential growth. The key issue was not the number of posts but the rate of increase in the numbers. The exposure of corporate and consumer brands to third-party comment was changing (Figure 10.1). This third-party influence is adding coverage at minimal cost.

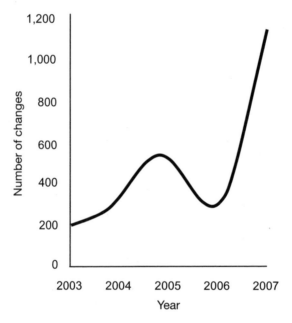

**Figure 10.1**  *Average rate of change in blog posts for five non-technical companies – a random but typical profile from David Phillips' eFootprint™ research*

Triangulating the results of Google, Yahoo! and MSN in 2008 revealed that the low-price airline easyJet had a website with 14,300 pages, and 150,000 other web pages had hyperlinks into its site where the online community had made explicit relationship links with the company. However, there were 10 million other web pages mentioning the company that were available and visible to the normal user of the web. This online presence is a corporate asset. Seldom seen on a balance sheet, this 'goodwill' in-tangible asset is very significant for the company's future success. These millions of page impressions – far transcending traditional media coverage – provide a simple measure of the extent of reputation and are, for the most part, beyond the control of the company. Indeed such is their extent that it would be impossible to review each one. The speed with which this digital footprint had grown is astonishing, but common to most established brands. According to the search engine Alltheweb, 80 per cent of the mentions (page impressions) were less than four years old.

Online content mediates a huge part of commercial interactions.

For most retailers online interaction is their biggest sales opportunity, with the lowest overheard and highest ROI. Research by Hitwise (http://www.Hitwise.co.uk) indicated that social networking site MySpace is responsible for more traffic flow into the HMV website than both the Yahoo and MSN search engines. A study from DoubleClick (www.doubleclick.com) suggests that the web is the most influential medium in shaping consumers' purchasing decisions, with shoppers using it at every stage of transactions, from initial awareness to final purchase.

Among the 175 million websites in the world, some of the most visited are major retailers. For example Tesco is ranked number 32, Apple 33 and HSBC 39. These are staggering figures; we are talking of billions of online interactions, dwarfing the footfall of even the largest shopping centres.

Let us consider the investment in a store that delivers (let's say the industry average in 2007) 15 per cent of all turnover, an investment that costs less than all the other stores, has more visitors than any other store, and encourages people into every other store as well. It should be the focus for high investment, top management involvement and very careful PR. Well, that store, for Tesco, Apple and HSBC, is online.

In addition consideration should be given to the corporate site, or that part that is given over to corporate matters. This site will almost certainly be the busiest area of corporate interactions, far exceeding the footfall in the company headquarters. The financial implication is clear: the online corporate site should represent an investment commensurate with its importance if it is to have the impact on reputation that a good headquarters has.

The commercial significance of the internet is evident from the knowledge that four of the 15 members of the Tesco Board are technologically savvy and two have first-hand experience of online commerce.

In 2007, Enquiro Search Solutions published the results of a business-to-business purchasing survey of 1,086 B2B participants seeking to purchase online in Canada. Its findings were striking, and are supported by other, less complete, research. The Enquiro study found that 51 per cent made their purchase online:

- 55 per cent of purchases were under $10,000.
- 31 per cent were for over $100,000. (That is still a large percentage of big purchases.)
- Over 70 per cent of B2B purchasers started out by using a search engine.
- Only 12 per cent of purchasers had their vendor-of-choice website bookmarked at the start of their search.
- By the purchase phase, 80.7 per cent were able to type the vendor website URL directly into their browser or had it bookmarked.
- The internet was used by the majority of respondents at every stage of the transaction, including initial awareness, product research, during negotiation and in the purchasing process.

---

It was once said that some retailers would always be immune from the need to be involved in online shopping. Fashion houses in particular believed that people still wanted to try clothes on in shops. How wrong they had been became apparent as Tesco joined House of Frazer to sell clothes online. The UK-based internet fashion retailer ASOS defied the weak consumer-spending environment of 2008, reporting a 176 per cent increase in full year pre-tax profits that year. As most retailers bemoaned falling sales in traditional shops, ASOS made underlying pre-tax profits of £8.2m for the year to 31 March, compared with £3m for the same period in the previous year. Overall revenues rose 90 per cent to £81m. This was around double the rate of the overall online marketing and was set against an overall cut in annual retail growth of 2.2 per cent.

---

Fleishman-Hillard published research in June 2008 showing that the internet has roughly double the influence of the second-strongest medium – television – and roughly eight times the influence of traditional print media. In addition, the research indicated, consumers use the internet in different ways to make different decisions. For example, consumers are more likely to seek opinions of others through social media and product-rating sites when making decisions that have a great deal of personal impact (eg healthcare options or major electronics purchases), but use company-controlled sources when making transactional decisions on commoditized items like utilities or airline tickets.

With these changes taking place, there is an imperative for re-training in PR to take full advantage of the economic reality of media relations versus online interaction to optimize the financial returns of employers.

In the United Kingdom, online retail purchasing was making great headway as this book went to print. It was not as evident in other countries, notably the United States.

- The Pearson education and media empire has focused on technology developments for a number of years. During the economic downturn it achieved strong financial results that showed the strategy is working. Pearson, which owns the Financial Times newspaper group, Penguin publishing and Pearson Education, reported a growth in sales of 14 per cent and operating profits of £124 million in July 2008.
- TNS Worldpanel revealed that home shopping sales at the supermarket ASDA jumped 71.8 per cent year-on-year in the period to 15 June 2008. Tesco had a 31.3 per cent share of the market, Asda 16.9 per cent and Sainsbury's 15.9 per cent.
- Mothercare highlighted a 28 per cent jump in internet sales as one of the big drivers behind its 21 per cent increase in group sales in the 15 weeks to 11 July 2008.
- Fast-food takeaway chain Domino's Pizza UK broke the 20 per cent mark in online sales for the half year ended 29 June 2008 – meaning a fifth of its pizzas are now ordered over the web.
- Music, films and games retailer HMV reported that online sales made up 10 per cent of total sales by value in 2008.
- A Populus poll for *The Times* in July 2008 found economic concerns were forcing three out of five people to cut back on holidays, with a fifth cancelling trips. Yet the accommodation-only supplier Seligo reported a rise in online sales of 50 per cent.

The non-retailing sector is also commercially influenced by the internet, showing a trend across a wider range of internet influences on business.

A survey in June 2008 amongst NHS and private practitioners by Mobilis Healthcare, one of the United Kingdom's larger medical suppliers, revealed a trend towards purchasing healthcare supplies via the internet. Whilst 50 per cent still viewed catalogues as their main source of product information, while occasionally searching the web for specific purchases, 32 per cent viewed technology as integral to practice, using the internet as an important means of sourcing information and purchasing supplies.

According to the IPA Bellwether survey in the second quarter of 2008, 19 per cent of companies reported a rise in their internet promotion budgets, while 12 per cent revealed they had cut their spending on this area. This is set against 15 per cent of firms reporting a rise in overall budgets and 27 per cent showing a decrease.

B2B publisher Centaur, which publishes titles including *The Lawyer*, *Marketing Week* and *The Engineer*, recorded double-digit growth in digital revenues in 2008.

Political campaigns are driven by wide-ranging, informed and (even globally) connected constituents. Political PR is being affected by the internet.
Success in politics is now highly influenced by the online activities of
political institutions, but services to support practitioners are comparatively
cheap compared with a decade before.

---

Dods, the political information, public affairs and policy communication
company, at its website http://www.epolitix.com, provides free to access
to leading political magazines such as *The House Magazine* and *The Parliamentary Monitor*. It has information about political figures and provides
up-to-the-minute political and parliamentary news – covering events in
Westminster, the Scottish parliament, the assemblies in Wales and London,
and the European parliament, as well as developments in Northern
Ireland.

It is a platform for exchanging views on all the latest political developments, inviting the public to add their comments on its blog, and it hosts
specialist public affairs websites for companies, charities and other organizations that want to put across their latest public affairs messages.

In the past a public affairs department would need a significant research
capability and would only get a fraction of the content available on this
site.

Because the service is an aggregation of many sources and because a
lot of people need and want to contribute content, high-value and (comparatively) low-cost content is now available to a much wider market.

The commercial impact on PR services in this case is self-evident.

---

The commercial significance of CSR becomes evident when looking at its
application among leading companies. Corporate information, notably
about social responsibility, corporate policies and performance are accessed
online much more than from any other single source.

---

In their report for an IBM Institute for Business Value study entitled
'Attaining sustainable growth through corporate social responsibility',
George Pohle and Jeff Hittner provided analysis that led them to three
dynamics that companies should understand and act upon in dealing with
CSR. These dynamics are:

- impact on business – from cost to growth;
- information – from visibility to transparency;
- relationships – from containment to engagement.

---

In their introduction they point out that:

> Just as the Internet has triggered lasting change in the structures of industry and the ways in which industries can create value, the ubiquitous connectivity in place today has already caused an enduring shift in the relationship between an enterprise and its customers, employees, and partners. That's because massive amounts of information – and opinions – about companies, their products and practices, are available in every part of the globe, every minute of every day.
>
> And because the internet is now a place where people congregate to discuss and organize social actions, the balance of power between business and society has shifted toward society and away from business.

Pohle and Hittner point to the M&S CSR programme initiated by Dr Mike Barry called 'Plan A', an integrated strategy that has over a quarter of a million pages online, including online media coverage and YouTube videos, and notably comprising mostly stakeholder comment and contribution, a massive brand promotion for the company at a relatively low cost.

Discrepancies in information bring about loss of confidence, trust and reputation, and cause breakdowns in relationships. If this happens, the organization forgoes the potential to benefit from the advantages the internet offers. The commercial disadvantage brought about by conflicting information is exacerbated because of the scrutiny of many actors, not just a few inquisitive journalists. According to research by Lenny and Oppenheim, 'since 1990 the web has spurred the growth of more than 100,000 new citizen groups devoted to social and political issues'.[3] This is in addition to individual investigations by people using search engines.

Activism is now low cost for high impact, but in a way it is threatened. The coalescence of activist organizations into mass movements is now subject to the network effect. The message changes as it passes through the network even if the sentiment is the same. For some organizations, this dilution of a 'Four legs good, two legs bad' campaigning style into a myriad of conversations about the range of problems besetting constituents can easily be missed until the groundswell of opinion is unstoppable. Equally, it is very hard for activists to see how effective their efforts have been.

Trust is a key element in online relationships and there are two online elements.[4] One is the trust an online presence such as a website or a blog is accredited with by internet agents. For example a link from the BBC website, with the huge numbers of other sites (blog posts, social network links, etc) linking to it, will enhance a website's reputation more than a link from a lesser website, with fewer inbound linked and therefore less 'credible' sites. 'High-value' links into a website are very important and add to visibility in many ways.

Such metrics mean that a site referenced by the BBC gains placement in search engines like Google (the internet search engine and agent). There are many such agents and not all of them are search engines.[5] The quality of trustworthy content, links and search engine optimization of organizational presence brings organizations' values to the attention of more people and offers competitive advantage.

The other form of trust enhancement comes from people offering ratings and opinions about products or services online. Well-known examples include Yahoo, eBay, BizRate, Epinion and Amazon, and there are less mechanistic inputs by people whose online comments carry weight in praise or deprecation in online networks and social media. Because of the network effect, of which more later, the influence of word of mouth is very significant. A story by one person linked to a group online and thence to other groups can be all but invisible when none of the participants has a huge following. But the reach of such a story can be, and very often is, greater than any single on- or offline high-reach medium. The story spreads like a virus and often only becomes apparent by assiduous monitoring or when it moves from the online network to broadcast media.

The Chartered Institute of Public Relations' report on the work and re-search by the UK PR industry Internet Commission was entitled *The Death of Spin*. The reason for this title is germane. 'Spin', wherever practised, inevitably finds its way into the information-hungry, networked, internet and is thereafter a threat to relationships, a hidden canker in the network and latent threat to the survival of the organization. Untruths, half-truths, hype and extravagant claims become reputation time bombs.

---

WikiScanner is a relatively new site that will track the edits made on Wikipedia. The purpose of this service is to see who's behind edits that are made, and how these actions can be exploited by self-interested corporations hoping to promote and protect brand identities. Created by CalTech student Virgil Griffith, WikiScanner searches the records in Wikipedia and cross-references them with public and private domain information to identify the people making edits on the online encyclopaedia.

A number of PR practitioners were surprised to discover that these technologies had made their sometimes covert and often overblown changes for clients very transparent, at a reputational cost to both consultant and client.

---

This is why organizations and practitioners need to apply professional, ethical public relations discipline to relationship management both online and offline. Ethics in internet public relations is not a bolt-on, nice-to-have option; it is critical to survival. As Philippa Foster Back, Director of the Institute of Business Ethics, puts it: 'In an era when one ethical lapse can significantly affect an entire company's reputation, fostering a culture where ethical issues and challenges are openly discussed and dealt with is critical.'[6] This would imply that internal exchanges about ethics in organizations are important and, because of internet porosity, probably would benefit from being a public discourse.

---

GlaxoSmithKlyne is quite open about its ethics policies. Its website sets out very specific policies, including this statement:

> Through the programme the Corporate Ethics and Compliance staff provide oversight and guidance to ensure compliance with applicable laws, regulations, and company policies, and to foster a positive, ethical work environment for all employees (http://www.gsk.com/about/corp-gov-ethics.htm).

---

There are many ways an organization's public relations practitioner will communicate using internet technologies. Many are explored in some depth in this book. But the internet also brings public relations closer to the heart of corporate re-engineering, corporate governance, corporate and brand relationships, reputation promotion and issues management.

What will rapidly become apparent in this book is that there are very few, if any, methods for communication that are the exclusive domain of the public relations practitioner. Today, the internet has put communications tools and techniques, once the unique preserve of a few professions, into the hands of everyone with a modem and a computer. The concepts of one-to-one, one-to-many, many-to-many and many-to-one laid down in 'new PR' are very important to modern PR practice.

---

The range of communications opportunities available includes community media that give individuals and community groups a 'voice' they might not otherwise have had. These developments are extremely sustainable as they are supported by open source (mostly free) software applications developed at the University of Teesside, and other free or inexpensive solutions. Each community group takes ownership of its own content creation and provides sound and video archives, recovers old or lost content and makes it available online. All ages, both sexes and most cultures are included in the scope of this project (http://www.tvcm.co.uk/).

---

One of the reasons that practitioners need to be very proficient in their use of internet communication is that it is very competitive. Reports by Neilsen Online revealed that in the year to May 2008, Britons spent a total of almost 34 billion minutes on websites and internet-related applications on average each month, but, despite the diversity of online content, just 10 sites accounted for 30 per cent of all the time Britons spent online. The big communications problem is that the top 10 sites are different for each of over 30 million people. The commercial advantage of being evident has been shown above; the commercial cost of being effective is higher than most imagine.

According to a joint Department of Trade and Industry and Chartered Institute of Public Relations report, public relations is part of and affects a significant part of the UK economy.[7] To continue to be a significant contributor, the industry has to be part of the internet revolution.

---

### IN BRIEF

- Understanding the internet is essential for commercial success.
- It is pervasive and offers new freedoms to operate.
- The amount of information about companies on their websites and associated websites is dwarfed by content provided by third parties.
- The growth in content, and notably privately generated content, is accelerating very fast.
- Internet audiences are huge, questioning and inquisitive.
- There are very low barriers to entry to facilities for being a content creator, aggregator or commenter. As a result a high proportion of the population adds content.
- A high proportion of consumer and commercial purchasing is undertaken online.
- Online, commercial and consumer information affects purchasing decisions.
- Trust, ethics and transparency are very important.
- Communication and use of effective communication techniques are no longer the exclusive preserve of PR practice; they are publicly available to all.
- The commercial implications are significant to the practice of public relations.

---

# Notes

1.  Shaping policies for creativity, confidence and convergence in the digital world, http://www.oecd.org/site/0,3407,en_21571361_38415463_ 1_1_1_1_1,00.html (accessed 2008)
2.  IMRG Press Release (2008) IMRG/Capgemini e-Retail Sales Index July 2008, 17 July, http://www.imrg.org/8025741F0065E9B8/ (httpPressReleases)/4BEFF910677F5D27802574A3004F8FCE? OpenDocument&view=archive
3.  Sheila, M, Mendonca, L T and Oppenheim, J M (2006) When social issues become strategic, *The McKinsey Quarterly*, 2
4.  Chang, E, Hussain, F. and Dillon, T (2006) *Trust and Reputation for Service-oriented Environments: Technologies for building business intelligence and consumer confidence*, Wiley
5.  S. D. Ramchurn, C. Sierra, L. Godo and N. R. Jennings identified this trust, reputation and confidence combination in their paper 'A computational trust model for multi-agent interactions based on confidence and reputation', included in the Proceedings of the 6th International Workshop of Deception, Fraud and Trust in Agent Societies (2003), pp 69–75, Melbourne, Australia
6.  Institute of Business Ethics (2008) Surveying staff on ethical matters, a good practice guide from The Institute of Business Ethics, 31 July
7.  *Unlocking the Potential of Public Relations*, a joint report by the Chartered Institute of Public Relations and Department of Trade and Industry, http://www.ipr.org.uk/unlockpr/

# 11

# People's use of the internet as media

## HOW DO PEOPLE INTERACT WITH THE INTERNET?

To begin to understand how practitioners begin to optimize the commercial advantage opened up by the internet, it is important to have a view of the nature of these media and how and why they are important to publics. Put another way, how do people interact with the internet?

The major considerations are platforms for communication (Chapter 13), channels for communication (see Chapter 14) and the context for communication (Figure 11.1):

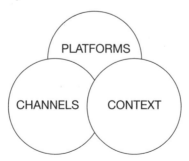

**Figure 11.1**   *The three elements of online public relations*

- Platforms are the devices we use to access the internet and its knowledge. These may be a mobile phone, PC, laptop, computer game, television set, in-car entertainment, e-poster, e-book or many other things now and in the future.
- Channels include the means by which we access information, like SMS, e-mail, instant messaging, websites, social networks (like MySpace and Bebo), blogs, Twitter (micro-blogs), wikis, virtual environments and dozens more (see Chapter 2).
- The context is important too. Is access at home, travelling, at work, in company, alone; when interactivity is easy or hard; in different moods; in different time zones and places and when time is at a premium or not?

What is more, as we discuss in Chapter 17, each of these three elements interacts with the others. For example, a web page will look different on a mobile phone from its appearance on a PC, writing an e-mail on a mobile is harder than on a laptop, and looking at an e-poster using in-car entertainment while driving is illegal.

## THE INTERNET IS ABOUT THE EXCHANGE OF INFORMATION – AND SO IS PUBLIC RELATIONS

The internet is creating its own society.[1] It reaches billions of people, each with a range of interests, and each with unprecedented connectivity.[2] Ordinary people can and do interact with each other and a whole range of institutions all the time.[3] They are also adding 'richness' to the information they exchange.[4] The internet is about mass audiences and small groups working, communicating and playing across many cultures that are at the same time both local and global.

Quite simply, the public relations practitioner may be involved in online public relations because the internet is important to people, as a report by Dutton, diGennaro and Hargrave has shown.[5] Their research found that the internet is either important or very important to a majority of people. More than seven in 10 people believe the internet is making life better. They say it saves them time, and 60 per cent of users multi-task (eg listen to music, watch TV or phone someone while online). People use the internet to get information (74 per cent), to e-mail friends (71 per cent), to get school information (51 per cent) and to shop (45 per cent), Almost half – 42 per cent – go online for work.

Only 3 per cent of users believe the internet is not important to their lives, while 70 per cent view it as important or very important (which is more than for even mobile phones at 41 per cent), and 76 per cent believe that people should be able to express their views online.

The work of three academics, Stephen Ward (Oxford), Rachel Gibson (Leicester) and Wainer Lusoli (Chester) has shown that while people are reading more news online, the UK audience for television news bulletins declined by 10 per cent between 1994 and 2005, with a 25 per cent decline among young people. Similarly, total national newspaper readership had dropped by 25 per cent over the previous 40 years, with one-third fewer people regularly reading a national newspaper now than 20 years ago. It seems that attention is moving away from the traditional heartland of public relations practice.

---

In 2007, the *Daily Telegraph* moved from Canary Wharf to Waterloo. The facilities are extraordinary. There are 500 journalists in a 67,000 sq ft open plan office with two screens per desk and a lot of technology beside. These facilities may be a revolution in their own right but, according to Chris Lloyd, who worked on the project from its inception to implementation, the biggest change was cultural. News and other content are published all the time and do not wait for the presses. The incoming content goes to the website immediately. In addition, journalists blog, proffer opinion on breaking news to 'Telegraph TV', record podcasts and use Twitter. The communications channels in use grow, morph and change all the time.

Other media houses are following suit. *The Guardian* and the BBC are both following this example.

---

Neil Thurman, a senior lecturer at City University, says that Americans make up an average of 36 per cent of the online audience for British news websites, with up to 39 per cent of readers coming from other overseas destinations. That means that as few as one in four readers hails from the United Kingdom (but UK online readership is nevertheless huge).[6]

Meanwhile online page views have escalated, with Guardian Unlimited in 2007 garnering 16 million each month, a trend that is now common across most newspapers, magazines and business journals.

---

The implications for press relations, that staple of the PR consultancy, are pretty stark. The medium that is their bread and butter is shrinking and is becoming a conduit for putting editorial, and by implication PR output, online. In addition, as we have seen, the online media encourage people to share their stories in social media information sharing websites.

As one PR consultant blogger noted:

During a recent wander round the press day of the British Motor Show, I kept coming across these well-groomed, smartly dressed people talking to one-man-band camera crews. Now the motor industry and the Motor Show in particular suffers from a distinct lack of mainstream media coverage – the boys from housewife's favourite *Top Gear* wouldn't be seen dead there. So who were these TV stars? Well, they were good old-fashioned journos from the car magazines. At the last Show they were slouching around in t-shirts and jeans, now they seem to own irons and have found the addresses of their hairdressers...

Remember they are not increasing budgets at these magazines to support this, just some serious multi-tasking – as an aside we have come a long way from the Wapping riots and what a journalist does nowadays haven't we? – So how can we help? Well first we need to appreciate that journalists are under pressure to get copy to website first, so the usual issues of speed, access and accuracy are key.

At the same time, the process of exchanging corporate information through the value network adds another dimension to many-to-many, many-to-machines and machine-to-many data, information and knowledge transmissions. We are seeing business-to-business (B2B) communication increasingly migrating to the internet for a host of reasons, and this is happening very fast. Beyond the commercial sector, a huge amount of personal and community information is becoming available through web-publishing platforms, and thus available at the click of a mouse.

# THE NATURE OF INTERNET PRACTICE

For a discipline that is all about communication, PR has been surprisingly slow to adopt the internet as a core component of practice. Some of the reasons why there is an urgent reason to make up for lost time are discussed here.

There are billions of web pages. Collected together they form millions of websites. This means that no individual can even begin to contemplate visiting all the web pages that may be of interest and relevance to them, still less to read or assimilate their content. And this is just what is on the surface – below this lies a wealth of information buried deep in computers that will be accessed only when asked for (called 'deep web') and that is said to multiply information available to internet users by a factor of 500! While technology is now used to access much of this information, most people choose to access the information in their own time and from their own research.

The internet is a 'pull' form of communication. People will seek information, action, fun and anything else at the time when they want it. Mostly, people use the internet with purpose. All other internet activity and promotion is clutter and some is irritation. Promotion may be 'tolerated', but for a public relations practitioner or marketer to believe that a message can be 'pushed' to an audience without the absolute and individual acceptance of the recipient is to be arrogant and naive. The Oxford Internet Survey shows that people are resistant – and are becoming more so – to spam and 'pushed' content.

Some believe that the currency of the new economy is attention; others argue that significant rewards lie in being an internet navigator whose role is to help people to find stuff on the web. From the perspective of those who argue that wealth is now measured in knowledge units, both positions may be right. Certainly the practitioner can aid this pull process and make it worthwhile for the user by offering advantageous exchanges across the internet.

One thing that is becoming apparent is the role of context. Different people in different environments deploy different values and act on them in accord with their ability to interact, and this changes from time to time. In *The Tipping Point*, Malcolm Gladwell points to a range of research that shows that people behave differently in different contexts.[7] Using a laptop at home, a mobile phone travelling or a PC at work are not untypically different physical contexts, and a need to find a plumber is a different context from a search for music. The practitioner has a need to know about the context in which publics will choose to seek online interactions.

Most internet users engage with the web by either visiting sites they know from habit and experience (often bookmarked favourites) or use search engines to find new content that matches keywords. They will also have habits associated with the platforms they use: for example, an iPod for music or podcasts, and a mobile phone to access a personal diary. In addition they are influenced by peer recommendation through the news and views of other internet users (information found on a favoured website or from online discussion) and their browsing is stimulated by referrals – links – from one site to the next. Online PR practitioners can build on the social, technological and psychological factors that drive internet navigation and access.

Making sure that rich content is known about is pretty essential if the aim is to encourage people to come to your organization's site, interact with your organization, identify with other offline activities and understand your organization better. This means that organizations reach out to their audiences via the internet, and through relevant platforms and channels offer the incentive in the right context for the audiences to want to seek the organization out as well. The digital footprint is important: those millions of online impressions are an asset but they need to be put to effective use. As we will see, they need to be used in online social interactions to gain a return.

Reach is at its best when each party has mutual magnetism. This convergence of values is complex, and many influences and much diverse information will lead to a relationship. Online there is no magic bullet channel for communication; the better analogy is golden buckshot. Advertising, in this context, has its place but is limited in the range of applications where it is the deciding influence. For example, context-relevant advertisements are much more likely to get 'clicked on' than a generic 'pop-up' window.

Conversely, the practitioner must be aware of the parallel factors that draw traffic towards information outlets that give exposure to competitors. Although the phrase 'surfing the internet' feels as old and clichéd as referring to the 'information superhighway', the phrase has some resonance – the ease and appeal of links mean that visitors have a natural tendency to skate over content, driven by almost subconscious forces that seem to carry them inexorably onwards.

It is not enough merely to pull; successful relationships are built on traction, and this means providing useful, relevant information and interactive capability in an accessible format – preferably in a form that people want to pass on to others in a place, circumstances and using a method of their choosing.

# AUDIENCE SIZE

We have already touched on reach as one of the key drivers of internet public relations. Practitioners will need to be able to convince clients that there is an audience with critical mass enough to make the effort worthwhile. Here are some basic facts:

- Online reach in the United Kingdom was 67 per cent – that's 31.7 million people – in 2006.
- 74 per cent of users accessed the internet at least once a week, 52 per cent daily.
- 55 per cent of users state that they would be lost without online access.
- Among internet users, 25 per cent of all time spent exposed to media is now spent online.
- 30 per cent of internet users were online for a minimum of 2 hours, 51 minutes a day.
- 60 per cent of users regard the internet as their favourite information source (compared with 49 per cent for TV, 47 per cent for radio, 34 per cent for magazines and just 24 per cent for newspapers).

Men were more likely to access the internet than women (71 per cent compared with 62 per cent respectively). Most people use the internet at home every day (60 per cent plus) for:

- finding information about goods or services (86 per cent);
- sending/receiving e-mails (85 per cent);
- using services related to travel and accommodation (63 per cent);
- obtaining information from public authorities' websites (46 per cent);
- internet banking (45 per cent);
- looking for information about education, training or courses – and using Wikipedia (36 per cent);
- playing or downloading games, images, films or music (35 per cent);
- reading or downloading online news and magazine content (30 per cent);
- other communication (use of chat sites, messenger, etc) (28 per cent);
- listening to web radios/watching web television (25 per cent).

(Sources: IAB/PricewaterhouseCoopers Media Audit, BMRB Internet Monitor Q3 2005, Oxford Internet Survey, TGI Q1 2006.)

There is a new player on the block: mobile internet. At the time of writing there were already two million people accessing the web using mobile phones. Mobile e-mail has long been an established channel for communication. And it has some interesting uses: e-mail, of course, chat in the form of SMS and more web-based information. In 2006, 70 per cent of active subscribers to mobile phone TV services (which was then only 9 per cent of the population) were tuning in at least once a week.[8] Web surfing on mobiles is now very significant and growing.

The most significant thing to take from these figures is that in the key areas users outnumber non-users. Put simply, in the United Kingdom, as elsewhere, most of us are doing it! The internet is fast becoming the medium of choice for many activities. It is even beginning to challenge the most used forms of entertainment.

The case for the internet replacing television as the consumers' medium of choice is strengthened by a 2006 YouGov survey that claims the average internet user in the United Kingdom spent 20 hours a week online. This figure excludes e-mail usage, which accounts for over three hours of our weekly internet activity, and 28 per cent of people in the United Kingdom say the internet has caused them to watch less television. Among all people in the United Kingdom, three in five of those who use the internet seek news and 20 per cent read additional publications online that they don't read in print – less the 1 per cent of people who pay for news online.[9] In addition, as we have already noted, people multi-task. For example they will use a PC online and watch television at the same time. The numbers of students who swap notes in Facebook or have multiple IM windows active among course group members while writing essays with internet-delivered music going in the background is probably a majority in the United Kingdom.

The internet's challenge to traditional media has become a lifestyle change for many. Ofcom, the UK communications regulator, revealed that television is of declining interest to many 16–24-year-olds; on average they watched television for one hour less per day than the average television viewer. Of the television they do watch, an even smaller proportion of their time is spent viewing public service broadcast channels.

In March 2008 the addiction to online video was evident. Twenty-seven million people watched more than 3.5 billion videos online in the United Kingdom according to comScore. The BBC iPlayer service accounted for 3–5 per cent of all internet traffic in the United Kingdom according to *The Guardian*. Research by Nielsen Online in 2008 showed that Facebook and YouTube were the two sites with the fastest growth, based on the number of minutes spent on each website by Britons. Facebook experienced a 387 per cent increase in the number of minutes spent on it by UK internet users per month to 2.2 billion.

The impact of the internet on where people spend time is affecting most social groups. Reports come in daily. For example, research by the insurance company Axa, in a 2005 survey, found the over 60s spent more time online than gardening or DIY, and 41 per cent said the internet is a favourite pastime.

As public relations is largely dependent on communication it has to follow the public appetite for media, and this is fast becoming internet based. What the practitioner can take from these figures is that it is important to monitor such trends.

# SOCIAL MEDIA ARE OVERTAKING THE TRADITIONAL WEB

A lot of people in public relations and marketing were wrong-footed when the first corporate and business websites started to emerge in the mid-1990s. They did not see how the internet had evolved in chat, e-mail and Usenet – that is, as an interactive arena. Even many of those who realized that the world wide web was going to be a lot more than a passing fad fell into one of two traps, and many managed to be snared by both. First, they saw internet and computer stuff as the province of the socially challenged characters in IT, and (usually simultaneously) saw the web as primarily a promotional tool. Their errors are quite understandable; back then, it was quite difficult to create a website. You had to learn a whole new language (Hypertext Mark-up Language) – which though less difficult than shorthand was beyond the scope of most practitioners' CPD, and you had to understand how to host, load and manage web pages. It was difficult, and anyway wasn't that what the IT people were there for? So they went on to make another mistake; instead of creating content that was suited to this new, interactive environment, they took the easy route of handing over brochures and other corporate outpourings and asking the IT chap to stick them on the website. Very often the result was soporific, dull and off-putting, or worse flashy and tiresome to load.

Web design has evolved very rapidly over the last 10 years, and today there is no excuse for an organization to maintain a website that is not attractive, accessible and user friendly. At the same time, the technology has advanced in another direction. Not only can it offer hugely powerful tools to professional designers, who with an adequate brief can produce wonderful results, but we have also seen the emergence of the 'writable web', the extended applications that have evolved from e-mail, chat and Usenet discussion lists. A whole range of applications have become widely available, which means almost anyone with a computer and internet connection can create their own online presence, perhaps uploading photos to a photo-sharing site, through a blog or a social networking site such as Bebo or Facebook. The speed of change has been phenomenal. When 10 years ago it took a great deal of patience to download (by dial-up modem connection) a relatively small photograph, broadband-enabled bloggers and social networkers can now embed their own video and sound into clean, accessible microsites that require little investment beyond time and creativity.

> Hitwise reported that UK internet visits to weblogs reached an all-time high during the week ending 7 June 2008, accounting for 1.19 per cent of all UK internet traffic, equivalent to one in every 84 website visits.

Such activities have entered the mainstream so quickly that many users don't really have – or need not have – much idea of what they are dealing with. Put simply, you no longer need to understand what happens under the bonnet, you just get into the virtual car, turn the key and surf. Most people can set up a blog within half an hour, and a Facebook account is up and running in a lot less time than that.

Looking at how much time people spend online, one can see that this has appeal (remembering of course that surfing can be concurrent with other online and offline activities). The activity that accounted for most time spent online in 2007/08 according to Nielsen research was instant messaging, followed by shopping on eBay. Facebook was the next most favoured use of online time, followed by search, e-mail, music and video; of the top 10 all the rest were in social media sites. Intimate conversation, shopping, group interactivity, communication and entertainment are all very human activities enjoyed across the millennia and are reflected in this research.

The fastest-growing use of time also reflected this appeal of social media. The fastest-growing time consumers were in order: Facebook, YouTube, Second Life, Google Search, Google Maps, Wikipedia, Asda, iTunes, Club Penguin and Veoh (another video-sharing site). Six out of 10 were social media, that is, Web 2.0 sites.

It is such data that has prompted us towards our emphasis on the social web in this edition of this book.

# WHAT IS WEB 2.0?

Web browsers such as Internet Explorer, Firefox, Chrome and Opera offer most people their window onto the web, but is worth remembering that other tools exist that can allow people to do much more, and make their experience ever richer and more exciting. In less than five years, a movement has taken hold that is having a profound effect on public relations. Called web 2.0 by Tim O'Reilly of O'Reilly Media in 2003, it heralds the evolution of the web from a repository of information and communication technologies into a space for symmetrical communication: a platform that aids the transfer of knowledge and conversations and a place where people can easily mix and match both. This has immense implications, and is nowhere more evident than in the sudden significance of channels like Facebook, Bebo, Wikipedia and blogs.

Web 2.0 is bandied about by a lot of people as being new. It is really an evolution. The network that was until recently primarily a repository of information through interlinked but essentially static websites, and complemented by channels for interaction such as e-mail, discussion lists and instant messaging, has evolved to create a seamless platform for all three. It is now possible for almost anyone to create a type of website that not only provides an information resource but also offers the means by which people (and machines) can add, change and share content with others; blogs are a common and now widely recognized example of this new phenomenon.

In Chapter 2 we listed many common channels for communication, and most of them combine the dual functions of information provision and information exchange.

Web 2.0 has another aspect. It allows these new channels to be integrated ('mashups'). This development allows one channel of information and its associated content, plus contributions by third parties and the associated sharing capability, to be integrated and absorbed into another channel. For example, a Bebo page can include YouTube videos, Google Maps, surveys, podcasts, slideshows and much, much more.

Another significant addition is the ability to index content in a new way, known as tagging. Content generators can describe content by using keywords in a format that can be read and aggregated by other people's computers. For example, the tag 'public relations' included in a blog post will be picked up by a search engine like Technorati, Google, Yahoo! and MSN to allow anyone to search for those blog posts (or other web pages) that have this tag. Called *folksonomies*, these are user-generated taxonomies that help to link or aggregate different content into common themes, and are powerful in helping people 'pull' content they find relevant.[10] For example, the social bookmarking site Delicious uses tags to offer taxonomies as a way to work with an underlying folksonomy. As Quintarelli shows, this allows structure to be added without the need for direct collaboration between classification experts and content consumers.[11] Adding a tag requires either an embedded capability (a box where users can add tags) or some html code, for instance rel='tag'>folksonomy</a>. (It is worth remembering that because such tags are user generated they do not have the quality or structure of more formal and disciplined listings.)

One of the principal drivers of the 'web 2.0 era' is an XML-driven capability to share information. There are two basic systems: RSS and Atom. They allow people to 'subscribe' to a site and be informed when its content is changed or added to. All practitioners should examine their own online content to assess whether it should include an RSS feed. A very simple description of RSS is available on the BBC site. Most newspapers, TV and radio stations, blogs and many websites offer RSS subscriptions (all free) to their content. RSS heralded the mass use of 'many-to-one' communication. Anyone can now accept content from many people all the time. Being one of the many requires high levels of ethics in communication. Once an organization has lost the confidence of the user and is 'unsubscribed' it is, in effect, on a blacklist forever.

Because web 2.0 has brought the 'conversation' into the web and spawned high-profile mass interactions in sites like Facebook, Bebo and Wikipedia, and has facilitated the blogging and other communication phenomena, it has spawned a range of off-putting expressions like 'PR 2.0'. It is important to look beyond the shiny new labels to assess where its true significance lies.

# THE TRADITIONAL WEB HAS A CHANGING ROLE

Despite more time being spent online, faster internet connection, high penetration of broadband and huge sums being spent on websites, traditional websites do not seem to be attracting a lot more users. In 2006, students at Bournemouth University used alexa.com to view the reach of a range of 'traditional' websites. In every case, they showed a decline in popularity (Figure 11.2).

**Daily reach (per million)**
ebay.com ——— microsoft.com ‑‑‑‑ amazon.com ▯▯▯▯▯▯ bbc.co.uk ——— guardian.co.uk ∞∞∞∞

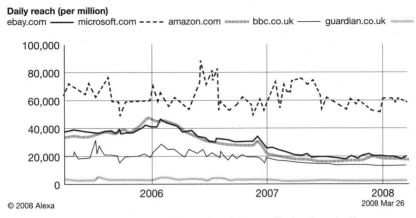

© 2008 Alexa

2008 Mar 26

**Figure 11.2**   *Traditional website traffic in slow decline*

There was obviously something going on that needed further investigation. The slow decline of the websites shown in the figure might have occurred because there are more websites, but the evidence the students found suggests otherwise. Social media sites such as blogs, file-sharing community sites and interactive shopping (eBay is the best known example) were not only competitors for the biggest reach, page views and dwell time on each page, their popularity was growing at an astonishing rate (Figure 11.3).

**Daily reach (per million)**
wikipedia.org ▯▯▯▯▯ facebook.com ▰▰▰▰ myspace.com ∞∞∞∞ youtube.com ‑‑‑‑ blogger.com ———

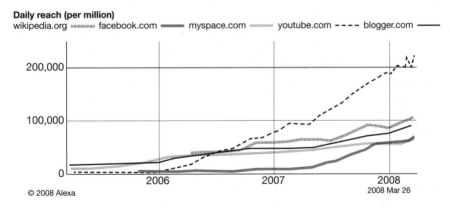

© 2008 Alexa

2008 Mar 26

**Figure 11.3**   *Reach among social media sites showed a strong upward trend*

At the point where the downward trend for traditional sites and the upward trend of social media sites intersect, it becomes apparent that there is a new paradigm of online communication that in part is about information (traditional websites) and in part social content sharing and commentary (social media). This was, the students discovered, new territory for communicators.

The findings at Bournemouth were born out in other surveys. An American survey by Piper Jaffrey showed the number of minutes online devoted to social media (primarily social networks) had moved from 3 per cent to 31 per cent between April 2005 and October 2006,[12] a change reflected in other data in the United Kingdom, where time online is even greater. It was evident that there was something that appealed to people and it was not traditional websites.

Heather Hopkins of Hitwise offered year-on-year evidence of social media sites' growth in popularity compared with 'traditional' websites in January 2007:

- Adult websites were down 20 per cent in market share of UK internet visits, comparing December 2005 and December 2006.
- Gambling websites were down 11 per cent.
- Music websites were down 18 per cent.
- Net communities and chat websites were up 34 per cent.
- News and media websites were up 24 per cent.
- Search engines were up 22 per cent.
- Food and beverage were up 29 per cent.
- Education (driven by Wikipedia) was up 18 per cent.
- Business and finance were up 12 per cent.

(Source: Hitwise, 2007, www.hitwise.com)

Some online community providers like MySpace (www.myspace.com) attracted 1.5 billion page views in a day. For the practitioner this is a tempting target. It has the feel of a 'mass audience'. In reality MySpace, Bebo and Facebook (among many other social networks, it is important to note), not to mention blogs, are closer to the conversations that might be overheard in all the locations of a chain of pubs, restaurants or nightclubs. To influence such communities PR activities need to be 'invited in' as part of the conversation.

The BBC reported in November 2006 that:

> the rapid rise of digital media like the internet, mobile phones and MP3 players is splintering people's media consumption and making it harder for conventional ad campaigns to make an impression. The online video boom was starting to eat into television viewing time, an ICM survey for the BBC has suggested.

Social media sites are not just growing in popularity; many of them are among the most used internet properties.

Every form of triangulation of what is happening online points in one direction. The use of the internet is moving towards social media (Figure 11.4), which are popular, different and have huge appeal. We believe there

| In 2007 the top online destinations monitored by alexa.org were: | |
|---|---|
| 1. Google UK | 11. Wikipedia |
| 2. Yahoo! | 12. Blogger.com |
| 3. eBay UK | 13. Microsoft Corporation |
| 4. Google | 14. Bebo.com |
| 5. Microsoft Network (MSN) | 15. Thefacebook |
| 6. BBC Newsline Ticker | 16. The Internet Movie Database |
| 7. Myspace | 17. Orange |
| 8. YouTube | 18. eBay |
| 9. Amazon.co.uk | 19. Argos |
| 10. Windows Live | 20. Msn.co.uk |

are very powerful drivers behind the rise and rise of social media, and in a later chapter examine the human and psychological drivers we suspect are behind this change in the use of the internet.

On this evidence, there is every reason for PR practitioners to get to know more about a genre of communication that has in just a few years changed the way people spend their time, communicate with each other and consume information.

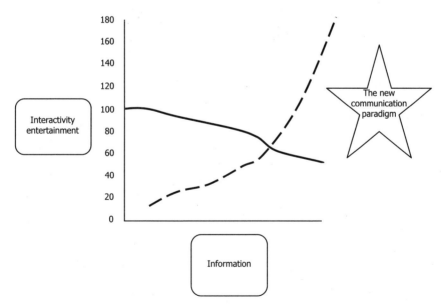

**Figure 11.4** *As traditional websites become less used by comparison with the interactive and social internet, a new paradigm of internet use has become established*

---

**IN BRIEF**

- The internet is creating its own society.
- It has massive reach to the majority of the population.
- The internet is important to people.
- The way people use the internet has changed dramatically in the last four years.
- The context for interaction is very important.
- All forms of communication are migrating to the internet.
- The internet is a pull form of communication.
- Video, social networks and social interaction are consuming a lot of people's time.
- Web 2.0 is an expression of the evolution from static information to interactive relationship-based information sharing.
- New forms of ordering information are emerging.
- Social media are emerging as a challenge to traditional online media consumption but are also dependent on it as a source for information.

---

## Notes

1.  Trio, N R (1997) Internetship: good citizenship on the internet, *OnTheInternet*, May/June, **3** (3); Phillips, D (2000) *Managing Your Reputation in Cyberspace*, Hawkesmere
2.  1.2 billion people, http://www.internetworldstats.com/ (accessed April 2008)
3.  The Office of National Statistics reported that in 2007 15 million households had internet access; half used broadband. Most people use the internet at home every day
4.  Phillips, D (2000) Blazing netshine, *Journal of Communications Management*, **5** (2), pp 189–204: 'Text-based e-mail will be perceived as archaic by 2005 as video e-mail and personal rich media sites take over.'

    Forrester Research reports that 92 percent on online consumers will communicate with one another using personal rich media and 57 percent of US households will use personal rich media at least once a month. Camera companies are already allowing for the widespread adoption of digital cameras and camcorders by providing websites that digitise 35 mm film, store photos online and offer their customers tools to create online albums and slide shows. Similar facilities will soon be available for home video productions. (http://www.forrester.com/ER/Press/Release/0,1769,247,FF.html)

5.  Dutton, W, di Gennaro, C and Hargrave, A (2005) *The Internet in Britain*, The Oxford Internet Survey

6.  Thurman, Niel (2007) The globalisation of journalism online: a trans-atlantic study of news websites and their international readers, *Journalism: Theory, Practice & Criticism*, August, **8** (3), pp 285–307
7.  Gladwell, M (2000) *The Tipping Point*, Abacus
8.  Ofcom.com, http://www.ofcom.org.uk/research/cm/cmrnr08/uksumm ary.pdf (accessed October 2008)
9.  Dutton *et al, op cit*
10. Fichter, D (2006). Intranet applications for tagging and folksonomies. *Online*, **30** (3), pp 43–45
11. Quintarelli, E (2005). Folksonomies: power to the people, http://www. iskoi.org/doc/folksonomies.htm (accessed 7 May 2007)
12. Piper Jaffrey & Co (2007) *Internet Media and Marketing Report*, Piper Jaffrey

# 12

# What lies behind the internet as media

In this chapter we touch on the diversity of applications that now affect the lives of people and that affect the PR profession. The impact of these influences is far reaching, and we sum them up at the end.

First, it is reasonable to identify what the internet is and how its convergent technologies affect message delivery.

## WHAT IS THE INTERNET?

In reality there is no such thing as 'the internet'. We use this term to describe the interconnection of millions of computers that are linked, usually by cable, satellite or wireless telemetry, in order to receive, re-route and transmit data. Then there are computers that just transmit and send, and even a few that just receive.

A very large part of the internet is not normally visible to the general public but comprises networks that are owned and run mostly by corporations, governments and academic institutions. Such networks that are important to practitioners exist, largely because the communities involved offer a 'walled garden' domain for communication, mostly just data but often for internal communication. It is not an area of practice we cover in this book.

There is also a huge volume of information that is held in databases that are not normally visible (deep web) to the public. For some practitioners, the security of these data is important. The information about people held by organizations is one such part of the hidden web. Exposure of such data is very damaging to reputation and can lead to legal sanction.

---

So worried was the UK Government about data security lapses that a prime-ministerial statement was issued in 2008 saying:

The Prime Minister announced that he had asked the Cabinet Secretary, with the advice of security experts, to work with Departments to ensure that all Departments and all agencies check their procedures for the storage and use of data. An Interim Report, published on 17 December, summarised action taken across Government, and set out initial directions of reform to strengthen the Government's arrangements.

---

Most of the internet is not visible to most people. But what is visible is still mind-bendingly large. Our realm is the 'visible internet'.

Internet computers are polite to each other. Their good manners are based on internet protocols (IP). The etiquette of IP is expressed in the form of digital greetings at the beginning of small digital packets of information and a proper farewell at the end. Sometimes the greeting is such that the computer politely sends it off to a neighbour, and sometimes it recognizes it has come to stay. This is called packet switching, and it is the most used technology for both data and voice communication worldwide. It is relatively new and has replaced the old 'telephone' type of communication that was based on the idea of circuits (creating a single end-to-end connection between sender and receiver, like an old fashioned telephone operator 'connecting you'). This meant that a dedicated circuit was tied up for the duration of the call and communication was only possible with the single party on the other end of the circuit.

With packet switching, a system could use one communication link to communicate with more than one machine by disassembling and re-assembling data packets. Not only could the link be shared (much as a single person posts letters to different destinations), but each packet could be routed independently of other packets. The network can optimize capacity and fill in the gaps that in another era might have been a pause in a telephone conversation, or more accurately the gap between syllables and frequencies. Enough to say that the leap in productivity of circuits is big.

The idea of networks for computers that are robust and can flow round obstructions applies at a technical level and, both logically and in practice, at a more human communication level. It copes with both broadcast information and networked communication.

The greeting description on each packet helps the receiving computer to decide what to do with it. When people talk of the internet network, this is what they are describing. What makes the internet so robust is that it does not depend on any one computer or even dozens of these hubs, and it can use any combination of cables, satellite and radio channels provided by a wide range of organizations.

Equally, no message depends on one channel for communication. It can move between channels.

Not all internet applications are significant for public relations, but many are. Examples of internet protocols you may have heard about include packets of information with a greeting that could be a telephone message (Voice over Internet Protocol – VoIP), or e-mail (Internet Message Access Protocol), a web page (using HTTP – Hypertext Transfer Protocol), file transfer (File Transfer Protocol) and eXtensible Mark-up Language (XML), which is an enabling protocol for many of the important new web-based tools used in online public relations. Knowing this helps us to realize that although different 'protocols' seem to offer the same thing, they are really quite different. For example, e-mail is not the web.

Which leads us to the concept of 'convergence'.

# CONVERGENCE

Internet protocols can be interpreted. E-mail can be interpreted into web applications. This means that people can send an e-mail from their e-mail software client (eg Microsoft's Outlook) and it can be read from a website like Yahoo Mail, MSN Hotmail or Google's Gmail, and from these web applications passed to e-mail clients. The internet protocols seem to be interchangeable from the users' perspective. They have 'converged'. This convergence does not stop there. E-mail from a client software or the web can also be transmitted using cellular telephony and can be read on mobile phones, or it can be transmitted via online games and many other devices. Indeed, most internet protocols can be made to interact in this way. For PR practitioners this is both a challenge and a fantastic opportunity.

In August 2006, the European Union agreed that internet protocol would become the standard used in radio and television technologies. This means that TV will become fully convergent with the internet, and digital radio and television will be seamlessly integrated. Internet TV is a reality in many more ways now that it uses an internet protocol.

These developments can optimize broadband copper and fibre-optic cable, radio, cellular phone and Broadband Over Powerlines (BPL) networks to speed applications such as streaming films and long TV programmes; this means time-shifting programmes to be downloaded at a convenient time for the user and, interestingly, allowing users to 'edit' the content they want to watch and then share their edited works with others.

Many of these capabilities are, of course, already available using services from cable companies and satellite broadcasters like Sky. They will become ever more ubiquitous and user friendly.

What convergence means to PR people is that it affects the way people use the internet. It means that more information is available on a wider range of devices and platforms and that messages are no longer constrained by the media they were designed for. For example, a press release can now be published by a newspaper, by the client website and the online media for reading on a PC, laptop, mobile phone, television and gaming machine, or even a TV set or in print.

## THE NETWORK EFFECT

The internet is a physical and electronic network. It is also a network on a much more human scale.

In the 18th, 19th and 20th centuries, the power and capabilities of mass media developed through the distribution of news sheets, newspapers, radio, film and television. In many ways traditional forms of social distribution of news and information took second place.

The internet has changed all that. Mass media and mass communication are still very important but there is a challenger: network communication. The simple example is blogs. Anyone taking a look at blog posts delivered by any web search may well agree with the prominent PR voice who said, 'blogs are ill-informed, rambling descriptions of the tedious details of life or half-baked comments on political, sporting or professional issues. They read like a mixture of the ramblings of the eponymous pub landlord and the first draft of a second-rate newspaper column. The concern of some public relations people as they worry about this new media for consumer comment, engagement and reputation destruction is a bit overdone.'

This is to take a mass media view of this network genre. If one takes a closer look, the reverse is the case. These blogs are comments on a personal level. They are of the culture of the author and his or her friends. Some do have a mass audience but most do not.

What one sees is something extraordinary. People with passion about their subject are expressing their views, passing on their perspectives and commenting on friends' blogs from their own perspectives. What happens is that from time to time they focus on a subject, product, brand, company, issue or person (and sometimes all six at the same time). They will provide hyperlinked evidence to support their case and will refer to other blog opinions and insights. These networks are mostly tiny. They allow community interaction, debate and new approaches to the subject matter. In the process the subject matter morphs and changes – the product, brand, company, issue or person changes from explicit reference to generic comment and back in a flow of conversation. This will appeal to other bloggers who will join in the conversation, add their own insights and thereby engage their own small group in the discussion.

There is one other driver: RSS. As bloggers comment, what they say is quickly picked up by others and the subject spreads fast – sometimes called the viral effect. It is spontaneous and human; it sometimes spreads like wildfire and sometimes dims to a flicker in cyberspace, never completely forgotten (it's on the internet and so is available, in effect, for all time) but smouldering, awaiting a breath to liven it up at another time. Because it is personal, with all the effort and emotion involved, it has a power and strength that a corporate boilerplate lacks.

The analogy works for all social media, whether they be video-sharing on YouTube, a comment in Facebook or an amendment in Wikipedia. Knowing the reach of social media and understanding that such content can, because of convergence, hop from one medium to another with ease, it is not difficult to understand that these small groups have immense power. They are not mass media, they are network media.

Clay Shirky, in his brilliantly written book *Here Comes Everybody*, explains the phenomenon well with some powerful case studies.[1]

---

Market Sentinel CEO Mark Rogers argues that:

The ideas espoused by Malcolm Gladwell in his book *The Tipping Point* work in social media but not as some suggest. The first idea is that some people are 'hubs' – they are well connected. (True, as far as we can tell.) The second idea is that some people are influencers. (Also true, as far as we can tell.) The third idea is to spread an idea – any idea that is 'sticky' – you target the influencers, who are gatekeepers to the mass market. (This is an idea that is false, in our experience.)

The third idea does not follow from the first two. The reasons for this are to do with how networks assign authority. Authority is – in our metrics – topic specific, it is the characteristic of being disproportionately linked by other authorities on that topic. Authorities are, by their nature, hard to target. A communicator wishing to influence an authority must tailor their message, sometimes at great pain, to make it relevant to that authority. Once it is relevant to the authority, the authority will further shape it (they are, after all, authorities) and pass it on to their network, but in their own time and manner.

People count, and the voice of some people seems to strike a chord with a wider public. Examples in PR include the Hobson and Holtz Report (www. forimmediaterelease.biz), Steve Rubel (http://www.micropersuasion.com) and The New PR Wiki (http://www.thenewpr.com/wiki ). Most people and a majority of practitioners will not know these media but their influence on speakers, writers and teachers is profound, far reaching and important.

This then takes us to the role of traditional websites when social media have such sway. Whereas websites were once widely regarded as primarily online corporate brochures, they are now increasingly functioning as information repositories, online shopping checkouts, and portals for dialogue and relationship building. The traditional website has become a place of record and commercial exchange. The new social media web is a place for interactions. Many organizations have incorporated the interactive nature of the social web into their websites to good effect. Examples include Amazon and eBay.

The technologies that lie behind the internet as the practitioner and consumer know it are powerful facilitators for the daily practice of public relations as it was known in the first decade of the new century. The knowledge that internet protocols are creeping into so many electronic domains seems very technical, but for practitioners with imagination, it means that there are whole new ways of communicating.

---

**IN BRIEF**

- The internet is made available through interlinked computers.
- Messages are split into small components, are transmitted via many routes and brought back together at the receiving computer.
- There are many internet protocols, each with a specific role to play.
- Internet protocols can deliver content derived from other protocols in a process called convergence.
- The internet is an array of network technologies and is also effective when people use it among networks of groups.
- Networked groups are very effective in spreading messages and concepts that sometimes spread like a 'virus'.
- The traditional media remain powerful because they combine traditional news-seeking capabilities with the network effect.
- To compete in an internet-mediated era, news outlets are changing the way they collect and disseminate news.

---

# Note

1.   Shirky, C (2008) *Here Comes Everybody*, Penguin

# Part 3

# Building blocks for online PR

# 13

# Communications platforms

In Chapter 2 we discussed a range of channels for communication, and we deal with channels in greater depth in Chapter 17. In this chapter we explore the nature of the platforms those channels use.

There are many ways that people engage with the internet and, naturally, they are available to practitioners too. As well PCs and laptops, devices like television or radio sets, mobile telephones, game machines (yes, Xbox and Play Station are included too) and static and mobile VoIP sets (let's call them Skype phones for ease of understanding) are all platforms for communication.

We use communications channels such as e-mail or blogs on platforms, and we often use a range of platforms to deploy different channels. For example we can send SMS messages (using the SMS 'channels') from a PC or laptop as well as from a mobile phone.

We need not stop there. There are many other platforms available to the consumer, including, for example, e-Paper, a flexible sheet that can be digitally updated, which has a place alongside newsprint and books, and internet-enabled e-posters (posters that can be digitally updated), which have a place alongside posters, signage and even computer and TV screens.

It is not unusual for platforms to offer capabilities they were not designed for. SMS messaging from mobile phones was added for occasional use. The extraordinary success of SMS was not anticipated and yet has become one of the most widely used of all modern communications channels. It has evolved too. It is now possible to send photos by SMS. Until very recently PCs were not designed to deliver video or television programmes but today this is one of their most common uses.

It's actually quite easy to turn your Sony PlayStation into a fully fledged PC, which is great for adding media and productivity and flexibility to the black box beneath your TV. If you dig into the Settings, then System Settings menu you'll find an option to Install Other OS. Then by following some simple instructions (at http://psubuntu.com/wiki/InstallationInstructions) you can download a copy of the operating system, burn it to a CD or DVD, and then install it onto your console's hard drive.

Practitioners with the imagination to deploy platforms in new ways will be among the most effective communication pioneers. Such applications might come from technologies such as near-field electromagnetic ranging (NFER), real-time location systems (RTLS), radio-frequency identification (RFID – the most sought-after tickets to the opening and closing ceremonies at the Beijing Olympics were RFID-enabled) and contactless 'smart' cards (like the Oyster card used by London Underground). They allow small amounts of data to be transferred between smart devices and receivers. These channels mean that there will never again be a need to register at an exhibition because the embedded technology in the tickets will have all the information and can transmit it to computers for visitors to gain admission. In retailing, such technology will mean that the supermarket checkout is, well, on its way out.

Viviane Reding, Member of the European Commission responsible for the information society and media, at the 2008 OECD Ministerial Meeting on the future of the internet economy in Seoul, Korea, noted that: 'RFID and sensor technologies embedded in products will not only significantly impact on business organization and efficiency, but also impact our daily life.'

There are new platforms on their way. The mobile phone is due for a major revolution, with iPhone and its more advanced cousins already in the shops.

Speakers at the 3rd Mobile Pricing Symposium, organized by research firm Tariff Consultancy in 2008, forecast that mobile data services will continue to be the main driver of growth in the mature markets until 2012. Mobile broadband pricing declined by more than half in real terms between 2004 and 2007, with more broadband capacity being available for the same price.

The recent availability of easily portable mobile data connections (such as the USB modem – usually called a 'dongle') means that mobile data services have become a mass market consumer item.

---

### MOBILE PHONES ARE PIGGY BANKS

Two hundred Manchester City season ticket holders trialled a system through which they 'show' their Nokia 3320 handset to an automatic reader to get into a game, instead of handing a card to a gate attendant.

In Estonia mobile phones can be used in a similar way to pay taxi fares and bar bills. Many people use satellite navigation in their cars. These devices can also be used to provide a wide range of information about routes, local restaurants and beauty spots, and already 'talk' to mobile phones and thence to the rest of the internet.

---

These platforms can be linked using internet protocols by traditional phone cables, by radio in many forms, including wireless local area networks (WLAN – often known as WiFi), infrared (often used in phones and the cable-free computer mouse), Bluetooth, cellular telephony, broadband over power lines (BPL) using the grid and domestic power cables, and the simple Universal Serial Bus (USB) devices and cables.

Microsoft Surface is a new platform that offers web and internet services without a keyboard or mouse but with flat touch screens.

---

A ring, necklace, watch and earring set announced by IBM will look like standard jewellery but has a difference. The ring flashes to alert you to an incoming call. The caller's number is displayed on your watch and you can answer the call by pressing a button on the same watch. You can hear the caller through a tiny speaker in the earrings and the necklace holds a microphone to speak into. From almost any organisation except IBM this would sound far-fetched. The company is also working on emotion sensing, monitoring body temperature, heartbeat and moods. This information can then be transmitted over the internet and others can gain access to it.

---

We are all used to getting money from an ATM on the street. These internet-enabled platforms and the information kiosks to be found on many a street corner are part of this mix of channels.

Most people, for the most part, do not notice these changes taking place. They are gradual and quickly form part of daily life. How many Londoners now find the Oyster card strange or think of it as a channel for communication? Oyster cards are getting very clever.

---

Working with Transport for London, researchers at the Imperial College Internet Centre are using tag devices, a technology used in Oyster cards, to process and send information about delays and engineering works to commuters to aid them in their travels. This tag technology can be embedded into items such as railway posters or billboards at tube stations, so travellers can access the latest transport information wirelessly transmitted to their mobile phones. The same technology can be used for transmission of other PR messages, of course.

---

Practitioners can think of these platforms in the same way that they might think of newsprint, magazines, radio, television, film and other platforms for communication.

For PR practitioners, the use and application of communications platforms is limited only by the extent of their creativity. Imagine a satellite navigation device that offers a story about a company as the driver passes by – such devices are already being deployed at the hi-tech end of online PR but one can imagine a wannabe celebrity broadcasting her presence in the street to mobile phones nearby, and shops offering discounts to passers-by when footfall drops off in store.

---

Ofcom predicted in May 2008 that the Bluetooth wireless technology that allows people to use a hands-free earpiece while making a mobile telephone call could soon alert the emergency services when someone has a heart attack. The communications regulator said that sensors could be implanted into people at risk of heart attack or diabetic collapse that would allow doctors to monitor them remotely. If the 'in-body network' recorded that the person had suddenly collapsed, it would send an alert, via a nearby base station at their home, to a surgery or hospital. A similar application can alert carers when people have forgotten to take medication.

However, Ofcom also gave warning in its report, *Tomorrow's Wireless World*, that the impact of such technology on personal privacy would require more debate.

---

Is there an appetite for all these platforms? A 2006 Best of Stuff survey suggested that 60 per cent of UK consumers spend £5,000 on gadgets every year, with 30 per cent of those surveyed saying that they have 15 gadgets in total.

What is really big about these devices? It's unnerving. Many of them can be used for a range of two-way communication. We know this of the ubiquitous PC and mobile phone, but what of an e-poster? One that can interact with a mobile phone. In Japan a user can already 'pull' information from them! Progressively, this interconnectedness of these platforms will engage the consumer in ever more one-to-one, one-to-many, many-to-many and many-to-one forms of interaction. And while we are pondering these developments (and sending an e-mail from an Xbox games console as one of the authors did when writing this book – and got a reply!), it is worth noting that many of these platforms do not have a keyboard or even a mouse; many do not use text, but use touch, pictures, graphics and sounds.

The creative practitioner may find applications for voice-to-text in applications such as Twitterphone that allow the user to make a phone call and dictate a message that will almost immediately appear on the Twittersite, a blog, web page or wiki, and can of course be downloaded to a mobile phone.

Many practitioners will imagine that these platforms are not part of the PR repertoire; many of them were doubtful about PCs; the mobile phone was not considered a PR channel and the BlackBerry was thought to be a toy until each in turn became a more or less essential part of working life.

Mobile devices like the iPhone have morphed away from being a telephone to become fully fledged hand-held computers.

Between the first edition and the time of writing this book many new platforms have emerged. We cannot predict what will happen in the coming months and years but we can stay in touch with developments.

Constant evaluation of platforms is a structured activity. It should be one of those activities that are the subject of investigation and brainstorming at regular intervals. There are 10 practical measures practitioners can apply to do to keep up to date with the current, emerging and new platforms for communication:

- Assess whether current campaigns can be executed on most relevant platforms.
- Decide what current activities can be enhanced with developments in platform technologies.
- Watch out for new channels and be a little curious about them.
- Keep an open mind about these platforms.
- Use imagination and creativity to seek relevant, sometimes innovative, applications for these tools of our trade.

- Re-examine who is using different devices (fashion changes).
- Old platforms should always be considered. Is fax really dead?
- Watch out for evolution such as photos and the web on mobile phones (PCs being used like televisions).
- Be aware of existing and emerging multiple applications like voice and e-mail for games machines, near-field applications for mobile phones, applications run from USB sticks, CDs, DVD and MP3 players, and many more devices.
- Reach. Some devices are only used by a few people and some are used by many. Is the fashion for use changing?

---

**IN BRIEF**

- Information is transmitted and received using a wide range of devices.
- These platforms can broadcast and deliver information using a wide range of channels.
- Delivery of information on different channels can be interpreted differently by the receiver.
- Many internet communications-enabled devices can be harnessed for use with the internet.
- The range of applications that evolve and can be used for different communication purposes is largely untapped.
- The range of platforms is growing all the time.
- Evaluation can be structured and should be ongoing.

---

# 14

# Channels for communication

In the previous chapter we briefly described some of the devices people use to communicate and build relationships online. We touched on the many forms of communication that can use these internet-mediated platforms

Once upon a time, communication channels were letters and newspapers, conversation and the town crier. The platforms were paper, ink, meeting places and the market square. Now, there are many more channels. The most common are e-mail, websites, instant messaging (IM) and recent entrants like blogs, and photo and video-sharing sites.

The old channels have not gone away. Most communication channels don't. People still even use fax! As the American internet PR guru Shel Holtz puts it: 'New media does not kill off old media, but it does influence and change it.' Online PR is not an alternative to other forms of relationship building, communication and interaction; it is an extension of what has gone before.

Very few people use all the modern channels for communication. In fact there is doubt as to whether anyone could. But most people use a few. They will probably use SMS on a mobile phone, e-mail, websites and then some others. This does not mean that communicators can only focus on these few. The professional communicator needs an understanding of a very much wider array of channels and needs to be able to deploy most of them directly or through a specialist third party. For example, knowing that multi-player online games are a hugely popular form of communication does not mean that the average PR executive has to be a level-10 player. What is important is that s/he needs to know about these games, how they work and why people find them absorbing as a means for communication in small groups or across the world.

As more people have spent more time with faster online connections, new channels have appeared. Some of them have become bywords for communication, including search engines like Google, encyclopaedias like Wikipedia, online diaries such as blogs, social media portals like Facebook, Bebo and MySpace, online games and virtual environments. Fashions come and go for these channels. Relatively few people now use Usenet, one of the early social media channels, and traditional websites are less sought after, but some social media channels are gaining popularity at an exponential rate.

People are routinely using many different communication channels, and often using them concurrently.

Avid fans of the early *Big Brother* programme are reported to have followed the television programme, conversed about it using blogs and instant messaging (IM), found out stuff about the participants on websites and voted 'housemates' on and off the programme using mobile phones. This was all done while the programme was live on-air. This adds a new dimension to reach. It means that reach can be and often is multi-channel, and indeed can be multi-channel at the same time (synchronous) and at different times (asynchronous). This means that the user can choose a range of channels, of which a number can be interactive, allowing communication with other people who are also interested in the programme/activity. Whether the practitioner can also claim the attention of the public is a mute point. Did members of the audience glance at the television or did they watch the PC screen, or did they toggle between the two, picking up the mobile phone as light relief from such intense activity.

While we offer insights into channels for communication – and there are many – new ones emerge all the time. Students of communication have to be able find ways that help future-proof their professional knowledge and understanding of channels. In Part 3, which deals with planning and management, we present methodologies for identifying and strategically applying channels tactically, for communication and relationship building. Many of them also provide information to inform the strategic relationship and communication process of public relations planning.

First we need to know about these means for interaction. How do we identify existing, emerging and new channels for communication? Some simply come from lists in books like this, or are featured by PR bloggers like Steve Rubel (http://www.micropersuasion.com/) or on podcasts such as For Immediate Release (http://www.forimmediaterelease.biz), but others enter the consciousness of communities and migrate into the mainstream by what seems to be a magical osmosis. For example, at the time of going to press, the game World of Warcraft (a massively multi-player online role-playing game – MMORPG ) had a 9-million community of players who not only can interact online with each other but also pay to play it. Games as a communication channel offer deeply immersive environments for communication and yet, beyond the genre, are not well known as an internet channel for communication.

Since 1995, the research company Gartner has used 'hype cycles' to characterize the over-enthusiasm or 'hype' and subsequent disappointment that typically happens with the introduction of new technologies.[1] The social software hype cycle (Figure 14.1) highlights the most important technologies that support rich social interactions, which is a useful indication of emerging and maturing channels for communication.

As new channels arrive, there are a number of things that PR practitioners should know and master and that are needed as part of the processes involved in planning and management (see Chapter 16). We have identified that there are 20 things practitioners need to know about channels for communication.

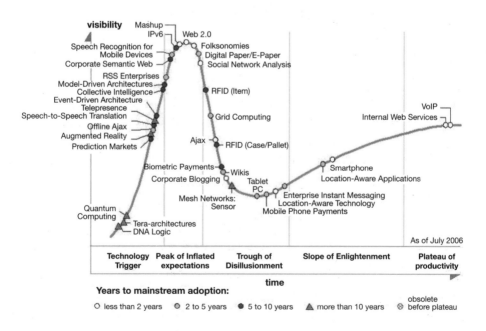

**Figure 14.1**  *The Gartner social software hype cycle*

It is well beyond the scope of this book to provide definitive data about all media (we identified some of them in Chapter 2). It would be a tome if we were to attempt to view every channel from every potential application, and would require the combined imagination of millions of people seeking new ways to communicate every day.

Some platforms and some channels for communication will be and are relevant to some domains of practice. The BlackBerry, is already part of the dress code of crisis management PR professionals.

One's perspective of social media in politics will be very different from an approach for application in business-to-business PR or internal communications.

Using communications channels has seven elements:

- the medium;
- interactive elements;
- application;
- policy and optimization requirements;
- monitoring and evaluation;
- buy-in;
- planning and implementation.

# THE MEDIUM

| The media | |
| --- | --- |
| Title | The generic name, eg e-mail, wiki, etc. |
| Definition | A description such as: 'Printed newspaper publication issued periodically, usually daily or weekly, to convey information and opinion about current events' or 'A blog, an online, regularly updated journal or newsletter that is readily accessible to the general public by virtue of being posted on a website'. |
| Brief history | From wikipedia or another resource. |
| Fast facts | How the practitioner would explain this channel for communication really quickly. For example: 'About 1,500 printed local, regional and national mass media, with 21 million people reading national newspapers each day' or 'Interactive, personal interest web communication channel published by about 4 million people in the UK'. |
| Communication platforms | eg Paper, PC, laptop, mobile phone, print, TV. |

The key here is to create a brief explanation that can be useful for the practitioners and will enlighten people who are not professional communicators. The nature of media and the nature of communicators will dictate how different media are described.

# INTERACTIVITY

| Interactive elements | |
|---|---|
| How do people (the public/s) contribute to this channel? | To what extent is this common (past/now/future)? Is this interaction predominantly exercised by the publisher or user? What is the context for use? |
| How does the public share knowledge of content in this channel, using this channel and across other channels? | To what extent is this common (past/now/future)? What is the context for interaction (eg must it be using a PC or mobile phone or specific channel, or will it use convergent channels)? |
| Risk analysis (nature of the risk, likelihood of occurrence, extent of potential damage, mitigation procedure/s extent of amelioration achievable) | Risk can be to a publisher, user or third party, and one person's risk can be someone else's opportunity. Of which more later. |

In PR, where much of the activity is focused on social motivation, this analysis is important, and never more so than in evaluating the medium for efficacy in reaching relationship and communication goals.

# APPLICATION

| Application | |
|---|---|
| What services are available to help the practitioner set up/deploy this channel (software; suppliers and/or contractors; expert people that the practitioner could employ on behalf of a client)? | Services to aid communicators (such as lists, technologies and vendor applications) can be very diverse and can be implemented using convergence to good effect. The lists of such services and lists of vendors who can help is relevant, as is training and CPD. |

| How is the technology implemented (ie the steps involved)? | It is important to have access to detailed learning about how many of these channels work and what is required to implement them. In some consultancies, internal wikis offer detailed advice to employees on implementation. |
|---|---|

Applying channels for communication is not something to take lightly. We already know that it takes time and training to be good at press relations or conference organization. In just the same way, the use of social media requires acquisition of skills and capabilities in addition to an understanding of the advantages of one medium over another to achieve specific goals or how the mix and match of various media combine to be more effective together than when used in isolation.

## POLICY AND OPTIMIZATION

| Policy and optimization requirements | |
|---|---|
| Internal/external policies (examples of such policies will be needed if the practitioner is going to use this channel) | All communication deployed for organizations will be guided by policy. For social media, which by their nature are more personal and more direct, there is an overriding mantra: 'Everything you do online can be seen by anyone for the rest of your life and beyond – is this activity how your family, peers , friends or employers do or will judge you now or in the future?' |
| How does the practitioner optimize this channel to help people find/use it? | This may seem like a simple SEO question but it goes much further. Optimization may also include context, content, tone of voice, frequency of activity, online community interactivity, added value online advertising or integration with a convergent coms channel. |

The combination of policy and optimization is important. Policy can be a list of rules read once and soon forgotten, or it can be an ongoing and fresh debate. The latter is important because policy will evolve as the media evolve, and that can be quite rapid.

An approval policy for a media relations campaign with every last full stop subject to senior management scrutiny is just nonsense for Twitter (Twitter.com), where communication occurs in fast, short, spontaneous 140-character utterances. The extremes between a press release and a telephone conversation require flexible policies in terms of approval of corporate statements. Social media need the same kind of flexibility.

# MONITORING AND EVALUATION

| Monitoring and evaluation | |
|---|---|
| Monitor: what is there out there that can help monitor the effect of work using this channel? | For example, can the practitioner set up an RSS feed or a search engine monitor? Can the practitioner monitor how this channel is affecting its audience? Does the practitioner need to use a monitoring company, and if so who has the expertise and how much will it cost? |
| Metrics: What numbers are available in the public domain? What numbers are available in the private domain? | Is this best measured as page views or is it by the number of references it generates in a medium like www.digg.com? Or by a combination of measurements? Or are the metrics completely different? Do they include the actual context, and the brand values of users or those of the organization? Is Google Analytics really relevant? |
| Evaluate | How does the practitioner set realistic targets and outcomes? How can the practitioner measure how good s/he is at using this/these channels for communication? How can the practitioner evaluate the effectiveness of using this channel for communication as part of a relationship-building campaign? Is the range of media/channels so extensive that they can only be evaluated in aggregate? |

There are a lot of media to monitor and the available systems are not comprehensive. Practitioners have a long way to go, and a starting point may well be to look at an article based on a press release in most newspaper online content.

---

There are a lot of monitoring services available to the practitioner.

- Google Advanced Search provides an overview of news, blogs and Usenet discussion. It is not comprehensive but is fast and free.
- Services from Factiva and Lexis Nexis provide online news monitoring more comprehensively. CyberAlert has a very comprehensive list of UK publications it searches daily.
- The press clipping companies also monitor online publications and traditional print publications' online content.
- Technorati.com and blogsearch.google.co.uk are search engines for blogs.
- There are also search engines for Second Life, social networks, and microblogs like Twitter, Pownce and Plurk, as well as aggregators such as Alert Thingy.

---

The big issue is in sorting the most significant details from the mass of commentary.

In the past, a PR person might have been judged by the volume of coverage generated for a client. The key today is not volume but influence: that is, how deeply into the networks did the story reach and for how long did it actively set the agenda in the online 'conversations'?

There is a long history of smart clipping books being part of the PR scene, but if a company has 10,000 (or 10 million, as many do) web page impressions all live at any one time, the size of the 'clip book' is not very relevant. The active use of brand values in conversations across many channels, by contrast, is much more relevant.

Using the services provided by most online media for monitoring can be quite daunting and such facilities are by no means perfect, although many organizations are now offering a range of good services. This is dealt with in Chapter 24.

# BUY-IN

| Buy-in | |
|---|---|
| Overcoming objections to implementation | What are the practitioner arguments? How are they supported with real and verifiable evidence? Can the practitioner call on quantifiable evidence and reasoning supported by case studies? |
| Relevance to organizations and practice | Case studies of good and bad practice. Can the practitioner find case studies and look at the best examples and the worst, and then identify the risk mitigation or opportunity optimization policies when using this channel for communication? |

As this book is going to print, there remains a considerable reluctance among PR people, their organizations and managers to get stuck in to developing online strategies by committing to the new media landscape. This is not because there is no evidence that the internet is a pivotal part of relationships and relationship building. Every day new research is published and it all points in one direction. However, assembling this information (checking out on the way that it is not just another half-baked, self-serving survey – regrettably a much-abused PR tactic) is only part of the process. Being able to present it effectively requires good communications skills. Even then, there will be difficulties. Fear of the unknown, horror stories and demand for return on investment are typical responses.

Just putting a tentative toe in the water is not an effective option. The smell of amateurism, short-term commitment and a stilted approach in media predicated on community will not help any practitioner. The very idea of a 'campaign' in social media when 'engagement' is the norm is unlikely to lead to stunning success – even if there are a few cases of high-profile achievement. But to aid the practitioner, help is at hand. For nearly every form of social media, there are good strong case studies where success is evident.

# CASE STUDY: HOW TO BUILD UP A CASE STUDY LIBRARY

In 1996, one of the authors of this book needed to create a library of case studies to show students social media in action.

He created a number of Google news searches and – using the UK news option (where, in 'Advanced news search' it says 'Return only articles from news sources located in...' and return articles for the last day) for subjects such as 'blogger', 'wiki', 'podcast', etc – he created a 'news alert' for each of them.

Each day, he read through the top returns to see if the stories published showed examples of people and organizations using these channels in new or interesting ways. In two months, he accumulated over 60 case studies of successful (and unsuccessful) deployments of these, then relatively new, channels for communication. These case studies were posted to his blog, which was available to students (and anyone else with an interest) to see at first hand contemporary use of the new media. Using the capability to tag stories made the case studies easy to find by channel, subject, PR genre, industry sector and so on.

The total time invested in this activity amounted to an hour per day. An excellent ROI.

## PLANNING AND IMPLEMENTATION

| Planning and implementation | |
|---|---|
| Training | Training resources, training examples, etiquette. |
| Risk management | A structured, dispassionate assessment of the opportunities and threats. |
| Timescale for implementation | A Gantt chart to identify processes and time taken to implement. Well-structured social media campaigns actually take longer to implement than most. They are also more time consuming over a longer time if they are to be really good. |

This kind of structured approach to online communication channels offers the practitioner a number of advantages. It allows one channel to be compared with another to help identify the most suitable combination, it provides the elements needed to allow the channels to be implemented tactically into PR programmes and, finally, it means that as new channels for communication emerge, they can be evaluated in comparison with existing ones.

In creating analysis such as this it should be noted that this process does need updating, as the internet changes the relative significance of channels to people. FriendFeed is emerging as a possible new channel as this book is being written. Its use and application will be different by the time you read this book. It may not even still exist.

What communication channels can be included? Here are a few:

> Blogs, chat, e-mail, games, instant messaging, message boards, mobiles, micro-blogs, new media releases, online community portals, online conferencing, podcasting, SMS, surveys online, Usenet (Google Groups), video-sharing, virtual environments, websites, widgets, wikis, VoIP.

In addition, the practitioner will need some knowledge about search and monitoring and RSS. While we offer analysis of some channels using this approach, the practitioner will need to add others from time to time.

---

**IN BRIEF**

- The internet has spawned many new channels for communication.
- Most channels do not cease to be available but they do change.
- New channels for communication do not replace old ones, which remain significant in the communication arsenal.
- There are now so many channels for communication that it is unlikely that any one person could be expert or even proficient in all of them.
- People use a wide range of channels for communication.
- Many channels for communication are used concurrently.
- There is a technique for assessing the relative value of different channels for different applications:
  - the medium;
  - interactive elements;
  - application;
  - policy and optimization requirements;
  - monitoring and evaluation;
  - buy-in;
  - planning and implementation.

---

# Note

1. For an introduction to the hype cycles concept, see 'Understanding Gartner's hype cycles', http://www.gartner.com/

# 15

# How social media impact on strategy

As we have seen, the power and ever-growing influence of the internet and social media across all aspects of organizational development are remarkable. Now we need to look at ways in which communications strategies can be re-evaluated, redefined and developed in order to succeed in this new environment.

When one looks at the profile of most organizations in websites, on mobile phones, through digital television or in online media, there is one striking impression. It's a mess: inconstancies; for most, appalling search engine optimization; orphaned legacy content exposed online; lack of continuity between platforms and channels; intrusion of competitive or derogatory content; often stilted and static information on websites that are years out of date; a culture of not sharing in a era of sharing; and so the issues continue. Most organizations do not have a corporate internet strategy.

With the imminent prospect of 50 per cent growth in online retail, similar growth in online public purchasing, and more than 70 per cent of business-to-business purchasing decisions mediated by the internet, there is an overwhelming case for improving capability to strategically manage online presence, interactions and stakeholder relations by organizations.

Public relations, at its most senior level, has to establish board commitment to online strategy. Its significance is greater than executive board roles such as human resources, marketing, product development and supply chain, because each of these is deeply dependent on an effective internet strategy. In addition the web management functions and IT have to relinquish their grip on design functionality and on data. These are now often the stuff for building relationships.

In corporate communications strategy, there are big changes afoot. The readers of a book like this may come from a range of practices, from the most senior corporate manager to a first-year student of PR. This poses a problem. At one level, we are discovering that the impact of the internet, because of its mediation in transparency, porosity and agency, richness and reach, is changing the nature of economics, politics and culture. It is changing the way organizations are managed and is changing the management of activities. In part these are subjects for management titles, but, because the internet is so significant in communications and in relationship mediation, this change is a PR issue from top to bottom. At the other extreme, the significance of a Facebook profile on a potential employee's reputation brings home the reality of the internet to the student.

The platforms and channels and contexts and their many applications for communication and relationship building affect practitioners, the practitioner community and practitioners' organizations. PR should play a central role in this transformation, but this requires both a thorough, professional understanding of what is happening and an influential voice at the core of strategic development. One of the most effective ways for practitioners to gain acceptance for their work and ideas is through detailed and professional planning.

In its simplest form, PR management consists of planning, execution and monitoring. In traditional PR, little more is needed to represent a client than a clear brief, accurate data and sufficient practitioner time – leavened, of course, with a creative approach to knowledge transfer. Mostly it is a two-step (press agency, lobby or event-based) activity. It is assumed that human planners (seldom even using formalized planning and risk management tools) will generate the 'best' network of activities. The execution is expected to be the same as the plan – but this is seldom what actually happens! There is a fundamental difference between having a plan and executing it. Inevitably, emerging events will alter the execution, and never more so than when using social media.

The one thing we know for sure in 2009 is that we do not know what communication platforms, channels and contexts will be relevant in 2010 or 2020. Our experience over recent years shows that looking even a relatively short way into the future is beyond all but the most creative and informed minds. The rate of change will continue to be extremely rapid; although we cannot say how the way people communicate will change, it is still vitally important that we plan for that change.

Who, for example, would have predicted in 2003 that in 2008 (only five years later) broadcasters, newspapers and magazines would accept (solicit) video news clips from the public to publish on their own online TV channels. Equally, who would have predicted that chief executives of major corporations like Tom Glocer, the CEO of Reuters, would open up their thinking on blogs, knowing that they would face very open and often critical and public exchanges?

Part of strategic planning for corporate public relations requires a significant element to plan for change. For the practitioner this means that communication and relationships internally and externally will consider how the internet will affect five elements of corporate strategy development:

- *Business purpose.* Will it be changed by public environments, platforms for communication and channels for communication in a foreseeable time frame?
- *Organizational goals.* Will they be changed as people's lifestyles change? Do the devices people use to access information and interact with others affect the organization, and will emerging channels for communication influence the goals or access to them?
- *Strategies for reaching each goal.* There is almost an inevitability here. The strategy for reaching even simple goals will be changed and therefore have to be kept under review.
- *Action plans to implement strategy.* The PR plan (as opposed to PR campaign) might have a life of as long as a year.
- *Monitoring plan implementation.* The range of ways that business strategy can be monitored is growing rapidly and the shifting eddies, currents and tides of commercial influences brought about by communications technologies need close monitoring.

There are now a number of organizations that use social media to influence more traditional media.

Andy Lark, Vice President Global Marketing at Dell, is on record as saying:

The social media stuff is probably the most important thing we do today, from a marketing standpoint. The other elements of marketing mix have sort of become more and more transactional and more and more tactical in nature. Social media stuff is much more strategic... Use social media to power the fundamental of the business. That's what we're focused on.

HSBC Bank changed its strategy of ending interest-free overdrafts for students leaving university in 2007 when thousands of students on Facebook threatened to boycott the bank.

The media are aware that journalism's strategic model has changed too. Darshna Soni, a reporter for Channel 4 News, wrote in 2007: 'Citizen journalism has completely changed the way we cover the news... citizen journalism can be very powerful, a way for people to contribute to and even influence the news agenda, surely no bad thing?'

The effect of social media outreach on strategy can be felt in many areas of the media, government, business and academia.

On a shopping trip to Oxford, 16-year-old Laurie Pycroft staged an impromptu protest to counter a much larger demonstration by Speak, the group that led a high-profile and partly successful campaign to halt the building of a new animal research laboratory in Oxford in 2005. Pycroft and two friends chanted 'build the lab' and scrawled a placard reading 'Support Progress, Support the Oxford Lab'. They were shouted down and went home. He blogged about the experience, was surprised by the volume of support and so built a website that was receiving 300 hits an hour within two weeks. After a short campaign, and a shift in public sympathy that spurred government action, the new lab was built and is in use today.

The context and environment in the use of platforms and channels affect the planning of strategies and tactics.

The changing media environment is changing social habits. Of course, buying online is a significant change in behaviour; it now common to see a computer in the same room as a television, both working at the same time. The great news about a newborn child is flashed by SMS through the family network, while our daily agenda is dictated by an enterprise-wide diary on an intranet. The news about a fellow student's post-graduation world travels is on Facebook as the journey happens. Once, everyone wore a watch; today many people will take out their mobile phone when asked the time.

# CASE STUDY: THE INTERNET AS AGENT OF SOCIAL CHANGE

In the United States large numbers of internet users hold such strong views about their online communities that they compare the value of their online world to their real-world communities, according to the sixth annual survey of the impact of the internet conducted by the USC-Annenberg School Center for the Digital Future. (An 'online community' is defined as a group that shares thoughts or ideas, or works on common projects, through electronic communication only.)

Among a broad range of findings about rapidly evolving methods of online communication, the 2007 Digital Future Project found that 43 per cent of internet users who are members of online communities say that they 'feel as strongly' about their virtual communities as they do about their real-world ones.

The Digital Future Project also found that involvement in online communities leads to offline actions. More than a fifth of online community members (20.3 per cent) take actions offline at least once a year that are related to their online community.

Source: http://psychcentral.com/news/2006/11/29/the-internet-as-agent-of-social-change/ (Accessed July 2008).

We are aware that internet-mediated communication channels now form an integral part of managing relationships with large parts of the population, not least employees at work and at home, customers, suppliers, business partners and journalists. Indeed, for many it is now the dominant protocol for interaction.

# THE ESTABLISHED ORDER UNDER THREAT

The change is happening, but what makes it hard to grasp is that the internet, and notably social media, is shaking many long and deeply held customs and beliefs. As we saw in Chapter 1, the established order is under threat.

The idea that an organization is the nexus of contacts, espoused by Coase, is now significantly challenged by what we know of how communication inside (and to the outside) has changed.[1] At one time organizations were managed from the top down in departmental silos. Inter-departmental communication had to take place via a senior manager (Figure 15.1). The advent of e-mail, instant messenger and other channels for communication has changed that (Figure 15.2). Anyone can communicate with anyone.

This means that any group of people in the organization can come together to achieve their objectives, and on occasion those objectives will challenge senior management. The nature of network communication inside organizations changes the dynamic of management. Decisions can be made faster and can be made without reference to the senior management team.

Professor Feng Li at Newcastle University Business School articulates the model like this:

At the organisational level, a wide range of organisational innovations have been introduced across different sectors, resulting in both incremental and radical changes in the structures, processes, work organisations and inter-organisational relations of many organisations. From a structural perspective, for example, despite repeated predictions about the demise of the hierarchy

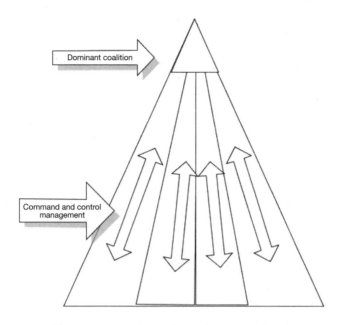

**Figure 15.1**  *The traditional organizational structure*

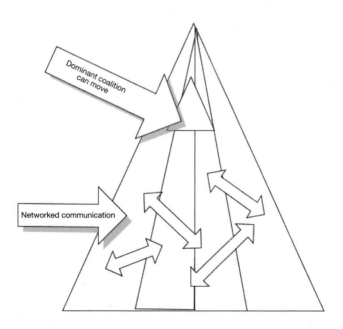

**Figure 15.2**  *The changing organizational structure*

and the continued search for alternative organisational configurations, today almost every large organisation remains hierarchical. They have become flatter, more flexible, more responsive, and they increasingly deploy project-based or virtual teams to address traditional problems associated with the hierarchy, but so far nobody has been able to identify an organisation that is not a hierarchy. This is not to say, however, that the characteristics of the hierarchies and the way these hierarchies work have not changed. The wide-spread adoption of ICTs has significantly improved the transparency of the entire organisations to business leaders and managers. This on the one hand leads to further centralisation of power, but at the same time it enables senior managers to have the confidence to delegate responsibilities and activities to operational managers and frontline employees without worrying about losing central control. The shape of the organisation may have not changed beyond hierarchies, but the way the new hierarchies work is radically different. ICTs have enabled some organisations to resolve conventional problems inherent in the hierarchy, allowing radical structural changes to take place within the parameters of the hierarchy. These changes are increasingly reflected in the changing principles of organisational designs. (Source: http://professorfengli. blogspot.com/2008/05/second-e-business-boom-how-internet.html, accessed October 2008.)

In the meantime we have seen how these changes are affecting other types of organizational structure. The influence of Facebook for UK librarians was written up by Jane Secker for LASSIE (Libraries and Social Software in Education) in 2007 and demonstrates how a number of communities provide a new infrastructure for the sector.

Managing internal relationships, and by that one can only mean a strategy for optimizing the environment for empowerment, availability of platforms for communication and awareness of threats and opportunities available through using different channels for communication, is now high on the internal PR practitioners' job description.

At a PR functional level, the political economy approach to media and communications described by Andreas Wittel has evaporated.[2] It is no longer credible to regard culture, communications and media as objects that carry symbolic value that can be produced, distributed and consumed. The production and consumption of media, culture and communications were once viewed as being distinct practices (especially in newspaper publishing), but in an era of citizen journalism (and in this context we can include internal e-mail as well as the posting of millions of photos by millions of people in the United Kingdom on Facebook), practices such as blogging, wiki-editing, video production and sharing mean the consumer of editorial content is also the producer. In traditional theory, those who controlled the means of production and distribution of media, culture and communications possessed greater power than consumers, but now the balance of power has shifted in favour of the consumer. In this world, interventions by organizations to develop business have to be at a strategic level because almost everything they do is under the intense and critical gaze of the growing online community and of those with which it interacts.

Potentially every word online is open to scrutiny by a billion people in this generation and the next. The theory is that the power of a minority will always be under scrutiny, whether that minority is a government or the local cricket team wiki. Equally, this scrutiny can at any time now or in the future be used to mediate knowledge and interaction. In discussing this in detail in Chapters 3–5, we noted that there are three major elements: the increased transparency of organizations, the extent to which organizational boundaries are breached – which increases porosity – and the extent to which people and technologies act as agents for transaction and interaction.

Until recently it was (relatively) easy to offer content to a wide audience through a strong media sector. Targeting messages at a range of print titles or a few dozen TV and radio channels was manageable. Today, reaching an audience is more complex. The proliferation of new channels presents a problem, but this is magnified by the rapid expansion in the range of platforms that can carry reputational messages.

One can speculate that most press relations managers are not fully aware of the extent of the coverage of their stories. In fact, it is probable that, even for the most knowledgeable search specialist, tracking all stories in all media as they are interpreted in pasting from channel to channel is impossible. But for the informed few in interested groups, their knowledge will be nearly complete.

Each platform offers a different experience, which means that reception and interpretation of the same message may be perceived differently at the point of consumption. The context for relationships is now more important in strategy development. For example, on-demand TV has a wider and more fragmented set of social uses than before. It is becoming increasingly interactive, and viewers themselves are gaining the ability to both time-shift and repackage content to meet their individual needs and life patterns.[3] Once watching television in the garden was not easy; today it is a simple matter of using a wifi-enabled laptop.

Equally, it is unsettling to realize that even in a traditional medium such as television, the PR message may be edited out by the consumer! A newspaper article or magazine feature might once have been read at home, on a train or at work. But the reader needed to have the publication to hand. Now the article is available wherever there is a PC, laptop, mobile phone or TV. The publication is always to hand on an array of platforms.

This means that even older forms of mass communication reception are now changed. This range of platforms and frequently convergent channels for information exchange means that relying on communication 'silver bullets' to reach any segment or group of people is no longer enough.

The compounding effect of new channels such as Facebook, YouTube and Twitter, plus wikis, podcasting and all the rest, adds complexity to relationship and behaviour motivation planning. Even the channels can be part of the message; the use of an un-editable PDF file suggests that further debate is not encouraged; if the same information is carried on a blog, the implied message is entirely the opposite, with content development by the audience positively encouraged.

In addition, as we have seen, online media encourage people to actively bookmark their articles and share them with others. Circulation of stories from the *Daily Telegraph, South Wales Echo* or *Heat Magazine* can be shared with friends and the world using common bookmarking sites (typically, at time of going to press: Delicious, Digg this, Stumbleupon, Newsvine), often with user-created tags and possibly including comments of the publication's site and/or the sharing site. Often the commentary and sharing is about content provided by a press office.

The evolution of the internet from a platform for data communication to an application that encourages data manipulation (not just through human intervention but by internet-enabled technologies that act as agents – internet agency) is now very apparent. This would suggest that a comprehensive operational strategy should consider how best to harness this power of sharing, and internet agency.

The need for timeliness of intelligence about what is happening is, as for many other PR activities, already changing the news monitoring strategy. For example, a web widget that combines RSS with automated keyword search (and is able to take information from web pages that do not even have RSS feeds) embedded into a blog, wiki or website can be the equivalent of an old-fashioned press clipping bureau. It is completely automated and can monitor in near real time newspapers and magazines, radio and TV sites, as well as social media. The cost is low (often free) and not only disintermediates the clipping bureau but provides a newswire and clipping service to the general public, subsuming an area of PR practice once the preserve of the PR department or agency. Perhaps the strategy has evolved into being the facilitator.

> There are a lot of people who provide a range of RSS news monitoring services to the general public. Dave Cross of Director, Magnum Solutions Ltd, has http://dave.org.uk/newsfeeds.

The opinion feedback that newspapers once had in the form of letters to the editor now includes e-mail, online comment, recorded comments and much more. Monitoring such interactions is now important. The strategic decision to focus on online monitoring, often at the expense of traditional paper clips, is a big change and no doubt some print coverage will be missed in some organizations, but if its reach is limited to walled gardens of subscriptions or print-only content, it may be deemed of lesser significance.

Things are changing, but experience shows that new media do not kill off old media. Old media tend to adapt. Newspapers are now also broadcasters, the BBC is using Twitter (http://twitter.com/bbcnews) and interpersonal telephone conversations include text, pictures and video from home phones, computers using Skype and mobile devices. Legacy channels also remain available long after they fall out of fashion (eg fax and Usenet) and/or morph into new forms (eg Google Groups) and should not be forgotten.

Internet strategies at a corporate level, functional level and operational level are, we have now established, all changed because of the internet 'new PR' effect.

# LOCAL VERSUS GLOBAL COMMUNICATION

There are further devils in the detail. The nature of local versus global communication online is a consideration.

There is a notable tendency for publics (or market segments or stakeholders) to give way to online user-generated social/consumer segments. Here, users gravitate to each other and engage on their own terms. Very often these users do not conform to the profile identified by the originating organization that once might have thought it 'owned' the product or brand. Online community portals offer rich evidence of this tendency. Groups form that defy their market geographies, age profiles, incomes and anticipated interests.

---

Using a Microsoft search analysis engine (http://adlabs.msn.com), it is possible to identify the use of a website by social demographic. This showed the demographic profile of Wikipedia as being mostly female oriented, with a ratio of 30 per cent male to 70 per cent female users; it had an age distribution of 27.2 per cent 25–34-year-olds, 26.8 per cent 18–24-year-olds, 23 per cent 35–49-year-olds, 13.2 per cent over 50 and 9.8 per cent under 18.

It may come as something of a surprise to find that nearly one in 10 users are children, and it is interesting to note that the most inquisitive people are 24-year-old women.

Using the same methods one finds that a quarter of the people interested in Formula One are women aged 18–34 and 36 per cent of people using Handbag.com are men aged 25.

---

> For brand sites this can be a revelation. Appletiser is a fizzy apple drink aimed at 'funky' young women. That is where the brand is pitched, but 55 per cent of the online audience is male, with 63 per cent of visitors over the age of 24. It is the consumer who is defining the demographic makeup for the brand's appeal.
>
> What is evident is that user segmentation online is of the public's choosing rather than by traditional market or PR segmentation methods. Perhaps these can be called user-generated market segments.

The words that are associated with the brand reflect brand attributes. Suppose one used a tool like Google Adword to find keywords for some brand of drink. This might show the keywords to be 'drink', 'advert', 'logo', 'orange' and 'orange juice', well before key brand values such as 'fruit drink' or 'soft drink' which the organization might claim. Here we see evidence of people defining the brand or values of the drink.

Another approach to identifying the interests of people is through the traces left as they use the internet. In 2005 Seth Goldstein coined the term 'MyWare'. He explained that sites we visit reveal what we like and do not like, and this activity leads to a form of segmentation called *behavioural targeting*.[4]

The idea that it is not only the brand manager that decides who the market will be, or indeed what the values of the brand are, is a revelation and it applies elsewhere.

> Using David Phillips' semantic analysis software, an analysis of a month of blog comments about public relations revealed that, worldwide, the concepts that were of greatest interest among the online community were, in order: press release distribution services, press release distribution, graduate advisers, internship experience, Google, the PR industry, event marketing, communications strategy, PRSA, concerted effort, creative design, media relations, new opportunities and a number of PR agencies. Tapping into the global interests of the industry using this methodology, we find that the big drivers for the industry at the time focused on press relations, students seeking experience and the power of Google.
>
> With this kind of intelligence, it is possible to develop communications tactics for social media outreach that can be directed to user-generated 'PR industry brand values' of the moment, as opposed to other values that may hold no current interest for the sector.
>
> Other methodologies in use include analysis of search terms drawn from search engine optimization techniques and analysis of inbound links to key websites.

Using techniques that are freely available, we are now beginning to understand what interests publics about organizations and what they think about them, from what is explicitly written and said about them online.

Even those sections of the population that never use the internet are influenced by it, albeit at one step removed. They can also influence those who are online, and the 'have nots' do have online advocates.

As a lot of information is user generated, this brings a symmetry in communication that influences both organizations and their publics. Here we have the unusual phenomenon of engagement by proxy, where individuals attempt to engage directly with both the organization and those believed to be able to influence it.

As argued earlier, the cherished (if flawed) belief that messages can be 'controlled' is largely a thing of the past. There is inherent agency in and of the internet, where messages are changed by human and machine interventions as they hop from platform to platform, channel to channel. An organization now competes with a wide range of other actors in the development and dissemination of information, inexorably contributing to what now becomes the development of value systems, across a network of authors, platforms and channels. We deal with this in detail in Chapter 17.

Because internet users are now also contributors, they cast searing 'net-shine' deep into organizations that are increasingly transparent – whether they like it or not. These new critics have the tools – and the inclination – to explore what organizations represent, do and say. With their enhanced access to online content from sources like governments, ombudsmen and regulators, and trade associations, and the comments of the wider online and offline community, ordinary people can question the values and value systems of organizations. And they pose – and answer – these questions in public, on blogs and social networking sites, through wikis, podcasts and YouTube videos.

Organizations have to be able to defend their values in public like never before. Spin, bling, hype and exaggeration as well as ethics and practices will be questioned and challenged, and any dissonance between the values of users and the organization is made very publicly evident (see Chapter 26).

In developing communications strategies at a corporate level, it is evident that there is an online view available from online interactions that also affect brand and other reputations. The manifestation and changed behaviours are not always evident from simple cause and effect analysis. They are the accumulation of small 'straws in the wind' blown through cyberspace.

# NOT WAVING, DROWNING...

This sea, this universe of information, has a downside. There is just too much of it. The sheer volume of 'facts' and messages means all players must confront the issue of attention deficit. People once did not have to multi-task when interacting with data or knowledge. Now, when people acquire knowledge, it comes to them as a constant, always updating stream of images and texts. The posters, newspapers, TV and radio images are more than matched by internet-driven content. It is a phenomenon described by Linda Stone, former executive at both Apple Computer and Microsoft, as 'continuous partial attention'.[5]

Once, to compete in such an environment, attention was gained by dominating channels. Huge poster campaigns and mass-media advertising offered a sure-fire, if expensive, magic bullet. Now, there is resistance. People 'tune out' these attempts and either select channels that are less intrusive or compromise by accepting a little interference for cheap access to what they want. They pull information and select personal strategies that will help them to stay informed without dedicating valuable time to reading advertisements or searching for information. Portals, filters, news alerts and RSS are just some of the techniques that help knowledge gatherers keep their heads above the surface of the data tidal wave. Other services that pull together RSS feeds, Twitter tweets, Facebook activity and e-mail (and much else) and display this in a constant stream in the corner of the computer screen (current examples being Twirl and Alert Thingy) serve to provide instant awareness of what is going on across the globe among important publics. They are also intrusive and distracting.

These facilities help practitioners stay in touch; they also provide equally fast information to stakeholders.

Strategies are required to manage this flow of information, prioritize it and respond to it. The implication is that the development of initiatives, responses to events and all the mechanisms needed to keep mangers informed and involved is becoming more difficult and at the same time more important.

---

### IN BRIEF

- Development of internet strategies requires planning.
- There is a difference between having a plan and executing that plan.
- Strategies need to be developed to accommodate changing communications platforms and channels.
- Strategies need to consider the social and behavioural changes wrought by the internet.
- Vertical silos for information sharing belong to the past.
- The dominant coalition can be the nexus of communicating groups.
- The production and consumption of media, culture and communications are now available to the majority of the population.

- Targeting using media selection is now more complex, with a wider range of platforms and channels.
- Different platforms for communication offer different experiences of channels and messages.
- Channels for communication can be an implicit part of the message.
- The range of platforms and channels requires development of multi-channel strategies.
- Old media are adapting and adopting new media.
- The internet is allowing people to cluster round products and brands (and issues), making segmentation difficult for traditionalist brand managers.
- People are selecting their own brand values (corporate, product and service), which are nearly always different from brand values expressed by brand managers.
- Behaviours also define interest in products and values.
- Some people affect the internet and its content by proxy.
- People can question values and value systems, and this requires a strategic approach to removing content that can cause dissonance between an organization and its constituency.
- Planning has to include consideration of attention deficit caused by fast-moving, ever-changing and always-on content passing in front of the public.

## Notes

1. Coase, R (1937). The nature of the firm, *Economica*, 4, pp 386–405
2. Wittel, A (2004) Conference of socialist economists winter, http://findarticles.com/p/articles/mi_qa3780/is_200401/ai_n9366252 (accessed July 2007)
3. Lash, S, Lury, C, Wittel, A and Bachmann, G (2006) Broadband project: a paper for the PACCIT broadband project, www.goldsmiths.ac.uk/paccit-broadband/paccit.pdf (accessed June 2007)
4. http://en.wikipedia.org/wiki/Behavioral_targeting (accessed Oct 2007)
5. http://continuouspartialattention.jot.com/WikiHome (accessed Oct 2007)

# 16

# Management approaches to planning

The evidence would suggest that optimized relationship development practice needs to adopt and develop a range of management skills so as to be able to deal with complex communication systems, taking account of a high level of uncertainty and change.

Put simply, we need to be able to plan for surprises in this fast-changing world. The past practice of copying what went before as a planning guide for PR is obviously unreliable. There is no 'before' online. It is all evolving all the time. Trying out a new channel on a client without careful planning can mean exposing a PR activity to ridicule, or worse to the derision of a billion people. So a 'bright idea' needs to be considered using the best management tools and skills we have before being put into practice.

Such management skills come from a range of disciplines. For the most part, they do not replace existing practice but add and extend it.

This means that the practitioner must know, understand and deploy the management practices needed for planning and implementing complex programmes in order to be able to develop effective online strategies. These are no longer mere options. Being conversant with such techniques is now a basic skill. The idea that one can run a 'PR campaign' is now flawed. A 'campaign' once had time limits and could thus be dropped after the event, but this does not apply today. The unforgetting internet will leave traces and possible interactions for years. Indeed, some campaigns can come back and haunt organizations decades later, fully referenced and naming time, place, event and those involved.

---

As New Orleans' residents fled the city after the city's mayor ordered an evacuation ahead of Hurricane Gustav's expected landfall, newspapers and bloggers round the world created hyperlinks to content created three years earlier when Hurricane Katrina devastated southern Florida and Louisiana. The BBC, USA Today and CNN all resurrected past coverage and, notably, amateur video of Katrina victims and storm chasers, complete with criticism of state and federal responses and the people involved in the 2005 disaster.

The content was as vivid in 2008 as it had been in 2005.

---

Of course all the management techniques used in corporate planning are needed as part of planning online public relations, in much the same way that they should be deployed for all management activity. This is not a management school textbook and thus we will take Pareto and grid analysis for granted.

Change management is a bit of an exception. There are two aspects: Individual Change Management and Organizational Change Management. In both cases, practitioners must be aware of the ways that change mediated by the internet is affecting both individuals and organizations.

It is a fundamental part of public relations where a project is introduced to individuals to include: awareness of why the change is needed; desire to support and participate in the change; knowledge of how to change; ability to implement new skills and behaviours; and reinforcement to sustain the change.

---

A range of recent research supports a form of change management that recognizes that individuals do not have access to absolute knowledge or reality, but rather refer to a set of beliefs they have built up over time, about reality.

Developed by Chris Argyris, and subsequently presented in Peter Senge's *The Fifth Discipline*,[1] a model referred to as the 'ladder of inference' helps to explain this phenomena.

The ladder of inference model from action science is a representation of different ways that individuals make sense of and deal with everyday

---

events. It posits that individuals select and process certain aspects of events, and introduce elements from this processing into their thinking, feeling and interactions.

The steps in the process are described in terms of people, beginning with real data and experience (verbatim words, specific actions, factual content). Individuals then choose a set of selected data and experience to pay attention to. To this selected data experience they affix meaning and develop assumptions, come to conclusions, and finally develop beliefs. Beliefs then form the basis of actions, which create additional real data and experience. It is beliefs that influence the selected data and experience people pay attention to.

This offers an insight into why social recommendation, comments, votes and other icons that suggest something is worthwhile do so well online. A lot of Web 2.0 is composed of belief-driven selected data.

This means that communication of change using relevant platforms, channels and contexts is presented in such a way that people have access to data (including different interpretations suited to the publics in multi-channel, multi-touch communication) from which they can use beliefs to identify with the 'facts' as presented to them. All PR programmes affect a range of people in different ways and they each need to be 'kept in the loop'.

Thus, in introducing the New PR, and the change it imposes on organizations, the means for developing internal strategies have to include elements of internet PR. The difference is this: thinking of the internet as a channel for communication (or several channels) or thinking of the internet as the foundation upon which the business stands.

We have to be ready to face the needs and responses of a wide range of internet users, without necessarily being able to predict how they will select and use our information, but in the knowledge they will make their own decisions on which channels for communication to pull content from and on how they will participate in the relationship dynamic. The nature of the internet means many processes that were once adequate now need to be updated.

In the next chapter, on planning, we propose a number of techniques.

Because of the combination of the mass communication model and the 'network effect model', there is a lot of information available to the practitioner to explore the context, the online environment, in which an organization is or can be regarded.

---

## THE NATURE OF THE NETWORK OF NETWORKS

Huber, in his *Theory of the Internet* in 1995, said that:[2]

> Normally metaphors are used to describe the Internet like the concepts 'path', 'information highway', 'data highway', 'architecture'. But these metaphors, unless understood in a new and extended meaning, suggest that the internet is like car driving on a highway. But what for instance are the tires of that vehicle? Or what is the 'gas station' of the internet? The term 'architecture' of the net suggests a three dimensional building with an entrance door, windows and certain levels. But what is the roof of the Internet and what is the staircase to its cellar? No one knows.
>
> So what we have to do is to develop a new theory and new concepts for the description and understanding of a complex structure like the internet, which are no metaphorical uses and which are already developed for the description of large, complex and interrelated phenomena. I mean the theory of social systems, the second order cybernetics as developed in the writings of Ranulph Glanville and Heinz von Foerster, the theory of knots (topology) and the theory of social networks.

The various dimensions in the new 'network' do include platforms, channels and contexts, but also include geography, time and time-shifting in the use of internet properties and the nature of juxtaposed data and 'mashups' that bring different forms of data together to create new and novel, often dynamically created, knowledge and insights.

The network effect model is beyond the scope of this book but the practitioner may need to consider that corporate information, once it is beyond an organization's direct control, is potentially (probably) subject to these influences.

---

In social media, there will be commentary about the organization, its competitors and their associated issues and values.

The explication of values goes to the very heart of an organization. It is the public reflection of the board's and employees' values. It is here that ethical management and ethical practice is tested.

Values and value systems are important for two reasons. First, values are explicitly expressed in an organization's websites and those that are closely associated with the activities of the organization. These values are picked up by search engines as part of the semantic analysis used by their algorithms. These techniques contribute to the results people get when searching for information about the organization or its core values. Second, the values expressed by and about organizations and their range of activities are the subject of commentary either directly or indirectly by people using the internet to express views and opinions, often in social media. These interpretations of corporate activities and values are also picked up by search engines and contribute to the view presented to the public.

Online, there is no hiding place.

People seek organization values and form implicit or explicit relationships with organizations that have values of interest to them. For example, when booking a holiday, internet users will form an affinity with organizations that provide particular types of holidays and related services, and will form relationships with those organizations that offer values in the form of services and advice relevant to their interest at the time. This is not just for big organizations. Such is the power of search, and especially those search engines that use semantic analysis of websites (and all the big ones do), that a private holiday-cottage owner has just the same chance as a travel company when the values involved chime with the needs and values of the holiday seeker.

Websites and online media form a 'cloud' of information that puts the organization and its values in context. Alan Jenkins, in his comment for the Coutts report 'Face value' on reputation in March 2008, put it quite succinctly: 'Your brand is no stronger than your reputation and will increasingly depend on what comes up when you are Googled.'[3]

---

Values expressed by organizations can provide added value to relationships between people and organizations. An excellent example of an organization addressing the values of its myriad stakeholders in its website is to be found in the CSR pages on the Tesco investor relations website http://www.investorcentre.tescoplc.com. Here the company explicitly explains its values alongside financial information.

In this case the company has built a defensive wall against criticism of its practices because it provides all the information that internal and external stakeholders need to understand the Tesco viewpoint. The Tesco value system creates an understanding of the organization to attract people who have an interest in it.

With these values in mind, discovering the response to the Tesco values and those of its competitors, suppliers and customers is a relatively easy if painstaking exercise: one can provide a situational analysis by using the range of services provided by search engines.

---

This principle applies as much to a small organization as to a giant, and also applies to brands, people and issues.

The role of most online activity is to build relationships. As we point out in previous chapters, there is no single magic component, and no single channel for communication that will achieve this. Online PR is about mutitouch, multi-channel relationships, often with tiny, but networked, groups.

There will always be a set of values or range of concepts that are involved in any public relations campaign. This stretches well beyond the snappy brand strap line and 'three core messages' into what they truly represent. They can be synthesized into a number of statements and then can be compared using a similar technique to that used for comments in websites linking to the organizations, the websites that are near the top returns derived by using search engines, the online press, social media and other channels. The more these concepts converge, the closer the organization is to reaching its PR objective of mutual understanding. It is a great technique for both setting objectives and measuring results.

---

### FINDING OUT HOW CORE VALUES RESONATE ONLINE

The practitioner can practice this technique by feeding one or more value statements into a search engine (in double quote marks if it is expressed as a slogan) to see what the results look like. For example the search string for the Tesco slogan "every little helps" in Google blog search shows the extent to which the company's value statements are associated with its most used strap line. Among the top 10 returns at the time of writing were a YouTube video, comments from *The Independent* and *The Guardian*, an anagram fun site, two blog posts and two traditional websites, as well as two pages from the company's own site. Here is evidence of a corporate value (one of its marketing slogans) reflected in a range of media and notably mostly beyond the company's control. These page impressions will be a legacy asset long after the slogan has been expunged from the corporate lexicon, and the strategy the company uses to sustain this value will be interesting to see.

---

Of course, there will be divergent views, and some of little help to the reputation of an organization, which is why such techniques are so valuable. They expose weaknesses as well as strengths.

In the previous chapter, we discussed how people are using the internet to define themselves. In many ways, these people conform to a Grunigian interpretation of publics.[4] They form around values (Grunig postulates that publics form around issues). While this will always happen, there is also a need in online PR to attract relevant audiences. Effectively identified and explicit expression of values is a must or there will be no reason why a target audience should pay any attention.

For some time to come, organizations' websites will be a cornerstone of their online presence. Experience in public relations practice suggests that many such websites leave a lot to be desired. Many may look good, but all too often they lack reasonable capabilities to really add value. This is the biggest shop window any organization has and it deserves as much care and attention as the head office or flagship shop. Many look like a pretty poster pasted over the front door and, notably, the door handle.

Of course, websites need to be designed to be search engine friendly from the start – long before anyone offers a design. The web site plan has to be designed to manage visitor interaction, navigation and gratification. Things like e-mail addresses, phone numbers, addresses and maps are just so easy to add and so often not available, limited in scope or drab. Perhaps they lack the means to instant message (IM), comment on a blog post, add to a Twitter stream, share the content of a page with the world or a few friends using Delicious, FriendFeed and Facebook, or perhaps to allow visitors to take information to add it to their corporate library or network behind their firewall.

There has to be some form of customer management systems (CMS) to allow people inside the organization access (which can include e-mail, voice, video, avatar or a virtual reception room) to visitors, and this has to be in the context that the visitor wants to enjoy. Then there are the many hygiene elements.

It is worth looking closely at the website from a reputation perspective. Simple things need to be considered against this checklist:

- Is the website easily available, or does it work slowly or, worse, go down under pressure of a lot of visits?
- Is it well constructed or does it have some pages that are not accessible (the dreaded 404 result when a page is called up)?
- Has it got lots of pages, microsites and other content with different URLs that confuse the visitor and search engines?
- Has every page got proper descriptions for search engines (called 'metadata') and is it regularly updated to optimize its visibility to search engines?
- Has it been changed so that there are orphaned pages that do not tie back to the site?
- Are web pages that were once available but no longer exist still indexed in other pages online (legacy content), thus reducing the value of the online asset?
- Does the site comply with disability rules that are mandatory in the EU?
- Does it provide facilities that allow visitors to monitor changing content (like press releases) by using RSS?
- Can users index or share pages by using social media?

The forgoing is a brief list and each of the points is a reflection on the quality of the organization's public relations.

The World Wide Web Consortium Accessibility Initiative (WAI) published an updated Working Draft of WAI-ARIA, the Accessible Rich Internet Applications technical specification, for resolution in September 2008. It is a matter of corporate social responsibility for organizations to monitor these developments at http://www.w3.org/WAI/ as well as to comply with the Disability Discrimination Act 1995, which is proscriptive as to 'access to and use of information services', including the web.

When, for whatever reason, a website performs badly it reflects on the organization as a whole. It sends a message to users that the organization is poorly run. It does not matter to the users that the website is the responsibility of some other department. All they know is that this organization does not care about their interests.

Most organizations have used websites for half a decade. These sites are important, and should now be integrated into the part of the organization responsible for relationships with internal and external publics.

---

**IN BRIEF**

- Online interaction requires a capability to plan for surprises.
- Planning online PR strategies requires the application of stándard planning practice.
- There are other considerations in planning because internet mediation impacts on change management.
- Presenting online PR strategies requires presentation to accommodate different belief systems so that publics can access the information.
- Much of online exposure is based on explication of values.
- Values expressed about an organization online are a reflection of the values of the organization.
- Values are brought to the fore by search engines and social commentators.
- Affinity of values creates relationships.
- 'Your brand is no stronger than your reputation and will increasingly depend on what comes up when you are Googled.'
- Explicit expression of values is a helpful defence strategy.
- Convergent values between an organization and its online publics give a measure of the effectiveness of the PR objective of creating mutual understanding.
- Publics form around values.
- Websites should be checked to ensure they are performing to optimal standards.
- Websites should be optimized for search engines on a regular basis.
- Websites need to be made social media friendly.
- Websites reflect on the public relations of the organization.

## Notes

1.  Senge, Peter M (1990) *The Fifth Discipline: The art and practice of the learning organization*, Doubleday Currency
2.  See: Huber, H D (1995) Theory of the internet, http://www.hgb-leipzig. de/ARTNINE/huber/writings/internete.html (accessed 2008)
3.  Jenkins, A (2008) *Face Value: Your reputation as a business asset*, http:// www.coutts.com/files/facevalue.pdf (accessed 2008)
4.  Grunig, James E and Hunt, Todd (1984) *Managing Public Relations*, Harcourt Brace

# 17

# Landscaping

There are loads of Public Relations planning models. In the CIPR PR in Practice Series books like *Planning and Managing Public Relations Campaigns: A step-by-step guide* by Professor Anne Gregory, *Public Relations: A practical guide to the basics* by Philip Henslowe FCIPR and *Public Relations Strategy* by Dr Sandra Oliver are all good examples.

They have in common an approach that can be summed up as: Research, Landscaping and situational analysis, Objectives setting, Identifying publics, Key messages, Strategy, Tactics, Timescale, Budget, Crisis issues, Management planning and Evaluation. However, there is variation to this model when planning and managing online PR.

Before any plan can be considered, the practitioner needs to know what already exists. Thus, before proposing an organization should have a blog outreach programme, it is sensible to know if there are people already blogging on behalf of the organization. Before proposing a change of corporate identity, it's worth knowing how much online legacy asset will be left orphaned in cyberspace (sounds sad, doesn't it?).

Most practitioners use a search engine to see what is available about their clients online. Looking at blogs is a different matter. A simple search at www.google.com/blogsearch or http://technorati.com will reveal the extent to which an organization is (admittedly often unwittingly) exposed by its (often absent) involvement in social media. After a quick look, there is a need for a more structured approach.

When landscaping the online opportunities for public relations, there are four major considerations:

- the platforms;
- the channels;
- the context;
- the content (which is the subject of the following chapters).

# THE PLATFORMS

It is an error to imagine that online content is not accessed by a range of different platforms. It is, and because various platforms exist, it seems sensible to test the extent to which different platforms are used, the channels that will be used and the context.

A simple example will explain how relevant this is. There is a world of difference between access via a PC and via a laptop. A PC is fixed, so the context for a PC might include a location such as home or office. On the other hand a laptop might be used in those same locations, but also in the train or garden, or at a client's office.

Access to information about the practitioner's organization, and all the rest of the information about it available on a wide range of devices, is important and the big three – PCs, laptops and mobile phones – should always be in the mind of the practitioner.

# THE CHANNELS

It is quite simple to dismiss the range of channels that might be used by the online community. Some information may not be designed to be included in a blog or embedded in another website or to be referenced in a microblog, but that does not mean that it won't be.

Reviewing what is available about an organization and how it would be presented through different channels, and perhaps mixed with other information, is part of effective landscaping and can be examined, in part, by examining the content and sources linking into a website (including sites like blogs, sharing sites and social networks).

For a quick look at your organization online here are some places to go:

- http://www.google.co.uk/blogsearch;
- http://technorati.com/;
- http://video.google.co.uk/;
- http://www.everyzing.com/;
- http://groups.google.co.uk;
- http://groups.yahoo.com/.

The practitioner who wants a comprehensive view will use a range of search engines. For example there are specialist search engines that can identify photographs and images (even when they have been altered) such as http://tineye.com. There is a comprehensive list at http://www.searchenginecolossus.com.

---

On August 18, 2008 Chrix Finne, the official Google Blogger, announced *Google Power Readers in Politics*. It purported to show what the leading political journalists and both US presidential campaigns using Google's RSS were seeing every day in their RSS feed. The post said:

> You can read what they read, and see what's on their minds as they share and discuss news. Each participant has created a reading list with a feed you can subscribe to in Reader (or any other feed reader), and is also publishing shared items. Here's the list of participants:

> Obama and McCain campaigns, Mike Allen, POLITICO, Chuck DeFeo, Townhall, John Dickerson, Slate, Mark Halperin, TIME, Arianna Huffington, The Huffington Post, Ruth Marcus, Washington Post, Jon Meacham, Newsweek, Patrick Ruffini, The Next Right.

The inference is that RSS, used as a channel for communication, can be made available about anyone to the whole world (in due course), which is a pretty powerful and different form of communication.

---

Identifying the channels used by people can also be done by searching in channels by means of their search facilities or by using in-site searches. Most search engines provide a site search capability.

---

In Google for example, adding 'site:cipr.co.uk' and then a keyword will reveal mentions restricted to the site, in this case the CIPR site. Thus a Google search: 'site:cipr.co.uk PR Week' will reveal 95 mentions of 'PR Week' in the site. The search 'site:myspace.com PR Week' shows the 549 times PR Week is mentioned in MySpace. This means we know that PR Week is mentioned in the social network site MySpace, and it follows that this is a channel for communication about PR Week.

---

The range of channels is significant and could include a web page, Wikipedia entry, online video, blog or Twitter among others. Perhaps the channel is a computer game, as in Second Life, or e-mail. Maybe it is instant messaging that offers the potent link. Of course, for the most successful campaigns it will all of these and more.

## Own site as a channel

In any landscaping, knowing about the organization's own presence is a good start. Who owns the site, where and how it is hosted and other simple basic information, these are the sort of things that anyone can check and are worth reviewing. Using sites like http://www.domaintools.com or http://www.who.is will reveal a lot of interesting stuff (and probably the name of the web master before the one who left three years ago, which of course needs to be updated).

The practitioner may have access to all the website statistics generated by one of the sophisticated software packages now available that give a lot of detail about site visitors and their use of the site, and indeed the data available by using Google Analytics.

Using Yahoo! and Yahoo! site explorer (http://siteexplorer.search.yahoo.com), it is not difficult to find out the number of pages on the organization's website that have been indexed by this search engine.

Of course many organizations have more than one site. There may be microsites and other properties such as blogs.

---

Many organizations have microsites. Some of these are provided by the organization itself; they may deal with a specific area of activity but link to the main site. Others will be provided and even branded by third parties. For example, the CIPR uses a lot of third party sites such as http://www.prshots.co.uk/ for its photo library, and http://www.prjobshop.co.uk/ for its recruitment activities.

The CIPR has two main URLs because of its name change when it was awarded Charter status: http://www.cipr.co.uk and http://www.ipr.org.uk. Web traffic is directed to the former from the latter, and care has to be taken to ensure that the method used adds to the presence of the primary website when it is indexed by search engines and, for the user, there is seamless integration. The classic mistake is when a company has many brands each with its own site as well as high levels of information that cut across the purpose of both sites.

---

## Channels that link to the site

The next information of value is to know who claims an affinity with the organization by linking to its website (called links in or back links). These links are valuable because they add to the credibility of the site among search engines, help point people to the site and provide intelligence to site owners about what is really important to the site visitors. Some sites linking to an organization (eg www.bbc.co.uk) have a high ranking, and a link from such a site would improve the rank of the organization's site. A link from www.anyoldrubbish.com website would have much less value and 'link farms' that link to everything in sight, normally for a fee, are of no value at all. Search engine managers are not daft. The number of pages linking back to a site will change quite dynamically as new pages index the site, are taken down or are edited.

Because the practitioner can see the URL of the pages that link back to their site, these pages can be identified and categorized by type (in all probability .co.uk = a UK website; the word blog in the URL = a blog post; .ac.uk is a university and so forth). Auditing this influential group of links will give an indication of the kind of organizations and people who find the site interesting.

One of the most useful tools available to practitioners is Google Analytics. By signing up and embedding some code on a website, the practitioner can have access to a lot more information. With between two and four weeks of data collected by the software, some significant information can become available.

## What kind of sites reference the organization?

A more detailed view of the sites that reference but don't link to the site is available by using Yahoo site/domains advanced search option. This allows practitioners to view websites by domain. So, for example, one can see which universities mention the site by selecting an advance search with the suffix .ac.uk, or government sites with the suffix .gov.uk and for specific types of blogs .blogger.com and so forth.

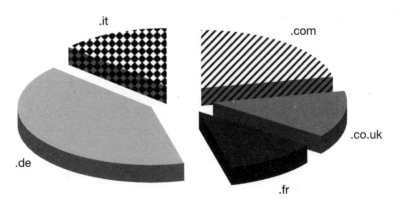

**The five big domains**
Mentioning easyJet in web pages

**Figure 17.1** *The different types of domain linking to a website*
*(Image courtesy eFootprint.com)*

This technique is really useful for identifying mentions in types of website with specific regular URL syntax. The suffix .blogspot.com will reveal all those inbound links from people using the Blogger service from Google and is a technique for many social media and other domains. (In tests for this chapter and using this technique, we identified the six people who most frequently reference the CIPR using Twitter – these are real people and we knew them all!)

---

Using website analytics software or Google Analytics will show a list of all the pages that link into the website and the pages that have referred traffic to the site. With this information there are three key elements:

1. The first is the sites that your organization has promoted by linking to them; you can see if there is a reciprocal relationship and see which of these sites have sent you traffic and which have not. This may prompt activity to build better relationships to promote such traffic.
2. The second is to see the sites that you did not realize are sending traffic. Practitioners need to examine these sites to see what kind of relationship is desirable. Perhaps it is a blog that posted a comment about your site. Look and see, and then make a plan of how to optimize the relationship.
3. The third thing is to look for potential joint initiatives. If someone has published your content or linked to your site, perhaps they will let you submit more content to their site. The next time you do a promotion, you can then send them an article to publish on their site as well.

---

## The page impressions

The total number of publicly available web pages that index the organization would seem to be quite simple to find. It is the number of pages indexed by the leading search engines that mention the organization, its people and its brands. This can be a bit misleading when the search engines say that they have indexed 1 billion page references about an organization but, in reality, only make a few hundred of them available. There is another measure, which is the number of pages indexed and publicly available that mention the company. As we have explained before, these pages are all assets. Most of these impressions will have been created without the knowledge, let alone involvement, of the organization. In addition some of these pages will have negative content (a form of asset liability). In the previous chapter we added another dimension to evaluating the online asset, which is to examine these pages for the extent to which the values expressed converge with the organization.

## Landscaping search returns

Using search in the first part of landscaping, the first 20 results are important because they show that, in the case of Google for instance, some returns are from other organizations and some may not be very complimentary (a case for improved search engine optimization – see below).

---

To find the numbers of web page impressions is simple if you can create a search for the organization using most search engines and then look at the results like this one:

Results 1–10 of about 27,100 for 'Chartered Institute of Public Relations'.

Of course, the search has to be appropriate, as in this case:

Results 1–10 of about 73,600 for 'public relations' 'CIPR'

---

People are becoming very sophisticated in the way they search. They are using phrases, phrases in parentheses and advanced search options. The key words that are often associated with a site or type of site can be identified by using online tools. These will include the kind of values that are associated with the organization.

---

### FINDING THE WORDS PEOPLE USE

Using one of the many online tools available (in this case http://www. webconfs.com/website-keyword-suggestions.php), one can discover the values that people associate and use when searching for the institute; we entered the CIPR domain 'www.cipr.co.uk' and the results were interesting:

- Of the top 10 returns, three were using the CIPR presence to enhance the visibility of their own websites (using SEO techniques).
- The value statements remaining were: public relations, public relations assistant job, PR, define public relations, public relations for law firms, measuring PR impact, PR contracts...
- It is notable that many of these search terms were phrases showing a sophisticated form of search (which are worth entering into a search engine to see whether such phrases would return the CIPR site or not).

---

The simple search or more complex search terms will yield a lot of page impressions. Who is providing all these pages?

- All the pages of the organization's website will (should) be listed unless they have a 'robot block' to ask search engines not to index the page.
- The search engine will probably find some pages that were provided by the organization and are out of date but still on the organization's site or are cached (filed) on other computers, called legacy pages.
- Many, if not most, will be from organizations with an interest in the organization.
- Some will have been encouraged or paid to reference or link to the site (sometimes known as affiliate marketing).
- Others will have a self-interest in being associated with the organization, and others will have other motives.
- Then there is the growing number of individuals who comment. For some organizations this can be a quarter of all web page impressions!

## Rate of growth in interest of the website

Some search engines, like http://www.alltheweb.com, show the numbers of pages that were added to their index each year, which gives an indication of the growth in popularity of a website over time. All search engines will show that there is an increase in pages indexed each year, just because of the growth of the internet. The best measures are against benchmarks such as competitors. Comparing the relative growth rates is instructive and provides helpful data.

# THE CONTEXT

The nature of context and environment, the values of the audiences and the ability for them to interact can be examined. If one anticipates the reach of the organization to be through a laptop in a living room and competing with television, its context will be different from that of a university library. In addition the context may be one that prompts motivations for the audience to select itself with the help of semantically attached, semi-detached or just passing acquaintance with the online concepts of the minute.

There is one other consideration. The content can be explicit, implicit, detailed; is it possible to reduce it down to just 140 characters for microblogs?

There is another form of context that is useful. Is the information on a website relevant to the context of visitors? One way of finding out is through examination of visitors entering the site (where from, when, to which page and from which website – what pages visited, how long did they stay per page and where did they go?). All this information is available from the web analytics software that is available to all web masters.

---

Getting lots of traffic is great but if visitors are not going where you want them to, there is a problem.

Website analytical software or Google Analytics helps you get a clear picture not only of where the traffic is coming from but also of what it is doing once it gets there. The steps needed to find such data include analysis of the top exit pages, 'time on page' and whether the page has a very low time on page. This information will identify the point where visitors have decided they have seen enough. It may be for the best of reasons or because they are disappointed.

If the average time on your top exit page is 20 seconds or less, then it may be reasonable to assume that people are landing on that page and leaving right away. This can be a because of a good experience, such as a 'thank you for visiting/doing something', or it could be that the message is just plain inappropriate and the visitor has left to find a better experience.

---

## Landscaping the competition

A similar exercise with competitors will yield similar results, and will also provide a benchmark against which to judge the relative presence of the organization. Competitor analysis is used to seek the context in which an organization is present online.

Analysis of competitors' sites is useful for another reason. The numbers that come from landscaping tend to be huge, and looking at other organizations helps one to get a sense of proportion.

## The (traditional) media

Most organizations are evident in online news media. The growth of online coverage in this form has been significant in recent years, and the rate of growth indicates that this is potentially an important area for PR to consider.

Online PR, of course, does not replace other forms of practice and, indeed, most PR activities help online presence a lot. Events, people profiles, product descriptions, case studies and application stories are all the kind of material that people like to share online. The media provide an area where such content can be made available and should be used because of the potential benefits and because it is a strong growth area online.

Links from media stories are very good for search optimization and site ranking, as well as being a useful third-party endorsement. Media relations are a considerable asset for building online presence.

Recent findings about the growth of online media coverage (Figure 17.2) suggest that that there is a valuable symbiotic relationship between online PR and press relations.

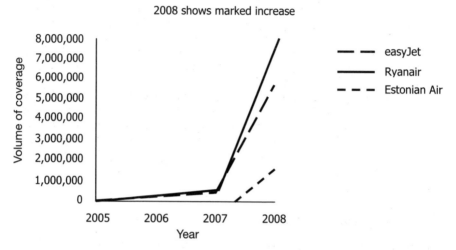

**Figure 17.2**   *Acceleration of growth in online news coverage after 2006 (image courtesy of eFootprint.com)*

---

**IN BRIEF**

- Landscaping of the online presence of organizations and external agencies and constituents is required for effective online public relations.
- When landscaping the online opportunities for public relations there are four major considerations:
  - the platforms;
  - the channels;
  - the context;
  - the content.
- In any landscaping, knowing about the organization's own presence is a good start. Be aware of:
  - who claims an affinity with the organization by linking to its website;
  - what kind of sites reference the organization;

- – the total number of publicly available web pages that index the organization;
  - – landscaping search returns.
- The nature of context and environment, the values of the audiences and the ability for them to interact can be examined.
- Landscaping competition is useful.
- The growth of online coverage in this form has been significant in recent years, and the rate of growth indicates that this is potentially an important area for PR to consider.

# 18

# Organizational analysis

Looking at the content that appeals to the online community, one sees that it comes in two interlinked flavours. The first is optimized content designed to appeal to search engines. Its elements include the important keywords relevant to the subject, which are part of search engine optimization. These words will be significant for metadata (of which more later), in the text on the page, and the way that other content like photos, drawings, video and podcast files are described (long URLs of unreadable numbers and letters are confusing for search engines as well as people).

The second rule about content is that it must be provided in a form that chimes with the interests of the prospective reader. To find what is the unique appeal of an organization, its products, brands and people, the practitioner has to look deep inside.

In preparing any public relations plan, there is a need to understand the organization. With the potential for unimaginable numbers of people to find and evaluate the direct and indirect statements made by the organization, this is key. In addition, these people have sight of information published by trade and professional associations, regulators, information aggregators, the media and social commentators online, which means that there is a need to be precise in statements about the organization. Claims served up with spin, hype, exaggeration or bling can draw a rich and often lurid riposte in cyberspace at a time and in circumstances not of the organization's choosing.

Value systems that are evident online need to be analysed and defensible. Wenstøp and Myrmel offer virtues, duties and consequences as three types of value systems that need to be identified about the organization, and it may also be necessary to modify unrealistic claims, common in another age, to be able to compete online.[1]

Such analysis will affect evidence and content published online, including the corporate backgrounders (history, financial and management structure, products, markets, associates, regulators and endorsers). Some of this will be provided by the organization (or it will point to it – often using hyperlinks, sometimes selectively using web widgets), but it is important to bear in mind that most organizations are not directly responsible for the majority of data that is published about them; in practice this might include government, regulatory and trade data provided by third parties, as well as website and social media content of varying degrees of accuracy. At this stage the practitioner will also want to check the organization's www.wikipedia.com entry.

As we have seen, all organizations have an online persona, partly of their own construction but increasingly shaped and defined by external comment and contribution. A useful method for examining the online image of an organization is to examine its website and selective commentary of the online audience for the values that are identified.

## CASE STUDY: AN EXAMINATION OF KEY VALUES ON WEBSITES

The Number 10 Downing Street website offered this front page content on October 2007:

> The EU, inheritance tax, Burma and flood defences were on the agenda at today's PMQs. The Prime Minister also took questions on the Royal Mail strike, the NHS and affordable housing.

There is an agenda here. The value systems of the site suggests it is for the well informed. The use of acronyms suggests the site is for a defined circle of visitors. This is a website for the 'Westminster Village', which includes very few chefs. However, the *New York Magazine* restaurateur's blog also showed interest in the Prime Minister's residence on the same day, telling the story that: 'Katy Sparks is on board at 10 Downing Street, stepping in for Scott Bryan.' 'But,' we are told, ' Sparks is not alone in creating the 10 Downing Street menu. A mystery chef, currently employed in the city somewhere, is onboard too' (http://nymag.com/).
There is no mention of Katy on the Downing Street site.

> Looking at the 14,000 web pages that link to the Downing Street site gives us a clue about who is interested (using http://www.google.com/help/features.html#link). We can see that the online community is adding its own content and that the interest in the organization goes beyond its own agenda and the online constituency indicated by the values it displays on the site.

This kind of analysis gives a good indication of the people and values that are important to the online community.

Because the online community is critical (and occasionally adversely critical), it will examine these value statements; where there is dissonance – ie the claim is unreasonable or unbelievable – it will expose such statements for wider user-generated comment online. Online commentators recognize hype.

---

Stories of hype provoking adverse response are legion and a couple serve to make the point.

- A blog comment about Nokia in http://www.gizmolounge.net read: 'Nokia is going [to] great lengths to hype up their future phone the Nokia N81 8GB Music Phone. So much so that they started a viral marketing campaign starting with the site http://www.070829.com.' The comment undermined the marketing proposition and campaign in a theme taken up by hundreds of people in blogs, Facebook and a number of other social media sites.
- Many companies have fallen foul of this form of online re-post. If an organization makes a claim on- or offline, it must be able to defend it or face criticism, as Kimkins did. In the blog http://allaboutkimkins.wordpress.com, the company's claims for its diet product were exposed and covered in 14,000 blog posts in a few days.

Hype and spin have a place, but have to be in context.

---

A typical value analysis profile would include analysis of:

- Company – product line, image in the market, technology and experience, culture, goals.
- Collaborators – distributors, suppliers, alliances.
- Customers – market size and growth, market segments (including internet user groups). Benefits that consumer is seeking, tangible and intangible. Motivation behind purchase; value drivers, benefits versus

costs. Decision maker or decision-making unit. Retail channel – where does the consumer actually purchase the product? Consumer information sources – where does the customer obtain information about the product? Buying process, eg impulse or careful comparison. Frequency of purchase, seasonal factors. Quantity purchased at a time. Trends – how consumer needs and preferences change over time.

- Competitors – actual or potential, direct or indirect, products, positioning, market shares, strengths and weaknesses of competitors.
- Organization's climate or context – the climate or macro-environmental factors are:
  - political and regulatory environment: governmental policies and regulations that affect the market;
  - economic environment: business cycle, inflation rate, interest rates and other macroeconomic issues.
- Social/cultural environment – society's trends and fashions. Technological environment: new knowledge that makes possible new ways of satisfying needs; the impact of technology on the demand for existing products.

The range of traditional landscaping processes outlined in the CIPR 'PR in practice' series book *Planning and Managing Public Relations Campaigns: A step-by-step guide* remain significant too.

Organizations are exposed in a range of channels for communication whose perspectives on values systems will differ. Television audiences will accept hype statements with little qualm, unlike the blogging community. The problem for the practitioner is that the TV programme can be transposed to video-sharing sites or blogs (sometimes legally and at other times not), and can easily be commented on.

One final test is useful, which is to examine how the online community regards online content.

The 'uses and gratification' theory, first put forward in the 1940s by Lazarsfeld and Stanton, attempts to explain why mass media are used and the types of gratification that they generate.[2]

Denis McQuail offers a schema to help establish the quality of websites.[3] When reviewing a site, this is a method that may be valuable in gaining insights into how people will regard and use a website (or a blog), and Morris and Ogan point out that U&G is a comprehensive theory and is applicable to internet-mediated communication (see also McLeod and Becker).[4]

Using McQuail, practitioners can create questionnaires to invite people to evaluate a website, blog, wiki or any other online property so as to identify its appeal as an online resource.

One means by which sites can be evaluated is by using focus groups to ascertain responses to four elements of a website/medium. An alternative used in some experiments with students was to create an online questionnaire. The respondents were asked to review a website and respond to four elements:

- The first was information. The question was framed to ask how the students used the site for information, and they were asked to rate it for its faculty to educate in certain areas, such as learning more about the world, seeking advice on practical matters, or satisfying curiosity.
- The second element dealt with personal identity, where students were asked if they identified with the content personally, professionally or for other reasons.
- The third part dealt with use of the site and how it integrated with the users' need to become involved, have social interaction or gain insight into the situations of other people, in order to achieve a sense of belonging.
- The fourth usage of the media identified by McQuail is 'entertainment', that is, using media for purposes of obtaining pleasure and enjoyment, or escapism. Not surprisingly, there were some websites that students found less than fun.

This kind of activity in situational analysis will show the potential nature of online interaction to inform strategy and objectives and may, tactically, result in changes to a website.

# SEGMENTATION

A quick glance at the 'Way Back Machine' (http://www.archive.org) shows that online there are no messages hidden from users. In addition information is kept (cached) on many computers in the network (even the humble PC does it). This might give rise to a view that there is little need for segmentation because anyone can find anything. This is a misleading view. Not everyone has the skill or inclination to use the capabilities that are out there. There are platforms and channels for communication, as well as types of content, written and semiotic, that are more significant for some audiences than others. Those people who have an interest in the values and value systems of the organization will be drawn to them, and where there is dissonance they will at some point take up the issue.

The use of segmentation techniques offered by Smith, Grunig and Hunt, and others – as described by Professor Anne Gregory and Alison Theaker as well as Freeman (stakeholder theory) and a multitude of others (not least the many market segmentation theorists and practitioners) – is now augmented by user-generated market segments we described in the last chapter.[5]

Users are now beginning to decide that they themselves will select issues, products and brands. This undermines the segmentation theory used by most organizations. The evolution of online behaviour whereby user-generated market segments (sometimes confined to closed communities such as Facebook, MyRagan and Melcrum) form around brands, issues and organizations makes discussion of these networked social groups (mostly very small groups) important.

There is nothing new or revolutionary about the concept. Small communities throughout history have behaved in the same way, aided by the normal discourse of daily lives leavened by gossip. The internet, a place, has many networked communities.

There is a temptation for many of us who are used to mass communication and mass markets to imagine that, because we can find references to issues and brands online, these sites and posts are a homogeneous market. The evidence suggests otherwise, and deeper analysis shows that comments about brands and issues are typically confined to relatively small, often transient, online social groups.

It is very common for people to use search engines to identify what the online community is saying. This is far too simplistic. The online community is predominantly active in small groups and cares little for views expressed across the whole internet unless seeking to selectively 'pull' new information.

Online social groups range from the intense and academic to those seeking hard news and simple family snapshots. To imagine that all comments about an issue, brand or event comprise a single sweep of comments across all such groups would be a mistake. This would be like listening to the hubbub of a virtual tower of Babel. It is only within the mostly small networks of linked individuals with common interests and language that any sense can be made of the vast majority of posts in blogs, social media groups of friends and Twitter followers. It is in these loose groupings that often rich interactions are to be found. In many cases they are very profound and often scholarly – and attempting to interject into, what are really quite private social groups, has to be very carefully done.

Clay Shirky applies this explanation of 'power law' to interactivity online, and notably to bloggers. He notes that they range from people with a lot of followers, who because they have so many cannot be very interactive with them all, to the blogs at the nexus of a few chums (who interact a lot with a few). This means that the 'average' blogger is probably a long way down the curve, and 'average' is a meaningless approach to identifying influence.[6] We come across the power law a lot in online activities. *Wired* magazine's editor-in-chief Chris Anderson, in an article in October 2004 where he coined the expression 'the long tail', shows a commercial interpretation.[7]

But the next part is also important. In Shirky's view, when we consider how to achieve connectedness (and enter the elusive 'viral' world of the internet), then media (like blogs) that mostly have very modest numbers of connections, nonetheless have community connectedness properties that make them extremely powerful.

This leads us to the conclusion that both the mass and the niche social media publisher are important, not least because both have reach, with the former having much more but diluted influence compared with the socially powerful latter, and because the niche commentator has all the potential for viral expression to the mass audience.

Segmentation is needed, not least because the platforms, channels and context – even the language – of different channels are different (for example, Twitter versus Times online). The channel is a message in its own right, and to be able to hold a conversation through such channels it is necessary to understand the culture of both the channel and the community. Barging in on someone's 'conversation' is rude in any environment, and nowhere more so than online. As part of landscaping, there may be a need to examine internal cultures that remain content to adopt the 'barging in on someone's conversation' model.

Historically it has been considered enough to frame key public relations communications in a few succinct messages. In the online conversation of the internet society, this is too simple. Statements need to be supported, users need to be able to explore further, and frequently seek to 'pull' more information.

This may mean that 'more' information is available using other online devices. The traditional website – the corporate repository of facts and information and some trading transactions – may be the repository for 'more', but the conversation and explication of values could well be found in much more transitory space like blogs, social networks and SMS exchanges. This means that the content needed needs to be made comprehensively available through devices such as hyperlinking. Where information is not provided by the organization, online communities will go elsewhere online to meet their needs. The attention to the organization is broken and the link lost. Value partners are valuable when they have all the information they need to hand. Identifying orphaned legacy content and the potential for its presence to create dissonance is significant for some organizations.

The practitioner can now have the best of both worlds: short, sharp and appealing content supported by the deep, rich content in the backgrounders and support content, all brought together because of the hyperlink. Examining the availability of such content as part of the inventory needed for development of strategy is quite important. Not having content can mean that it will be expensive to produce.

**MAKING AN INVENTORY AND CREATING GUIDELINES FOR INTERNET PR ACTIVITIES**

Consulting for a company with many big brands distributed through on- and offline retailers and a multi-million-pound budget for TV advertising proved interesting for one of the authors. At the time, online retailing in this sector had the potential to account for over 30 per cent of revenues.

The question of content inventory came up. There was no form of inventory control over online collateral and no set of guidelines for its use. The company did not know which elements of its collateral were in use or where. In addition, simple things were missing like product photographs and images, videos, TV commercials in web-friendly formats, podcasts and interviews, specification information, brief product descriptions for website references and so forth.

On advice, the company decided that that prior to considering any further online activity, an audit would be helpful and that resources should be directed towards developing platform, channel and context guidelines as part of the online strategy for the organization.

One of the more advanced and publicly available set of guidelines is available from the BBC at http://www.bbc.co.uk/guidelines.

---

**IN BRIEF**

- Consideration includes optimized content designed to appeal to search engines, and content that is provided in a form that chimes with the interests of the prospective reader.
- In order to provide content in a form that chimes with the interests of the prospective reader, it is important to identify the unique appeal of an organization, its products, brands and people.
- Value systems evident online need to be analysed and defensible.
- Analysis will include the corporate backgrounders (history, financial and management structure, products, markets, associates, regulators and endorsers).
- Because the online community is critical (and occasionally adversely critical), it will examine value statements and where there is dissonance – ie the claim is unreasonable or unbelievable – will expose such statements for wider user-generated comment online.
- Organizations are exposed in a range of channels of communication. Some have a different view of values systems from others.
- Practitioners can create questionnaires to invite people to evaluate a website, blog, wiki or any other online property to identify its appeal as an online resource.

- Segmentation is relevant.
- Analyse 'user-generated' market and social segments.
- There is a temptation for many of us who are used to mass communication and mass markets to imagine that, because we can find references to issues and brands online, these sites and posts are a homogeneous market. Evidence suggests otherwise.
- To achieve connectedness (and enter the elusive 'viral' nature of the internet), we should note that media (like blogs) with very modest numbers of connections may have community connectedness properties that make them extremely powerful.
- Both the mass and the niche social media publishers are important.
- Historically it has been considered enough to frame key public relations communication in a few succinct messages. In the online conversation of the internet society, this is too simple. Statements need to be supported, users need to be able to explore further, and frequently seek to 'pull' more information.

## Notes

1. Wenstøp, F and Myrmel, A (2006) Structuring organizational value statements, *Management Research News*, **29** (11), pp 673–83
2. Lazarsfeld, P F and Stanton, F (1944) *Radio Research 1942–3*, Duell, Sloan and Pearce
3. McQuail, D (1994) *Mass Communication: An introduction* (3rd edn), Sage Publications
4. Morris, M and Ogan, Christine L (1996) The internet as mass medium, *Journal of Communication*, **46** (1), pp 39–50; McLeod, Jack M and Becker, Lee B (1981) The uses and gratifications approach, in *Handbook of Political Communication*, ed Dan D Nimmo and Keith R Sanders, Sage
5. Gregory, A (2000) *Planning and Managing Public Relations Campaigns: A step-by-step guide*, Kogan Page; Smith, R D (2004) *Strategic Planning for Public Relations*, Lawrence Erlbaum; Grunig, J E and Hunt, T (1984) *Managing Public Relations*, Harcourt Brace College Publishers; Theaker, A (2008) *The Public Relations Handbook*, Taylor and Francis, 3rd revised edition; Freeman, R Edward (1984) *Strategic Management: A stakeholder approach*, Pitman
6. Shirky, C (2008) *Here Comes Everybody: The power of organizing without organizations*, Penguin
7. Anderson, C (2004) *The Long Tail*, Hyperion (Revised and Updated edition, 2008)

# 19

# Developing online PR strategies

Through landscaping and organizational analysis, the practitioner will now have identified the organization's aims, corporate objectives and extant mission statements. The latter cannot be changed. Once online, they are, in effect, there for all time. What is becoming a major driver is the immersive nature of the most popular websites.

The time spent on Facebook and Bebo, computer games, YouTube and even e-mail demonstrate the extent to which these technologies draw participants into a world that is beyond just instant gratification. They go deeper than, for example, a single beautifully executed advertisement into a world of involvement, participation and interaction. These channels and this interactivity, though still largely bounded by PC, laptop, computer games and mobile phone screens (although not for much longer), demand sentient engagement and response, often even at an emotional level.

The committed groups that surround some blogging communities show how powerful immersion by enthusiasts has become, which means that the practitioner will need to consider immersion (including close third-party interest) when developing strategy.

In addition, there will be a driver that prompts entry into the online world. It may be a brief or the practitioner's own initiative but it must be a conscious and purposeful decision. Furthermore, knowledge of the nature of online assets and inventory will help inform strategy.

The essence of online public relations is that it is a coherent organization-wide online strategy. There are no 'campaigns' on line. The internet time-shifts (it is part of the many dimensions in the internet's network effect). Few will remember that The Belfry Shopping Centre, Redhill, was awarded the BCSC Purple Apple Marketing Award, or the details of Tate Modern's opening in 2000 (the year the first edition of this book was written) but the award is still there for all to see online and so are the reviews of Tate Modern. This legacy content, part of today's reputation for both places, shows how today's public relations campaign will remain part of the reputation asset of the organization for years to come.

# SETTING OBJECTIVES

Thus aims and objectives for online activity have to be part of a strategic, multi-participant, multi-media approach, and if the aims are short term, one needs to be very explicit about duration.

Online activity might result from a corporate desire to be evident online, to extend its 'digital footprint', to add to its asset base (online presence and online relationships are significant assets) or to establish relationships offering products or services, knowledge, meeting of needs and satisfaction. The organization may be political, commercial, charitable, public sector or something else. The key is that online activity is becoming essential for most organizations.

What does the organization want to achieve? What does it seek to achieve? There is a difference.

An organization may want to sell more products yet it may also seek the collaboration of the online community to develop ideas, products or markets. The means may be a contribution to the ends.

Setting online objectives is not as simple as it may be in many other areas of PR. Online objectives have to coincide with organizational objectives and values, and to do so in ways that will make both transparent to the world. In addition, these ambitions need to chime with an online community that has plenty of other places to go.

There is a further consideration. The internet is interesting to people in the way they use it. Some people only use search engines and read what sites tell them. Others only go to sites that they know and feel safe exploring. Others are much more adventurous. Some add content in walled gardens like Facebook, and others publish websites and blogs. If one asks any audience what they use the internet for, the answers will all be different. Some people who use the internet are not even aware that the service they are using is part of the network of networks.

The internet is, for the most part, not a mass medium; it is 'me the user', and if this means 'I the user' will go to a website with huge reach, that is just what, in these circumstances, under these conditions and at this time, I will do.

The internet is also an experience and an emotion driver that fits well into what some consider to be an emerging economy when so many organizations offer so much that is so similar. Internet public relations allows the practice to develop completely new approaches to relationships and interactions. New PR is also about new thinking.

---

Professor Feng Li posits that:

Perhaps the age of the knowledge workers has come to maturity, and a new age is emerging. Daniel Pink called it the 'conceptual age', characterised by 'high concept and high touch'. Joseph Pine and James Gilmore called it the 'experience economy', because increasingly work is theatre and every business is a stage. C K Prahalad and Venkat Ramaswamy further developed this concept and called it the experience innovation, because the future of competition depends on co-creating unique value with customers. Shoshana Zuboff called it the 'support economy', because neither goods nor services can adequately fulfil the needs of today's market. Underlying all these ideas is a fundamental change that is rapidly taking hold in our society and economy: we are increasingly leaving the material and information age behind and entering a new, emotional age.

Back in 1973, Peter Drucker famously pointed out that '[w]hat the customer buys and considers value is never a product. It is always utility – that is, what a product does for him.' When a woman buys a lipstick, she is not buying a lump of coloured fat. Rather she is buying something that will make her feel more attractive. Think about the movie Calendar Girls. A group of middle aged women managed to achieve fame and financial success beyond their wildest dream, by evoking emotional responses from the public. Selling high quality products [is] important, but if you can evoke emotional responses from customers, the potential rewards will expand exponentially.

The notion of 'Making a Business of Emotions' is not entirely new. Harley-Davison (and Nike), for example, have for a long time promoted the image of being in the 'lifestyle' business rather than manufacturing. This not only added billions of dollars to their market capitalisation, it also means that Harley-Davison does not need to compete with Honda or BMW for the technical performance of their motorbikes. To a large extent, the success of Starbucks can be attributed to its focus on being the 'third place' which is neither home nor office, instead of a Cafe. The shifting focus towards experiences and emotions can often create exponential expansion of business value for all stakeholders.

---

Everyone is different and each person's use of the internet is unique to the individual.

This makes it interesting when setting out to develop strategies. The mass market/mass media mindset is hard to leave behind when the audience is reaching in and eschewing organizations that only reach out.

Setting online PR objectives requires risk and opportunity analysis and a view of how to manage the unknown. What, in other areas, can be a 'stand-alone' campaign will soon reach further both inside an organization and beyond it. Employees, customers, vendors and other partners must assume they will have complete visibility. It is an axiom that everything the practitioner and practitioner's organization does and says online is available to everyone – forever – however embarrassing that may be.

The aims need to be set as part of a continuum of objectives, and when set in a SMART context need to be relevant to the internet:

- Specific – objectives should specify outcomes and take into consideration the global, time-shifting, interactive, two-way and immersive nature of the internet.
- Measurable – across many platforms, channels and contexts; one must consider more than mass impact because of the network effect.
- Achievable and attainable – in context and bearing in mind that most online effects are best achieved because they are multi-dimensional, appealing to people through different platforms, channels, contexts and time shifts.
- Realistic – which usually means progressive because, unlike other activities, online adoption does not come as one 'big bang'.
- Time – in effect for ever, but also meeting outcomes as progressive milestones on the way.

To sum up: Do the practitioner's objectives chime with the organization's objectives? Are they compatible with the values held by the organization? Is the objective relevant to online constituents and defendable in any forum? Is risk and opportunity manageable? Are the goals SMART and agreed with the organization?

# STRATEGIES

At last! The practitioner is now in a position to get to grips with what actually needs to be done.

Online strategies have to be creative in concept. 'Me too' programmes have a lot of competition. There are so many platforms and channels for communication. There are no boundaries. The practitioner can use e-posters or SMS, blogs or wikis, podcasts and virtual environments, and all of them at the same time. The ability to mix RSS with point-of-sale devices or announce a presidential running mate via SMS, as Barack Obama did in 2008, can all be part of a timing strategy.

The programme should be part of a mix of activities for both new and old media. Online media (the sort that does not have a print version) and media online (the print and other media that are also made available online) can be part of a campaign that includes internet-mediated television or games machines. The key here is that if the practitioner does not include a mix of activities, there is nothing to stop the online community picking up the campaign and shifting it to different platforms or channels, with the initiative now taken out of the hands of the practitioner, organization and, often, the publisher.

Strategy is adaptable by nature. It will consider availability to both organization and external constituents to take the activity in different directions with the application of different resources (platforms, channels, contexts, finance, time, old and emerging technologies).

Strategy will consider skills and responsibilities. Allocation of responsibilities and reporting, with associated training and management infrastructure, are all strategy considerations. For example, if a blog is part of a campaign, there have to be people committed to creating good and relevant content, regularly and against a set of rules, with necessary training and reporting.

There is an imperative for good, clear employee communication inside the organization, and there is usually a need to involve internal 'stakeholders' because online initiatives will affect them; initiatives are visible and are better disclosed in a structured way. No employee likes to be wrong-footed by an outsider with 'insider' information.

Strategy will include methodologies for monitoring and reporting. Online activity can be slow to take off. It can also be explosive! Being able to monitor and report is critical, and sometimes it is monitoring the very ordinary that counts.

Strategy will be realistic and a reality check is always worthwhile. Timing, technologies, skill levels and vendor experience all need to be checked in advance.

The process will at some level in the organization consider the implications of transparency, porosity, internet agency, richness and reach, and will include risk and opportunity testing.

To sum up: strategy will need to consider a creative mix of activities. It will be adaptable and executed with relevant skills and responsibilities. The programme will have to include good, clear employee communication along with effective monitoring and reporting, and will be realistic and risk delimitated.

**IN BRIEF**

- What is becoming a major driver is the immersive nature of the most popular websites.
- Entering into the online world has to be a conscious and purposeful decision.
- There are no 'campaigns' on line because of the long tail effect.
- Legacy content is part of today's reputation.
- Online activity might be driven by a corporate desire to be evident online, to extend its 'digital footprint', to add to its asset base (online presence and online relationships are significant assets), or to establish relationships offering products or services, knowledge, meeting of needs and satisfaction.
- An organization may want to sell more products, yet it may also seek the collaboration of the online community to develop ideas, products or markets. The means may be a contribution to the ends.
- The internet is, for the most part, not a mass medium.
- Everyone is different and each person's use of the internet is unique to the individual.
- Setting online PR objectives requires risk and opportunity analysis and a view of how to manage the unknown.
- The aims need to be set as part of a continuum of objectives; when set in a SMART context, they need to be relevant to the internet.
- Online strategies have to be creative in concept.
- The programme should be part of a mix of activities for both new and old media.
- There is nothing to stop the online community picking up the campaign and shifting it to different platforms or channels, with the initiative now taken out of the hands of the practitioner and organization.
- Strategy is adaptable by nature.
- Strategy will consider skills and responsibilities.
- There is an imperative for good, clear employee communication inside the organization.
- Strategy will include methodologies for monitoring and reporting.
- Strategy will be realistic.

# 20

# Thoughts about tactics

Online PR tactics are a dream for creative people. There are so many variables, they can be creatively applied and there are lots that can be truly original and compelling.

Tactics need to be well understood if they are to be deployed effectively. For most professional practitioners, there is no substitute for trying things out. For most online channels of communication, there is a PR sandbox somewhere. If you hear of something like Second Life, try it, read what people say about it, and try to think why it has appeal now and how the appeal will change as it matures.

In Chapter 2 and throughout the foregoing pages we have mentioned a wide range of platforms, channels and contexts. They will be deployed to meet the strategic plan. There is no online PR campaign that only uses only one device, channel or context because the online community will, on its own initiative, shift channels, platforms and contexts. All tactics should, at the concept stage consider applications in different platforms, channels and contexts.

There will always be elements that will be included in tactical thinking:

- proactive actions and initiatives – to get the ball rolling;
- monitoring – in place before starting to see what the online community is doing with the campaign;

- publishing – the roll-out on platforms;
- awareness – what is done to guide the online community to the 'campaign';
- engagement – actions that are in response to the online community's actions;
- capability to respond to events and actions – just in case this is a peach or pear-shaped 'campaign'.

The order of interaction may start with being proactive, but equally with monitoring or even responding. In developing tactics, consideration of these six elements will ensure they meet the strategy objectives and will not leave important elements out.

All practitioners can play and get experience of most forms of communication long before they are presented as part of an online programme. There are some guiding considerations for tactics under consideration:

- Are they technically possible?
- Is there expert practice/guidance available to help and inform the execution of the tactic? (In most cases there is, and it's online.)
- Does the practitioner make or buy (use an existing service or develop the practitioner's own – who hosts, who has copyright, is the practitioner information confidential, is the practitioner sure about the nature, financial security, legal jurisdiction and nationality of vendors)?
- Can the practitioner sustain the activity for the duration?
- How is the practitioner going to test and evaluate the concept (eg platform/channel) and technologies?
- What are the risks and are there other opportunities?
- When does the practitioner deploy the programme and for how long?
- How will the organization launch the initiative?
- How does this tactic integrate with other tactics in the strategic plan?

It is not possible to cover even a small part of the opportunities available to the practitioner. But we can attempt to look at some generic activities that should be included.

# WEBSITES

The most evident form of publishing is in the use of web technologies and websites.

A visitor may be a prospective buyer of a product, service or content, or may be there for some other experience. Knowing what that experience is worth helps identify the value of every visitor and to identify the value of each event on the site.

A site needs to have clear goals, and these will be reflected in the way it is built. The site may be developed to do a range of things, such as offering sales transactions or attracting trials or sales leads; it could be developed to encourage interaction or community, or downloads, or it could be designed to promote awareness or for opinion forming or other purposes. Some sites are specifically made to work on mobile phones, others to be loaded on CDs, and so some sites are created to be platform specific. But they should all be designed to be optimized for search engines.

Websites should always be monitored to make sure they are available, are not slow to download, do not have broken links (the dreaded 404), work with all browsers (at least all the versions of Internet Explorer, Mozilla Firefox, Opera and Google Chrome) and are up to date. These are the basic elements of having a respectable reputation online. A failure of any of the above and visitors (well over half of all the people who will have any sort of relationship) will think much less of the organization.

Websites, e-mail and SMS are the last bastion of corporate control online, and for most organizations even that is tenuous. Corporate control can be a much-abused privilege, with many claims in words, graphics and sounds being hype, bling and 20th century corporate/marketing speak.

Most websites still have the feel and look of a brochure. They may be full of colour and design features but are not, in themselves, an experience.

Of course they should have good clear layout and should be well designed and will offer easy navigation. These things will be tested under controlled conditions, of course (won't they!).

But it's worth looking beyond the facade:

- The style and content of websites and the way they are presented need to be coherent.
- The design should allow the developer and webmaster to control the style and layout of multiple web pages all at once. Developers can define a style for each HTML element and apply it to as many web pages as they want. To make a global change, simply change the style, and all elements in the site are updated automatically. This form of design is called 'cascading style sheets' (CSS), and should be adopted for most websites.
- Every page of a website is potentially a 'landing page', the page that will be the first one people encounter, and all pages have to be presented as such.
- Every page will tell a story to visitors and to search engines (yes, search engines also read the text).
- Every page should be engaging and should offer an elegant exit, either to keep the visitor on the site or to offer a worthwhile place to go next.
- Every page will require explanatory texts in the 'meta data', the code that lies behind the page and is 'read' by a web browser and search engine, including a title and keywords.

**187**

- Most pages will have a capability to allow visitors to bookmark the page in social sharing networks. Many will facilitate interaction such as comment.

Put together, the pages should tell a coherent story. The values of the organization need to come out as an overriding theme, with key values more explicitly and frequently expressed. This does not mean that some slogan or pat phrase has to be on every page; far from it. If you really want to bore a visitor to death, add 'We value your custom' on every page. Visitors and search engines are quite capable of inferring such values from more rounded and interesting content.

Most online campaigns will have added content on the website (or microsites). This means that special 'landing pages' will be needed for the campaign to be coherent.

We think of websites in their traditional form, but of course there are many forms of website. Indeed, most of what we regard as social media is really another manifestation of the almost ubiquitous website. From YouTube to Flickr via MySpace, they are all websites, and most have generic equivalents available for the practitioner to copy, adapt or change. Some of them are available as open source software that can be adapted and changed.

When designing web pages, it is worth considering their application on different platforms. Does your new site look good on a mobile phone? Can it be used on a CD? Would you put it on a touch screen at an exhibition?

## ALL TACTICS WILL INCLUDE SEO CONSIDERATIONS

First stop is to ensure that, from the twinkle in the eye of the practitioner, throughout the build and publishing and on into use, any web-based activity is optimized for search engines.

Search engines have been about for a long time. They satisfy a deep drive in the human condition, which is that we are a very curious species; search engines are adept at meeting this need. In the past they have had manifestations as searchable directories compiled like an electronic library card-index system. At the time of writing, Google is the most used example in the United Kingdom. It has a lot of competitors, and among them is one that will change the way we find things out as profoundly Google did way back in 1996. Having a wonderful online PR campaign is jolly nice. If no one can find it through Google, Yahoo or MSN, then it will not have much of an ROI.

Finding the best way to present texts online, even in press releases, is a skill that practitioners can hone.

Some practitioners will be involved in optimization, and more than a few will recommend that organizations optimize their sites. Search engine optimization (SEO) is important. It is much more than adding keywords in the 'back end' of a web page or in the first paragraph of a press release. It's a big task. This is an area for PR practice that cannot be ignored. Bad SEO is like poor grammar in a press release, the mark of ignorance leavened with incompetence.

Not all the navigation or all the pages of a website are 'spiderable' by search engines. The search engine bots cannot read the pull-down menus, and many don't read javascript, hover effects or other special effects. Sites should have machine-readable (CSS) navigation to help the search engines index all the pages. This part of building a site is a competence issue for website designers. Most should know these things but, judging from a look behind many sites, even in some major companies, this is not always so. The practitioner should *always* make budget available for competent SEO design.

Optimizing the site begins with its goals. SEO begins before the site is constructed or any tactic is deployed.

Opinion-forming/informational goals are often best served with an organic search approach (the kind of search people do when they use a search engine to find websites by inputting keywords) though in some instances paid-for advertisements can be used, and so both approaches should at least be considered.

SEO will have very tangible, and occasionally financially measurable, objectives, so a set of measures of achievement can be put in place to evaluate SEO activity.

For website optimization, the best place to start is at the most used pages with the longest visitor dwell times. These are often the front page and then some very easily identifiable pages that appeal to visitors (these pages will change quite frequently, especially when a campaign is very successful). The top tip is to spot the pages that are already popular, with traffic coming from web search engines and the top referring sites (excluding link farms and affiliate sites).

These target pages will be the ones that already work. They can provide a template of detailed keywords to build on. There are a lot of services available, including ones provided by the search engines themselves (they offer this as a service to pay-per-click advertisers). Some keywords that emerge will be generic, some brand/product/service-related, some will be very specific to page content and some will be patently irrelevant. Specific page-related keywords should be reserved for the relevant pages and not peppered all over the site – folk just don't find it amusing to be driven to an irrelevant page, even by a search engine.

Where there are keywords that are not relevant to the site, take them out. Being irritating to the online community by attracting them to content irrelevant to their need is not good for reputation.

With the keywords in place in the metadata and in the leading paragraphs of text (without making the text read like taxonomy), the next job is to ensure that the pages are actually indexed in our target search engines: Google, Yahoo, MSN and the others.

For some organizations there is a case for developing a competitor matrix for the target terms.

With the keywords in place and the pages indexed, checking the website logs will show whether the process is delivering extra visitors from the search engines. The big search engines show the difference between the number of searches and the amount of traffic actually received, and there are other services that can do this as well, although none of the keyword research tools are precise about numbers.

At this point monitoring and evaluating the returns is worth doing. This will show the value of SEO and will offer insights into where future SEO activity can enhance the return on investment of the site.

SEO is an iterative activity. It needs constant attention and is best when really professional people are employed. That is not to say that an individual cannot achieve a lot.

In most cases, in the United Kingdom in the first decade of the 21st century most organizations could, with improved site optimization, increase the return per visitor by huge percentages.

There are some other tips that are worth mentioning. The URLs of many pages do not make sense. They are full of numbers and letters and are unreadable (meaningless). What is wrong with the sort of words and phrases that can be read – by people and computers? Collateral such as photographs, images, videos and podcasts can also add to the presence of a website online.

Finally, websites benefit by association. Links to sites count, and links from sites that have a lot of links count more. Inbound links affect search engine ranking of sites a lot.

In all tactics offered by a practitioner, there has to be an element of search optimization.

# THE SHARING TACTICS

The way people find out about stuff online is changing. Most proactively, the route to a website is through search but this is not the only way to get online attention. Many people follow links, some respond to advertising and others put themselves into environments where there is a lot of stimulus from which to choose. Helping people who seek is an important part of PR. Websites that 'recommend' other websites gain in authority and reputation among their users. Tactics that enhance sharing opportunities or embed them in the programme will gain authority and effectiveness.

For some websites, and increasingly, the content and the appeal to search engines depend on content provided by the public. Examples are blogs and social networks and folksonomy tags. Indeed, some very traditional sites are changing fast because of this user content that is changing their appeal. As an example, press sites have changed their profile for discovery through search or word of mouse. In other words we find the site because we are looking for a story, and the result takes us to a newspaper site we would not normally go to. This kind of discovery is powerful. It encourages people to share their findings and adds to reach. Helping people share content is a great way of getting attention. Helping the public become a contributor to the campaign is a tactical consideration.

For some, 'viral marketing' is the only way forward, but in one of the most robust experiments available to date the concept of viral marketing has yet to be proven. Jupiter Research reported in 2007 that just 15 per cent of viral campaigns are ever deemed 'successful'. Granted, success measurements vary by company, but that's still an extraordinarily low figure. Imagine if only 15 per cent of your other marketing plans were successful. It wouldn't take long before your marketing department or agency was out of a job.

In their paper 'The dynamics of viral marketing', Leskovec, Adamic and Huberman use big samples to test viral marketing.[1] Viral marketing focuses on leveraging existing social networks by encouraging customers to share product information with their friends. The research suggests that although word of mouth can be a powerful factor influencing purchasing decisions, it can be tricky for advertisers to tap into. This would suggest that public relations has a role in opinion forming, but advertising (and direct promotion) has a problem and there have to be a number of elements in place for an idea to 'go viral':

- Viral marketing does not spread well. In epidemics, high connectors are very critical nodes of the network and allow the virus to spread. In recommendations networks, a few very large cascades exist, but most recommendation chains terminate after just a few steps.
- The probability of viral infection decreases with repeated interaction. Providing excessive incentives for customers to recommend actually weakens the credibility of those links. The probability of purchasing a product increases with the number of recommendations received, but quickly saturates to a constant and relatively low probability.
- Viral effectiveness varies depending on price and category. Social context has a high influence on the potency of viral infection. Technical or religious books, for example, had more successful recommendations than general interest topics. Smaller and more tightly knit groups tend to be more conducive to viral marketing.

- The need for viral campaigns to chime with audience values is very important.
- Honey bees began dying mysteriously in the United States in 2006, which could be potentially catastrophic for the human food supply. Häagen Dazs considered this a highly relevant issue, as 30 of its 73 flavours use ingredients that depend on bees for pollination (eg almonds, blueberries, peaches).
- With help from Omnicom's Goodby, Silverstein, & Partners, the firm launched a multi-platform campaign that included TV ads, print ads that flower when planted, a microsite and philanthropic sponsorships.
- But it was the viral video Bee-Boy Dance Crew that generated the biggest impact. Inspired by a dance that bees do to divulge the location of nectar to hive members, a breakdancing crew, dressed like giant bees, competes on a dance floor. Targeted to youth thirsty for honey, hip-hop and a cause to support, the complex footwork of the bee-boys – a pun that plays on 'b-boys,' a street term for breakdancers – sparked the interest of kids that follow breakdancing culture.
- At the end of the video, only one bee-boy is left standing. He looks around, wonders 'Where my bees at?' and fades dramatically into darkness.
- The Los Angeles-based Feed Company spearheaded the initiative to put the Bee-Boys in front of digitally connected youth across social networks, video sites and blogs, acknowledging that their participation – and hopefully their desire to pass it on – was key to the video's viral success.
- 'Young people online are sharing content and issues that are important to their lives', said Josh Warner, president and founder of Feed Company. 'Using video to engage that audience on the web, where they hang out, is a great strategy for brands that are willing to take risks.'
- The pay-off was significant for Häagen Dazs, which isn't known for its youth appeal or digital-savvy. In two weeks ending 1 August, the video garnered 2 million views and 3,500 comments. It also earned a four-and-a-half star rating out of five on YouTube, was covered across 150 sites and blogs, and was mentioned in 11,000 forum discussions.
- Coverage in the *Huffington Post*, on Treehugger and CNN, which picked up the story and spread it nationwide, contributed to significant microsite traffic.
- Visits to Häagen Dazs' 'Save the bees' site spiked, reflecting heightened interest in the bee issue, and solidifying consumers' connection between brand and cause. While bees haven't yet been saved, intensified consumer interest in Häagen Dazs' ice cream – every pint of which sports the pro-bee message – suggests perhaps people have begun to care.

Many assume that setting up relationships with website owners that include an agreement to link into the organization's site (and thereby earn small amounts of money from 'click through') is a 'web marketing' activity. Affiliate marketing is really part of a genre of relationship techniques. It was very popular at the beginning of the century. It still has a role.

Essentially, these relationship techniques aim to set up hyperlink relationships. Some are very desirable, while others are less so. There are some sites that organizations do not want to be associated with, there are bloggers who do nothing else and really irritate people, and there are some sites where the commercial relationship is really worthwhile.

Building such relationships, called affiliate marketing, is important. Some publications seek such an agreement to add hyperlinks in press stories when they are published online. This is something practitioners need to know about.

Affiliate marketing uses other websites to become advocates for your site and increase online exposure. It can be as simple as a hyperlink in text or set up by a variety of methods, including creating banners that affiliates can include on their own websites. It can be through creating e-mail templates that affiliates can send to their database of users, or developing specific voucher codes for affiliates to use. There are many techniques.

An affiliate marketing initiative is only ever as good as your chosen partner sites. Thematically related web portals may be effective affiliate marketing partners for some, special interest niche sites for others.

There are a range of ways that affiliates are rewarded, such as: cost per sale – sales that have taken place; cost per lead/order – acquired customer contacts; cost per click – generated clicks; cost per impression – achieved page impressions (visits).

For some campaigns the use of affiliate marketing is a useful way to develop relationships.

Much link sharing is voluntary, and not considered affiliate marketing at all, and there are a lot of good reasons why. It is a very friendly gesture, and this is where the most powerful form of affiliation is today. Websites like Delicious, Flickr and YouTube do not only provide opportunities for online communities to share content with online communities; they are a way of sharing links and come with an inferred recommendation. The cost to an organization of encouraging this kind of sharing is low. Facilitating webpage sharing by offering simple ways for people to share the organization's web page information is simple and can be added to many web pages.

A phenomenon identified by Heather Hopkins at Hitwise showed that social networking traffic tends to be the greatest traffic driver for a pop band's early days, then a tipping point is reached as the band goes mainstream and individuals begin searching for more band information using search engines.

In developing tactics, practitioners will explore as many opportunities for sharing as possible.

---

**IN BRIEF**

- To be able to deploy tactics, there is no substitute for trying things out. Experience is valuable.
- There is no online PR campaign that only uses only one device, channel or context. All tactics should, at the concept stage, consider application in different platforms, channels and contexts.
- There will always be six elements that will be included in tactical thinking:
  - proactive actions and initiatives: to get the ball rolling;
  - monitoring: in place before starting to see what the online community is doing with the campaign;
  - publishing: the roll-out on platforms;
  - awareness: what is done to guide the online community to the 'campaign';
  - engagement: actions that are in response to the online community's actions;
  - capability to respond to events and actions: just in case this is a peach or pear-shaped 'campaign'.
- There are nine guiding considerations for tactics under consideration.
- Websites need to have clear goals, and these will be reflected in the way they are built.
- They should all be designed to be search engine optimized from the start.
- Websites should always be monitored.
- Most websites still have the feel and look of a brochure as opposed to being an experience.
- Good clear layout and design will offer easy navigation tested in advance of going live.
- Put together, the pages should tell a coherent story. The values of the organization need to come out as an overriding theme, with key values more explicitly and frequently expressed.
- Most online campaigns will have added content on the website (or microsites). This means that special 'landing pages' will be needed for the campaign to be coherent.
- All tactics will include SEO considerations.
- SEO will have very tangible, and occasionally financially measurable, objectives, so a set of measures of achievement can be put in place to evaluate SEO activity.
- Being irritating to the online community by attracting them to content irrelevant to their need is not good for reputation.
- Tactics will always include consideration to aid user sharing.

---

## Note

1.  Leskovec, J, Adamic, L A and Huberman, B A (2006) The dynamics of viral marketing, Hewlett-Packard Labs, http://www.communities. hp.com/online/blogs/kintz/archive/2006/09/17/HPPost1612.aspx

# 21

# Risks and opportunities

Public relations is a management discipline and as such has to apply management techniques to what it does. So far we have shown a number of such techniques used to optimize campaigning. We have also frequently mentioned the need for risk management.

Even today, many management teams are wary of the internet and many see it as a threat. For some, there is no doubt that it *is* a threat and needs management.

New channels for communication emerge and often with great speed; the internet is driven by many people and there is much presence that is not controlled by organizations. Much internet activity does not follow the usual linear models for management. The sequence of events can be as easily disrupted by the online community as by internal departmental interference from, for example the marketing or finance departments.

The lesson is obvious: plans have to be fluid. We need to be able to master the unknown. We have to grasp opportunities quickly and we need tools to help us make judgments – often at short notice.

The solution is to adopt practices from other disciplines in which 'management of the unknown' is common. Some of the greatest benefits to modern living have become possible because we know how to manage where there is uncertainty. There is a great deal of useful experience in this field, and De Meyer *et al*, for example, offer insights that can be used by relationship management practitioners. We offer an adaptation for use in online public relations.[1]

So what does uncertainty look like in the fast-moving online environment? De Meyer *et al* offer four uncertainty types: variation, foreseen uncertainty, unforeseen uncertainty and chaos.

Internet traffic data, displayed in time series (a sequence of events, measured typically at successive times, spaced at often uniform time intervals such as daily or monthly), have a number of characteristic properties, widely known as 'stylized facts', which are different from other kinds of time series:

- They tend to be long-tailed; in other words, there is a higher frequency of very extreme events that have a long life and tail off slowly.
- They tend to show long-range dependence; for example, search engines will find content that is old and present it today, people will remember and bring content to the fore long after it was news to another group and so forth (the internet has a 'long memory' and 'time-shifts' information – and reputation).
- They exhibit volatility; in other words, the apparent variance (from the plan or anticipated outcome) is not a constant but tends to fluctuate irregularly, something the internet has in common with traditional media that can bring back old news to support a new story.

These are challenging concepts, but can be visualized by thinking about books or recordings sold through an outlet such as Amazon. Traditionally, a band might release a single that was bought contemporaneously by a lot of people, making it a 'hit', before it slipped out fashion. Traditional record shops stocked the big sellers and knew it was not cost effective to maintain stocks when the song dropped out the charts. But the economies of scale offered by Amazon, allied with the infinite amount of virtual shelf space it commands, mean that songs that most have forgotten are still available. OK, they will sell in very small quantities but, they are sales nonetheless and the cost of storage and display is minimal on the website. This is the well-noted 'long-tail' effect.[2]

The same long-tail effect can be applied to news stories. Whereas once most people would read a story when it was splashed across the front page of a print newspaper and then discard it, such stories are now part of the digital archive, quickly accessible to search engines. An individual story may not be read by a huge volume of people on any one day, but its readership stretches down the long tail (the 'value' of the story has a very long 'shelf life'). This too has implications for PR, in that today the news never quite goes away. It may be forgotten by most readers, but Google has a long memory and is always ready to serve up scraps that organizations might imagine had long vanished.

In other words we are not quite sure where and when our online programme will pop up or in which platform or channel.

# RISK AND OPPORTUNITY

The practitioner can use some well-known techniques to second-guess what will be fashionable or will work (and those things that won't) using risk and opportunity techniques well established in other disciplines.[3]

One thing we know is that risk and opportunity changes are dependent on complexity. If a programme is very complicated there is more to go wrong, and online PR with its range of platforms, channels and contexts is quite complicated. But as we now know, the opportunities for considerable incremental success are greater.

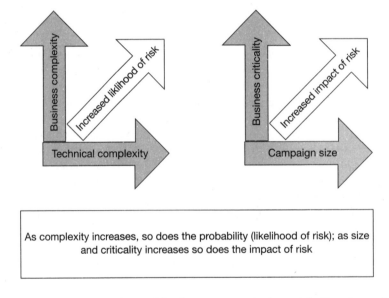

As complexity increases, so does the probability (likelihood of risk); as size and criticality increases so does the impact of risk

**Figure 21.1**  *The relationships between complexity, criticality size and complexity*

In most PR work there are risks and opportunities. To manage them we need to identify them. This can be done by an individual, a focus group or management team, or they can be established from research. It's a great opportunity for a brainstorm, with someone making notes!

In preparing a strategy for a programme, it is worth looking at where there may be influences that can affect it. In online public relations it is possible to second-guess many of the potential influences. The recession of

2008 is a classic case in point. For a number of companies, strategy had to change to maintain presence but at a much lower cost. Promotion budgets were slashed and PR had to take the strain. With reduced advertising, many publications just did not have the space for stories they would have run only months before. Online there were fewer constraints and so budgets shifted.

In PR there are some pretty well established influences that affect practice (see Figure 21.2)

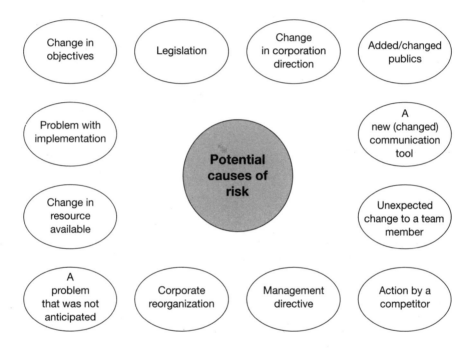

**Figure 21.2** *The range of known influences that can affect online PR programmes*

It is also possible to evaluate risk and asses its influence in terms of probability and impact. An example might be confidential product information that could leak out of the organization and into the public domain because an employee has a blog.

Having described risks and potential for effects, the practitioner (evaluation team) will assess each element in terms of likelihood of occurrence and impact. This helps put the risk or opportunity into perspective, and is a technique used by many voluntary and public sector organizations. It is the kind of matrix that might be used to assess risk for a school outing and is also used in project management (Figure 21.3).

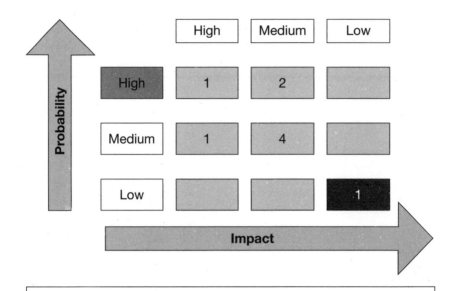

The Risk Matrix presents a pictorial view of the risk profile for the campaign and increases visibility and aids management decision making

**Figure 21.3** *Assessing the impact of events that can be estimated before any action is taken and again after mitigating policies are proposed to see if the potential for risk is lowered (acceptable) prior to implementation or exposure*

The next part of the process is to create a mitigation (or contingency) plan, process or protocol to reduce either or both of the likelihood and impact risks. This might be the introduction of, say, a company-wide blogging policy, or regulating the use of data on home computers.

Once a mitigation plan has been worked out, a new assessment is made of the likelihood or impact to see if the proposed actions for mitigation have had an effect that makes the risk acceptable within the campaign. The process is quite simple and effective and is valuable when attempting to identify competitive advantage versus doubts.

These methodologies can be used in making all manner of decisions, including those about the extent to which the internet should be made available during working hours (knowing that most people have access on their mobile phones anyway). The structured approach shown in Figure 21.4 helps inform such decisions.

Using such a process through each part of the planning process reduces risk to a manageable level and also helps to make precise projections of expected outcomes.

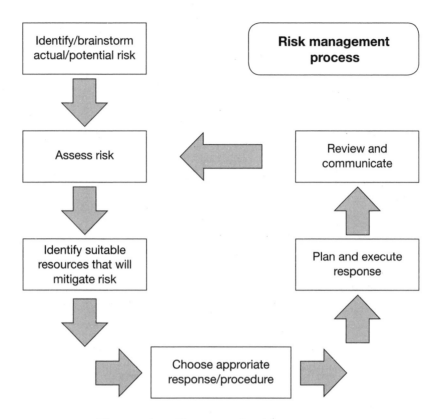

**Figure 21.4**   *The process for risk management*

Risk management is a process and can be applied to strategy as well as tactics.

Of course, for each risk there is an opportunity. By applying the same technique but looking for opportunities and means to optimize them, the practitioner can enhance the effectiveness of any approach to a campaign.

It is all too easy to imagine events in stark black and white answers. There is seldom only one solution and practitioners can work on contingency planning.

There are a lot of techniques that can be applied to ameliorate risk and optimize opportunity (Figure 21.5) and, affecting the programme strategy by using techniques adopted from other disciplines, PR can ensure greater certainty in online activities.

Disaster seldom comes unannounced for most organizations. There tend to be a number of indicators that presage the public event. The key is to be able to identify the stages as they present themselves. They are outlined below.

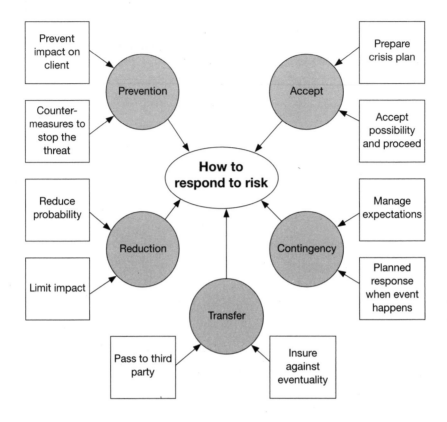

**Figure 21.5** *An amelioration matrix for managing PR risk*

## Variation

All plans have expected outcomes, financial budgets and timescales. These are often identified by using aids for project planning (see above).

Monitoring such plans will identify where plans are going awry. Often such occurrences are small. These are 'variations' to the plan. Good monitoring will give teams notice that remedial action has to take place, and contingency can be built into the plan. An example might be providing a contingency sum in a budget and allowing for some flexibility in delivery time.

## Foreseen uncertainties

There are some variations that are identifiable and understood but that the team cannot be sure will occur or when they might arise. To mitigate

foreseen uncertainties, the plan will need to include the capability to identify the event and to deploy a pre-planned contingency programme. An
example might be unscheduled maintenance of a computer that is running
the campaign blog. One big issue is website uptime, with issues such as a
slowing of response times of the organization's website or, disaster of all
disasters, the website being so overwhelmed that it stops responding (in
retail, this is the equivalent of one in 10 shops being closed).

When a website goes down, it is a PR problem. It is not an IT department
problem. Risk analysis is critical in identifying and mitigating these events.
Provision for such events has to be included in any plan. Who does what,
when and how? If they are not available or facilities are down, who else
should be part of such a plan?

## Unforeseen uncertainty

This kind of event cannot be identified during project planning. There is no
Plan B.

The team will be unaware of the event's possibility, or consider it so unlikely that there is no in-built contingency plan. To be able to manage such
events a comprehensive monitoring and alerting process is critical.

'Unknown unknowns,' or 'unk-unks,' as they are sometimes called,
make people nervous because existing decision tools are not applicable. Unforeseen uncertainty is not always caused by spectacular events or issues.
Unpredicted results can arise from the unanticipated interaction of many
events, each of which might, in principle, be foreseeable. The best management practice here is attention to detail and constant re-evaluation of
the plan and its application.

The model described here includes risk analysis at just about every point
in planning. Mature management of PR will have to begin to include these
more complex management techniques in the future, and this will take out
a lot of the management concerns that surround the use of social media.

Here are the key elements for reducing the impact of the unforeseen:

- Teams must go beyond mere crisis management and continually scan
  for emerging influences – either threats or opportunities. Practitioners
  should be scanning the horizon more than three months out to identify
  potential problems while they can still do something about them.
- Risk analysis must be an ongoing activity, with no potential hazard
  excluded because it seemed wacky at the time.
- With unforeseeable uncertainty, a lot of time and effort must go into
  managing relationships with key publics, often getting them to accept
  unplanned changes. Knowing who to approach and how to contact key
  publics is important. Good old-fashioned public relations to maintain
  good and effective relationships count when the unforeseen happens.

- Top-management support, negotiation techniques, team-building exercises and the practitioner's leadership can help resolve conflicting interests.
- Trust is a core element in managing the unforeseen, which means value systems and value system analysis are critical.
- Managing variance and planning to manage foreseen uncertainty assist in managing the unknown because contingency planning will be part of the organization's culture.

The unforeseen can be managed.

The US Institute for Crisis Management offers some insights into where to look for unforeseen uncertainty, listing the most common on its website (http://www.crisisexperts.com).

In an era when the internet is bringing great change in communication (as well as in the way organizations are organized and managed), being able to deploy these types of technique allows organizations to enter new areas of interaction with some confidence in their ability to gain optimum benefit at an acceptable level of exposure.

---

**IN BRIEF**

- Many management teams are wary of the internet and many see it as a threat. For some there is no doubt that it *is* a threat and needs management.
- The sequence of events of online programmes can be easily disrupted by the online community.
- Plans can allow organizations to grasp opportunities and manage threats with tools that can be deployed at short notice.
- The practitioner can use some well-known techniques to second-guess what will be fashionable or will work (and those things that won't), using risk and opportunity techniques.
- Online PR, with its range of platforms, channels and contexts, is quite complex. But the opportunities for considerable incremental success are greater.
- Risks can be identified and conform to a number of recognized variables.
- It is possible to evaluate risk and assess its influence in terms of probability and impact.
- Development of plans to mitigate risk before implementation will reduce threats.
- Risk management is a process and can be applied to strategy as well as tactics.

---

- There are a lot of techniques that can be applied to ameliorate risk and optimize opportunity, and intervening in the programme strategy by using techniques adopted from other disciplines, PR can ensure greater certainty in online activities.
- Planning for programme variation, foreseeable uncertainties, unforeseen uncertainty and the unknown is possible and practical.

## Notes

1. Pich, M T, Loch, C H and De Meyer, A (2002) On uncertainty, ambiguity and complexity in project management, *Management Science*, **48** (8), pp 1008–24
2. Anderson, C (2006) *The Long Tail*, Hyperion
3. Risk management literature includes: Chapman, C and Ward, S (1997) *Project Risk Management*, Wiley; Kliem, R L and Ludin, I S (1997) *Reducing Project Risk*, Gower

# Part 4

## Influences on present-day PR practice

# 22

# How the internet is changing news

Throughout this book we have talked about public relations in terms of sharing information, and one of the most obvious ways this happens is though 'news' – topical, interesting, relevant and largely factual information that is traditionally delivered by established news providers through a relatively small range of different channels. As individuals, we have been used to getting our news at set times in the day through scheduled slots on television and radio, through national, regional and local newspapers and (in specialist areas) magazines, monthly and weekly. All this is changing.

Media relations is a significant part of much public relations practice; many practitioners see themselves as the being the interface, the bridge, between their organization and news producers, usually journalists. Their many skills include the ability to spot a story, to use their appreciation of news values to package it in an attractive manner, and to identify appropriate news outlets to deliver organizational messages to target audiences. Such skills are complemented by an ability to understand what journalists will want and to respond to news enquiries in a way that reflects positively on their organizations; ideally they might hope to control who in their organization says what to which journalist.

But the internet is changing many of the fundamental assumptions that underpin this familiar picture. As we have seen, media consumption is changing; people are changing the way they use print newspapers and television, and are receiving their 'news' in many different ways, including from their computers through news websites, from news feeds driven by RSS, or direct to their mobile phone or PDA. For most people this is not either–or; many still love the relationship they have with print media and use the internet to source news as well. But we regularly ask university students where they get their news from; very few, perhaps two or three out of a class of 20, will read a local paper – if they do read print news it is usually a free daily; many rarely watch a television news programme, but most look at a news portal such as bbc.co.uk or Sky; in most classes a couple of students will say they haven't watched TV at all the previous evening, favouring YouTube for visual entertainment. This is not a scientific sample, but any PR practitioner who wants to talk to under-25s needs to do some careful market research.

The online presence of news organizations is changing quickly, too. A couple of years ago newspapers were beginning to experiment with websites and worrying about giving their content away free – and they still are worrying about how to derive serious revenues from their online activities. But the online presence of all national newspapers and most regionals has evolved to a remarkable degree; most 'nationals' include podcasts, video, blogs, message boards and forums. They encourage readers to 'share' content and to 'bookmark' it in social media.

Most, if not all, are now happy to break certain stories on the web before their print version hits the streets, work hard to provide online backgrounders, and are prepared to provide external links to other organizations in a way that would have been unthinkable a few years ago.

The flattening reach of the internet means that terms like 'national' and 'regional' are losing their significance; their content may still reflect geographical priorities but the user profile is broadening and evolving; a significant number of users of any regional newspaper website will be visiting from outside the United Kingdom. (Note here the choice of the word 'users'; we naturally think of newspapers having 'readers', but with so much visual and audio content available online that is increasingly becoming a misleading description.)

The BBC has one of the most widely used and most referenced sites on the internet. Newspapers like the *Daily Telegraph* and *The Guardian* count online readers in millions. They have devoted online readers but they also have one big trick up their sleeve. They tap into the network effect. These online media are quoted in social networks, blogs, wikis and websites. The online reach of the stories is huge and the traffic they generate to their websites is all the more rewarding. They offer their copyright and intellectual property freely to individuals and are rewarded when they visit the sites, check out the advertisements and buy added value content.

We have already discussed the issues of transparency and porosity, but keeping copyright in walled gardens is becoming harder. Not all copyright is offered freely but the nature of information flowing round obstructions is pertinent here.

A fledgling website called Mygazines.com encourages people to copy and upload popular magazines that are currently on newsstands. Visitors can read high-quality digital copies of dozens of current titles, including *People*, *Men's Health* and *The Economist*, in their entirety.

The site, with some 16,000 registered users at the time of writing, was a 'flagrant' violation of copyright laws, according to legal experts – but it is run by an offshore company of specious origin, making it difficult to shut down.

In 2007, the *Daily Telegraph*'s move from Canary Wharf to Waterloo co-incided with much enhanced use by journalists of offering content in blogs, proffering opinion on breaking news to 'Telegraph TV', recording podcasts and using Twitter.

In addition, like many publications, the *Telegraph* seeks to spread its stories – and by implication the stories of media relations professionals – across the internet. At the bottom of the story on the website, it is common to find a number of buttons inviting the reader to 'Post this story to:' and then there is a list of information-sharing sites such as (in the case of the *Daily Telegraph* in 2008) http://delicious, http://digg.com, http://www.newsvine.com, http://view.nowpublic.com, http://www.reddit.com and http://www.fark.com.

The big question is whether readers of the article take the trouble to add the story to these content-sharing sites. The evidence is that they do. Ordinary people act as agents to spread news, using internet agents that are designed to spread information.

Some PR practitioners are beginning to see the opportunities this broadening of content formats offers – or demands. It is tempting to argue that the last few years have been relatively easy for those engaged in standard media relations; newspaper pagination has been climbing steadily whilst editorial staffing shrinks, a combination that makes regional news organizations rely ever more heavily on content generated by public relations. Against tight staffing budgets, it is hard for editors to commit resources to producing time-consuming video and audio content; it is not just the editing that takes time; the video reporter actually has to leave the office rather than make a couple of quick phone calls or tweak the intro on a news release. Here is a golden opportunity for imaginative and creative PR to create valuable content that will be snapped up by video-hungry news editors.

# WHO IS A JOURNALIST ANYWAY?

Another assumption that underpins the 'traditional' view of media relation is that the 'press officer' deals with a 'journalist'. As we have seen, the designation 'press officer' is becoming as anachronistic as the notion of a 'press release', in that much of the content that they will produce or seek to influence will go nowhere near a printing press; more importantly, the person the practitioner engages with may not be what has long been seen as a journalist. The 'who is a journalist' debate is clearly of great significance to 'real' journalists who need to maintain their territorial rights, but it also has great relevance to the PR practitioner; the challenge is to try and establish who out there is worth engaging with.

For example, the practitioner needs to consider carefully the implications of news coming into 'traditional' news outlets from a much wider range of sources, and then being delivered across a much wider range of channels. Perhaps the most obvious example of this change is the way the use of mobile phones to take pictures is influencing the hardest of hard news stories.

On 7 July 2005 when four suicide bombers struck in London, the BBC received 50 images within an hour; on that day more than 300 e-mails containing an average of three images and about 30 video clips were sent to yourpics@bbc.co.uk. Likewise, as our case study below shows, when devastating floods hit parts of England in July 2007 a wealth of information was produced by people who used social media. By no means all of them would begin to consider themselves to be journalists. These examples are about one person telling someone else something that they find interesting. And through connectivity, that something may be passed on to other people.

# THE ECONOMICS OF NEWS PRODUCTION

At the same time, the economic model that shaped mass communications is being dramatically distorted; where once owning a newspaper was the privilege of a very rich elite, the advent of the writable web means creating a news outlet is now within the reach of anyone with a computer. The immediate response to such a claim is that although most people could launch their own news outlet, the vast majority will have no intention whatsoever of doing so. This is fundamentally correct, but it should not obscure two highly important implications for public relations. The first is that in almost any conceivable area of interest, somebody, somewhere is establishing a niche as a credible voice, as an opinion-former, as a node for focusing dialogue.

Second, while most people won't generate structured content on a regular basis, they are increasingly concerned with creating micro-content that when aggregated with other nuggets of micro-content can coalesce into something that might properly be called news and can definitely be called reputation. In real terms this might well play out as an individual, for whatever reason, creating social media content that is then picked up by the mainstream media; at the very least, traditional journalists do monitor blogs, message boards and other social networks to pick up stories.

Somewhere in between the unstructured opinion of the individual blogger or social network contributor and the work of those who regard journalism as their 'profession' sits a new genre, the product of engaged writers who are using the low-cost wide-access tools of the internet to create what some call participatory journalism, others citizen journalism, and Dan Gillmor, author of *We the Media*, 'grassroots journalism'.[1] Gillmor argues that blogs not only signal a change from mass to micro-media but also make it 'profoundly more grassroots and democratic'.

---

How and on what terms the PR practitioners should interact with grass-roots journalists is a matter for careful thought and judgement, as is the anecdote with which Gillmor describes his own groundbreaking contribution to the new genre. On 26 March 2002 Joe Nacchio, the Chief Executive of telephone giant Qwest, was talking at PC Forum, and complained about the difficulties of raising capital. Gillmor, who was in the audience, blogged about this and straightaway a lawyer friend sent him a link showing Nacchio had cashed in shares worth $200 million while the price was going down. Suddenly the audience turned hostile – they were reading Gillmor in real time, and they didn't like what they were seeing.

---

# ENGAGING WITH THE NEW JOURNALISTS

However fractious and grumpy they may be, and however reluctant they might be to admit it, most journalists and PR practitioners will privately concede that they work in a symbiotic relationship from which both sides gain. Sensible practitioners treat journalists like a friendly pit bull terrier whom they can usually get along with quite nicely, but take care never to forget that dogs have teeth; likewise the sensible reporter knows that most 'press officers' are reasonably decent individuals who will be as helpful as they can – as long as it is in their client or employer's interest to do so. These are the unwritten rules of the game, shaped by years of experience, passed down by generations of 'hacks and flacks' and underpinned by fairly robust 'cultural' assumptions (often strengthened by the propensity of many journalists to succumb to the better money and easier hours offered to those who move to the Dark Side).

But the vast majority of bloggers and citizen journalists haven't followed this route at all; they don't know the rules of engagement and in many cases have no intention of learning them.

# BEWARE OF YOUR FRIENDS

Journalists can often be seen as a threat (they like the opportunity to report things that go wrong!), but the wise practitioner also needs to be aware of people who like clients too much; fan sites created by users, customers, audience members or others who are infatuated with a particular subject can be a breeding ground for information with a potential to impact on reputation.[2] Promoters of movie, book, television and music properties should want to encourage such authentic forms of word-of-mouth endorsement. But many fan sites cross the line by misappropriating copyrighted material and by diverting traffic from officially sanctioned sites that generate revenue by selling products (eg branded merchandise) or services (eg downloadable music).

Although Hallahan is primarily concerned with protecting digital assets, he also touches on very important reputational issues.[3] He points out that fan sites also can pose problems because they sponsor bulletin boards or chatrooms where moderators and users can express derogatory comments. It is a tricky area, partly because it is not always easy to see where fair comment and criticism ends and defamation begins, but also because large organizations, major brands and celebrities will think carefully about the consequences of taking on individual critics, who may be customers, fans and supporters. It is one thing to launch a legal action against a national newspaper, quite another to do battle with a 17-year-old flexing her writing muscles, over a computer in her bedroom.

# INTERNAL CRITICS

In some of the more fanciful debate surrounding the emergence of blogging as an activity that should interest public relations, some commentators began to ask whether this heralded the demise of media relations or press officers and their ilk. In a nutshell, their argument ran along these lines: when everyone within an organization has access to social media they will have no need of the traditional conduits – if they have something to tell the world they will just blog about it.

It made for good headlines – 'PR is dead', no less – but makes little sense as a thought-through position; if anything, the advent of social media makes the PR practitioner, certainly in the role of relationship manager, more important, not less.

But there is a very significant shift that public relations cannot ignore. Although few organizations are going to give their employees *carte blanche* to write what they want on a platform that may appear to be officially endorsed, they will have to respond to a changing reality in which their workforce does have an enhanced voice that may be readily accessible to both mainstream journalists and the newly arriving citizen journalists. As is argued in Chapter 23, employers have a duty of care to ensure their employees have robust guidelines to help them though potentially damaging situations. Again, the point is that a combination of access to social media and the power of search engines is changing the dynamics of news gathering; chatrooms, bulletin boards and blog clusters provide useful and fertile hunting grounds for the inquisitive journalist.

## STORY-TELLING IS CHANGING

Melissa Wall argues that the emergence of blogs is leading to a new genre of journalism – offering news that features a narrative style characterized by personalization and an emphasis on non-institutional status; audience participation in content creation; and story forms that are fragmented and interdependent with other websites.[4]

This new journalism maybe distinguished by a lack of respect for normative behaviours such as fact-checking, an attempt at objectivity and some commitment to the notion of balance. Reporters are expected to remain uninvolved in their stories. The voice of the typical news blogger (and in this instance they can be found in Bebo, MySpace, Facebook and a range of other media) is personalized, opinionated and often one sided. It is also very often also distinguished by a more conversational and often less structured writing style. Some see this as good thing, with Dan Gillmor observing: 'Big media… treated the news as a lecture. We told you what the news was… Tomorrow's news reporting and production will be more of a conversation, or a seminar.'

Thirdly, blog narrative works to a different conception of time. With a 'conventional' newspaper, which in the strictest sense comprises news printed on paper, this news is locked on the page – nothing happens in the narrative until the next time the press rolls. (This model is under heavy challenge from 24-hour rolling news on television and radio, and in the press; deciding at what part of the day a daily newspaper should appear is a subject of vigorous debate.) As Steve Outing shows, the internet has also speeded up the news publishing cycle.[5] No longer is it easy for a news organization to sit on a big story and publish it at a set time, when all the dust has settled.

This constant stream of news provides a significant challenge for media relations managers who need to anticipate and respond to stories that are constantly moving and changing.

Blogs (and other social media) change the game again, in that very few work to a time schedule or subject themselves to limits or minimum amounts of content. Planning a newspaper is a complex operation based on a whole range of technical and economic factors, but once pagination is determined and advertisers accommodated, there is a finite amount of space to fill. Subsequent decisions on the different weightings and projections that individual stories merit follow directly from these initial decisions; there is no such limitation on online content other than the amount of time the blogger is prepared to contribute.

As Pavlik notes, the stories themselves are being delivered in structures that ultimately de-emphasize traditions such as the inverted pyramid (important facts at the top of the article, less important at its end) to re-conceptualized relationships between reporters and audiences as well as between reporters and news organizations.[6]

It is worth spending a little time thinking through the implications of some of these dialectics. The first three characteristics that seem to distinguish blog discourse from the traditional news story, that it is personal, opinionated

|  | Traditional journalism | Blog journalism |
| --- | --- | --- |
| Narrative style | Detached | Personal |
|  | Neutral | Opinionated |
|  | Both sides | One-sided |
| Approach to audience | Audience as passive recipient | Audience as co-creator |
| Story form | Structured format (eg inverted pyramid) | Fragments |
|  | Answers basic questions (who, what, etc) | Incomplete |
|  | Closed text | Open text |
|  | Sources and datelines for credibility | Hyperlinks for credibility |

and one sided, fit well with notions that link social media transactions with conversations – this how we speak to our friends and colleagues. (It is also how many newspaper and magazine columnists write, so this shouldn't be pushed too far.) Likewise, there are elements of magazines and newspapers that suggest some degree of co-creation, such as letters pages or advice columns, but as we have seen, the blogger can extend co-creation into areas where the original purposes and objectives can be completely lost; certainly, the blogger is expecting to generate comment that has an equality of status on the publishing platform that is not mirrored in print or broadcast media, and this parity is likely to be encouraged by the narrative style of the blogger (we are back to Gillmor's analogy of lecture and seminar). When the audience becomes active rather than passive, the shape of the discourse must change.

The really interesting changes come further down the list, when the values of the news pyramid – the need for a story to answer the five basic questions of who, what, why, where and when, and the necessarily closed nature of the text – are replaced by qualities Wall describes as fragments, incomplete and open. As all journalism students learn in week one, the intro is the most important element of a straight news story; it must be relatively short, 15–20 words max, it must be compelling and it must go some way towards encapsulating the whole story; facts are then delivered in order of descending importance, with a well-crafted story capable of being cut at the end of any paragraph (or sentence) and still retaining its coherence. Most non-news stories that we tell begin 'Once upon a time...' and compel us to journey to the end to learn the conclusion. News is different – whereas a story might end with the death of a character, in a newspaper the death would almost certainly be in the first paragraph. The blog posts of a citizen journalist may well incline more to the storybook structure than the news pyramid, and this tendency increases the less the tellers see themselves as journalists. This is important – the 'news items' being created by bloggers that aggregate into reputation may well not be intended in any way to resemble a conventional news story; many will take the form of comment or commentary.

One of the characteristics of a blog is that posts are displayed in reverse chronological order, the latest addition showing first. This gives blogs a lot of their immediacy and relevance but it also means that many readers will approach the content in reverse order. This will be particularly noticeable if the writer is posting frequently in real time on an issue or event that is unfolding contemporaneously. The effect of this delivery is to convey messages in an impressionistic way that can lack the context of a traditional news report, and this has implications for message delivery that should interest the PR practitioner.

The open nature of the texts combines with the blogger's desire to seek credibility by linking to sources outside the story (this is not necessarily a conscious process, or indeed the purpose of the links). Here again, the blog post is analogous to conversation – when we are talking to friends or colleagues about an issue of mutual interest or concern, and of which we are each familiar, we are unlikely to explicitly state vital elements of context. We don't talk like bad soap operas – 'Last night I went to the pub with Jill, who is the illegitimate daughter of pub murderer Crazy Ken' – or say: 'Look over there, I think I can see a rhinoceros, a large mammal of any of the five surviving species of odd-toed ungulates in the family *Rhinocerotidae*. Two species are native to Africa and three to southern Asia.' But, in effect, this exactly what newspapers do – because they have to. Bloggers take a different approach; rather than repeating information in detail to give necessary context and authority, they simply link to other posts, or to organizational websites, news portals or organizational blogs.

In a useful article entitled 'Think twice about that press release: you may have entered the Google zone', Jeffrey Geibel confronts the difficult compromise practitioners face when trying to balance market visibility with explaining past history.[7] Geibel suggests that before any information is distributed, it should be reviewed from two dimensions: how long you want it to be available, and how much control you will have over it.

This is done by evaluating everything you put out in terms of the nature of the content, its timeliness, and the method of dissemination. By thinking ahead, you can limit the amount of damage done by a thorough 'Google' of your company and its executives.

Is it an 'evergreen' topic, or can the event or item possibly turn sour in the future? If it can, but it has value now, might you want to be less than specific about the details, or conversely more specific? Geibel goes on:

> What do you estimate the shelf life of the announcement is? Ego aside, after just a few months – no one really cares that you have a new CEO. But if you have five CEOs in four years – that's news in itself – the kind your competitors like to use to create FUD (fear, uncertainty, doubt) about your stability as a company and a vendor. Also – most press releases should only hang around for about 12 months. Easy to do on your website – not so easy to do once they are out there on someone else's site.
>
> The most important aspects of controlling your information are to think about what you are sending out, and then how you plan to distribute it. Plain and simple – your website is your best tool for that – and the one you have most control over.

The word 'controlling', suggests there is control. Once published, of course, there is no control over any news story.

## CASE STUDY: WHEN THE FLOODS CAME

In July 2007, it rained. Across a swathe of England, first in Yorkshire and then in Gloucestershire, unprecedented monsoon weather created floods, disruption and travel chaos. Tens of thousands of households were inundated, water supplies stopped and, but for a massive effort, tens of thousands of households faced power cuts as the electricity distribution network was covered in water. These were rains of proportions not seen since 1789. It was a big story. Online, bloggers, social media, video-sharing sites, podcasts and micro-bloggers provided a mass of rich and human response. There were articles, links to where help was available, photographs, videos and commentary. The traditional media were stuck. There were just not enough reporters, photographers and film crews available to compete. Every newspaper, radio and TV station published or broadcast appeals for people to upload their comments, pictures and movies to fill the gaping void in their reporting. The engine of news had moved from the traditional media to social media, to ordinary folk using their mobiles and internet presence. The mass media were not able to compete with the human stories pouring out of these areas and beyond.

To discover what was going on among relatives and friends, people turned to the bloggers, who, district by district, gave local, germane news and helpful contacts and advice as the flood water gushed downstream. Human, timely, informative, multi-media coverage was provided by people sitting at their PCs or using their mobile phones.

The resources of big media brought in planes and helicopters to film swamped towns, roads and countryside. These too were dramatic pictures, but it was online that the real contexting was taking place. The international nature of the online community was able to compare and contrast not just visions of devastation at home but the inundations in China, India and Texas in the same month, debates about climatology, global warming, treasures at risk and a mass of context.

This event was a stark example of the changing nature of news and feature reporting. The internet won hands down, and in doing so provided a resource that was plundered by newsrooms that could never have found such a rich seam of content using traditional reporters on the street.

(See also Allen, S (2006) *Online News*, OUP.)

New media do not replace old media but they do change the dynamic of news. In the United Kingdom the engine of news is now in the hands of 37 million people online.

Stepping up to the mark, the PR industry recently began to offer video, voice and other content to match the digital needs of the media. The development of the social media release is one such initiative prompted by a blogger, 'The Silicon Valley Watcher', ex-FT journalist Tom Foremski, who expressed dissatisfaction with old-style press releases because they are not well suited to the editorial needs and style of bloggers.

On 16 June 2008, the Chartered Institute of Public Relations issued its first social media release. It evoked comments in the release itself and seven blog posts, and its content was used by journalists. It can be viewed at http://blogit.webitpr.com/?ReleaseID=8986.

Much may be said of the power of social media but the power of the traditional media holds considerable sway online too.

## IN BRIEF

- News is being shared.
- It is being shared by newspapers, magazines and other traditional media channels.
- People are changing the way they use print newspapers and television, and are receiving their 'news' in many different ways.
- National newspapers and most regionals have evolved to a remarkable degree; most 'nationals' offer podcasts, video, blogs, message boards and forums. They encourage readers to 'share' content and to 'bookmark' it in social media.
- Most if not all are now happy to break certain stories on the web before their print version hits the streets.
- The flattening reach of the internet means that terms like 'national' and 'regional' are losing their significance.
- These online media are quoted in social networks, blogs, wikis and websites.
- The 'who is a journalist' debate is clearly of great significance to 'real' journalists who need to maintain their territorial rights, but it also has great relevance to the PR practitioner; the challenge is to try and establish who out there is worth engaging with.
- Social media writers are different. It is one thing to launch a legal action against a national newspaper, quite another to do battle with a 17-year-old flexing her writing muscles over a computer in her bedroom.
- The internet has also speeded up the news publishing cycle.
- Online authors structure 'news' stories differently.
- New media do not replace old media but they do change the dynamic of news.

## Notes

1.  Gillmor, D (2004) *We the People: Grassroots journalism by the people, for the people*, O'Reilly Media
2.  Hallahan, K (2004) Protecting an organization's digital public relations assets, *Public Relations Review*, **30** (3), pp 255–68
3.  Hallahan, *op cit*
4.  Wall, M (2005) 'Blogs of war': weblogs as news, *Journalism*, **6** (2), pp 153–72
5.  Outing, S (2004) What bloggers can learn from journalists, http://www.poynter.org/content/content_view.asp?id=75383 (accessed 2007)
6.  Pavlik, John V (2001) *Journalism and New Media*, Columbia University Press
7.  Geibel, J (2003) Think twice about that press release: you may have entered the Google zone, http://www.geibelpr.com/googled.htm (accessed 2007)

# 23

# What is right and wrong?

Throughout this book we have argued that the rapidly evolving internet society is changing public relations in profound ways. But technological advance does not change what is right and wrong.

The principles of ethical behaviour do not change, so there is no need for public relations to develop a new code of conduct for social media. But at the same time the new PR brings a host of new issues and ethical conflicts, some of which throw the dynamics that underpin PR practice into sharp relief. Likewise, the practical changes flowing from new technologies are presenting new problems in interpreting the law and prompting changes in regulations that any practitioner would do well to follow carefully. (From the outset, we must make clear that this chapter is not intended in any way to be a comprehensive guide to the law or to be regarded as constituting legal advice. If in doubt, consult a lawyer.)

As we point out in Chapters 3–6, many of the key changes brought about by the move to online PR revolve around transparency, porosity, agency, richness and reach, and we can add timelessness. Crucially, social media bring greater possibilities for interaction with a wider audience, with different expectations, norms and vulnerabilities. The implications of these changes need to be considered in terms of managing both internal and external relationships.

Arguments around transparency usually develop from the belief that for public relations to be ethical it must declare its hand, often in the form of disclosures and health warnings. The most obvious example of transgression would include astroturfing – creating a website, blog or other platform for discourse that acts as a front for another, hidden organization, usually cast as the expression of a spontaneous grassroots movement. Recently, some critics have extended this definition to include much broader actions, such as making posts or comments that do not reveal the author's connection with a product or service. (Astroturfing is contrary to the CIPR code of conduct. There is a wealth of useful background on astroturfing at http://www.thenewpr.com/wiki/pmwiki.php?pagename=AntiAstroturfing.HomePage).

Some PR bloggers take the need for transparency in their own actions very seriously, and it is not unusual to see comments acknowledging that an article under review was supplied by a manufacturer or supplier, or that the blogger has a business connection with the organization being discussed. One of the reasons such declarations have been made is linked to the realities of online visibility; it is hard to hide on the internet and one of the best ways to avoid unwelcome exposure is to lay your cards on the table from the outset.

# SHOWING THE UNSEEN HAND

Before dealing with these issues in more detail, it is worth looking further into what is being said here. It has long been the convention for public relations practitioners to keep out the picture, out of the story; PR-generated quotes are attributed to a person with senior status within the client organization, spokespersons are often unnamed, and many organizations fear that if they were to be seen putting forward a named agency public relations practitioner for an interview it would lead to a loss of credibility. At a deeper level, there are many times that an experienced 'operator' will actually take pride in being the unseen hand that guides a particular message; that the majority of people outside the industry would struggle to name even a couple of practitioners beyond Max Clifford is indicative of the 'I'm not really here' nature of practice. One of the reasons that this behaviour is accepted is that until recently, in this media relations model, the practitioner was dealing directly with a journalist who knew the rules of the game. But things are changing; those who see advantages, sometimes even a necessity, in bypassing the gatekeeper have to establish some sort of revealed identity to carry credibility to their messages, and increasingly this means that the previously unseen hand is moving into fairly sharp focus.

This may be a highly pragmatic and ethically questionable motivation for openness (which is almost always seen as a virtue) but the desire to be seen to be 'clean' is certainly enhanced by the very real fear that exposure is almost inevitable; visibility is a great motivator towards transparency (for more on transparency see Chapter 3). The third leg of this structure is porosity (for more on porosity see Chapter 4). As has been argued on many previous occasions, the days when the command and control of messages was the fiefdom of the press office are disappearing rapidly; this model, unconvincing as it ever was, melts away when most employees have the opportunity to make their views known to the widest audience. Again, this is nothing new – employees have always had the opportunity to talk to friends and family about the products and services provided by their employer; if they felt sufficiently aggrieved they might write to a newspaper, or more seriously, become a 'whistle-blower' (which, incidentally, is usually seen as a heroic act). The difference is in visibility – comments on a blog or message are searchable and can be picked up by news organizations, or by bloggers, with a speed and reach that provides a real challenge to those charged with reputation management.

Reach helps us to contextualize the online world in geographical and social terms; we don't know where our audiences, our users and possibly even our independent co-creators will be in the world. Clearly, shared language plays a part, but it is increasingly difficult to tailor one message for one target group whilst simultaneously speaking to another group using a different voice – or worse, using different facts or value systems. Dissonance between messages almost inevitably erodes trust and questions one of the core territories of public relations, truthfulness.

Timelessness, too, has several dimensions that throw forward ethical and legal hurdles that might be familiar in the offline world but are cast into a sharper focus when played out online. Speed of reaction, the need to be 'always on' so as to monitor discourse in real time, is a distinct challenge, but a strong force is pressing in the opposite direction and can present equally challenging problems. Once something is out on the web, it stays there, and this permanence, the practitioner's powerlessness to remove or rework 'old' messages, is a real concern. The long tail may be a good thing for, say, a rock band or an author, but it can be rather different for a PR issuing statements and news releases, or, worse, who is trying to counter false or damaging information. This can manifest in at least three ways; the most obvious is that only organizations with the most disciplined of procedures can track and manage the content of their own web presence (it is a lot easier to overlook something in a virtual environment than, say, on paper); many communications can be multiplied and locked into an elaborate, aggregated network of cross-references in which positions are set in a virtual amber; and finally, because search engines automatically cache web pages, it is quite possible for users to retrieve content the originator believed had been deleted or erased.

# THE PRACTITIONER AS PUBLISHER

These last concerns cast the PR practitioner as publisher, a role that carries a range of legal and ethical responsibilities. In the symbiotic 'flack and hack' relationship that has long underpinned media relations, the practitioner was often shielded from the full impact of these responsibilities by the media gatekeeper. The internet and social media change this, with practitioners making raw news releases available through virtual newsrooms, and catalogued in online archives. The advent of blogs means public relations departments may well be publishing a greater range of texts that will not be passed through the filter of an experienced news editor. The word 'published' is used with care, to reinforce the nature of the communication and to underline the legal responsibilities that this brings forward. There is a potential danger here. It has not been common for an individual or organization to take legal action over a defamatory press release, partly because the complainant is unlikely to see the release in its raw form; it is more likely to come to attention when included in a newspaper or magazine item. Unethical behaviour erodes trust; behaviour that falls foul of the law brings potentially ruinous financial consequences.

Unhappily for PR, those practitioners who would position themselves as the 'conscience of the organization' often lack any training in or specialist knowledge of ethical thinking and frameworks; those who generate content that has the potential to be libellous or slanderous often have little or no legal training (the exception usually being those who began their career in a newsroom). These considerations will be brought into sharper focus if and when organizations become more porous, when more people can communicate externally without the guidance of those with such experience.

If it is a challenge to ensure that the content generated by the PR team or by other members of the organization is appropriate, the situation becomes considerably more perilous where user-generated content is concerned. The most obvious flashpoint is comments on blogs. An organization trying to build open and honest dialogue with stakeholders will be reluctant to be seen as 'censoring' comment and there is a tendency to argue that all comment should be allowed. A few moments thought suggest this isn't the solution – comments of, say, a racially offensive or clearly libellous nature can't be allowed onto an organizational website, so it immediately becomes apparent that some form of moderation is needed. But this decision brings two consequences: first of all someone has to do the moderating, and this requires time and personnel (visitors expect to see their thoughts published pretty soon after they post, and they don't always post between 9 and 5, and aren't necessarily from the same time zone). Second, moderating constitutes, in the eyes of the law, an admission that the comments are approved by the organization and have therefore been published by that organization, opening up all the legal obligations that this implies. At the very least this places something of a burden on the moderators, who may not feel they have the training to make such decisions. (It must be worth noting that this is presently a vigorously disputed area and legal opinion appears divided on the implications of moderation.)

# STARTING POINTS FOR ETHICAL INTERNET PR

The basic principles of ethical behaviour depend on the individual deciding whether to consider the nature of an action in itself, or the consequences of that action. Most people can very quickly come up with a list of things that are wrong, that we shouldn't do. We consider it wrong to lie, we consider it wrong to break promises, we consider it wrong to steal and so on. But almost as we have begun the list we can think of exceptions – there are times when we consider it acceptable, even praiseworthy, to lie or to break a promise. We believe that the 'good' outcome of breaking the promise or, say, telling a 'white lie' can outweigh the obligation to stick to one's principles. We quickly convince ourselves that bending the rules is of benefit to us and, better still, has benefits for other people. This position can be summed up as the end justifying the means.

All well and good, but if we are to adopt this consequentialist stand, we are assuming that we actually can foresee the consequences of our actions – which is quite a tall order. This inherent tension between duty and consequence is one of the main reasons why there appear to be so many grey areas in ethics, and why people who we find demonstrate 'goodness' and integrity will nonetheless have different ethical values.

There are two other areas that need to be borne in mind in any discussion of PR ethics: the nature of obligation and the nature of public relations itself – two rather big questions to unleash this far into a book!

We need to decide who sets the ethical compass. Is your ultimate ethical responsibility to yourself or to society, or is it to your organization, or to your client? Again, there is great scope for confusion, and for saying 'a bit of this, but in some cases mostly that...' An example might be someone working in the press office of a police force; one might hope that the interests of society and of the force would closely coincide, but it is not hard to imagine conflicts. Where then should the press officer's obligations lie?

This links with second conundrum: what is the function of public relations in this contested area of message exchange? Is it really about facilitating an exchange of information through a model of two-way symmetry? Or is it about persuasion through the projection of messages and partial truths designed to encourage behaviours and attitudes favourable to the client? This latter 'advocacy model' reaches its extreme in Max Clifford's

admission that his first duty is to the client and if that means telling lies, tell lies. Before condemning Clifford, it is important to note that, whether you agree with his choice or not, he does carefully select clients with whom he is comfortable working, and this declaration is important to any version of the advocacy model.[1] Although it is possible to imagine a website that presents information of a largely neutral nature – a document setting out opening times for a swimming pool, for example – it is hard to imagine a blog, which relies on its personal voice, that doesn't seek to influence perceptions; what other reason would there be to blog?

## TRUTHFULNESS

Telling the truth is seen by many as a basic prerequisite of ethical public relations – and it is the often the obstacle on which PR trips up. Even discounting those who would deliberately lie or deceive, there is a clear distinction within any advocacy model between the need to tell the truth (which most would accept) and an obligation to tell the whole truth when this would require volunteering information that might be unhelpful to reputation. We would argue that telling partial truths is inherent to PR practice, whether online or in any other forum or channel, and that deciding where the distinction lies between a partial truth and deception is an individual decision. But as we have seen, such is the transparency of internet-mediated discourse that such decisions are increasingly laid open for public scrutiny and comment amplified through social media. Yet, again the pragmatic response has to be openness.

## DUTY OF CARE TO EMPLOYEES

As we have seen, a significant proportion of the UK public engages in social media in one way or another, and it is very likely that this will include a significant proportion of employees of either your own organization or of your clients'. They may engage in work time or in their own time, they may on occasion blog about their employer, or simply mention their employer in what is ostensibly a personal discussion. People give their opinions about their workplace and work colleagues all the time to friends and casual acquaintances. These conversations may all may be replicated by repetition, as rumour or by peer recommendation, into something that begins to coalesce into reputation, but for the most part this information is passed on through discrete channels that are not readily accessible by others. The difference comes, as ever, when such comments are searchable and can be aggregated by hyperlink.

Some employees will be well aware that what they are saying has the capacity to impact on organizational reputation, and causing damage might be the desired outcome. But, as has been demonstrated on many occasions, many bloggers neither appreciate the level to which their comments can be exposed, nor do they necessarily recognize that the internet is blurring the distinction between the public and the private to a startling degree. Increasingly the activities of an individual employee can impact on organizational reputation. To make this more acute, many people who generate content – write blogs, comment on them, upload photos and videos – believe that they are anonymous. Unfortunately for them, that is not the way the internet works: both as a physical entity and as a social construct, internet use leaves distinct electronic footprints and it is remarkably easy to find out who is hiding behind an ostensibly opaque nickname or *nom de plume*. Even without following the tracks, it is in the nature of these searchable, permanent and interlinked texts that clues to identity will emerge; the individual scraps of identity may not reveal much but these small jigsaw pieces can quickly be assembled into a readily identifiable whole.

Clearly no organization can take absolute responsibility for the micro-behaviour of its employees, but this does not remove the duty of care it has to ensure that its workforce is at least aware of a clearly stated policy on internet use. It is worth pointing out that many commentators argue that there are fewer incidents of employees making errors in social media use within organizations that have a strongly defined organizational culture, and that the employees who overstep the mark are often the type of employees whose behaviour would cross borders with or without guidelines. The internet simply presents them with greater opportunities or temptations.

---

**IN BRIEF**

- The principles of ethical behaviour do not change, so there is no need for public relations to develop a new code of conduct for social media.
- Some PR bloggers take the need for transparency in their own actions very seriously.
- Dissonance between messages almost inevitably erodes trust and questions one of the core territories of public relations, truthfulness.
- Timelessness now has several dimensions.
- PR practitioner as publisher is a role that carries a range of legal and ethical responsibilities.
- What is the function of public relations in this contested area of message exchange? Is it really about facilitating an exchange of information through a model of two-way symmetry? Or is it about

persuasion through the projection of messages and partial truths designed to encourage behaviours and attitudes favourable to the client?

- Such is the transparency of internet-mediated discourse that decisions are increasingly laid open for public scrutiny, and comment is amplified through social media.
- A duty of care extends to the significant proportion of the UK public that engages in social media in one way or another, and it is very likely that this will include a significant proportion of employees of either the organization or its clients.

## Note

1. Fitzpatrick, K and Bronstien, C B (2006) *Ethics in Public Relations: Responsible advocacy*, Sage Publications

# 24

# Ethics in a transparent world

## WIDENING THE DEBATE

Many PR practitioners see themselves as the bridge between an organization and its publics, or, in the media relations function, as the intermediary between an organization and the media channels through which messages might be distributed. Traditionally, this relationship has largely been managed through intermediaries, often in the form of news organizations, but online public relations allows – even obliges – practitioners to engage directly with members of the public.

There is nothing new in PRs talking to ordinary people – they have long engaged in creating news by eliciting testimonies from satisfied customers, or promoting individuals as case studies. Likewise, they may send a bunch of flowers to a disgruntled customer. As ever, the difference is reach and access – and is made harder by the fact that it is not always clear with whom you are interacting on the internet.

Although blogs and other social media sites are inherently public, there is also a compelling temptation for the blogger to see them as personal. This is quite natural: the layout, fonts and colour scheme of the blog may feel analogous to our choice of clothes, and it is quite likely that the posts will be written at home on a personal computer. Some argue that anyone who posts to a blog is publishing to the world and should accept, indeed expect to receive, the attentions of both friend and foe, and have the courage to face criticism. Yes, there is legitimacy to this argument, but it is an unpleasant ethical position. A 14-year-old girl who creates a MySpace account and makes comments on her favourite band simply isn't creating texts of the same nature as a professional music critic working for an established news organization. Public relations practitioners who engage with the social media constructs of 'ordinary' people must consider carefully whether they are in fact invading what those people believe to be private space.

We have seen that a blog audience is hard to define – it can be anyone, anywhere – but that doesn't mean individual bloggers see it that way. As so often with ethical questions, the right behaviour is usually also the one that makes commercial sense. Look at it like this: although arguably legitimate, an unsolicited approach or intervention from a PR practitioner might seem highly intrusive – at best like when you have just settled down to watch a favourite television and are interrupted by a telephone call from someone trying to sell double-glazing, or when you are holding what feels like a 'private' conversation in a bar when a complete stranger walks up and intervenes with a hostile or personal comment. The bar analogy works quite well. Imagine you are having a drink after work in your usual meeting place with a half a dozen colleagues, some of whom you get on with better than others. You will have a general conversation about the day that is accessible and audible to all, but may want to confide something to a close friend in low whisper. Jill is showing holiday snaps from her trip to Barcelona, Jack is complaining bitterly about the service in that new restaurant round the corner, and Susan has seen a really good film that you really ought to see; Norman, as ever, is complaining about how boring his job is and how no one in the agency has any imagination.

As you are regulars, members of your group might interact with other groups. Perhaps there are two people you don't know well but have met once or twice before who are standing nearby, and can hear your group conversation. They may comment on your conversation, they may interject. And then there are a couple of other people nearby who are rather irritated to have to overhear your conversation, which they consider a little loud and intrusive, but they are keeping their thoughts to themselves. The evening wears on and the social mix changes, as more one-to-one conversations coalesce and dissolve; a few people from other groups have joined your party but a couple of others have left. You haven't really noticed him, but a man at the bar who has been taking notes on a beermat now joins you and asks a few questions that take you off guard; pretty much at the same time, someone else marches up to your boss and starts criticizing the colour of his shirt and ridiculing his hairstyle. The intervention isn't appreciated but all in all it's a pretty average evening, not one to stick in the mind.

The next morning, you start getting e-mails about a blog posting that says employees of a certain PR agency behaved rather badly in a bar last night... It includes video footage shot on a mobile phone, derogatory comments from Norman about the boss, and worse, unattributed quotes about the financial difficulties one of your key clients is facing. Welcome to the blogosphere.

Again this is particularly important when it comes to children. How old is 'jack123'? To what extent is 'jill234' able to make an informed decision on the facts available? What assumptions can we make about the nature of the discourse we can establish?

The answer is that you simply can't know who they are, or how old they are. Reports of music companies employees posing as teenagers on MySpace suggest a practice that is indefensible.

## SETTING GUIDELINES

Blogger Allan Jenkins has devised a Code of Blogging Ethics for his Desirable Roasted Coffee site.[1] It goes like this:

To write, publish, and be read is a privilege and responsibility. Being mindful of that privilege and responsibility:

1. I shall not barter my words or my silence.
2. I shall write and advocate openly and honestly.
3. I shall strive for accuracy, avoiding errors and correcting them immediately when discovered.
4. I shall strive for balance; even in advocacy, I shall not distort or suppress obviously relevant facts to bolster my argument.
5. I shall welcome and invite rebuttal, debate and discussion through comments, e-mail, and trackbacks.
6. I shall disclose my sources fully, through credits, links and trackbacks, unless the source, with good grounds, has requested anonymity; moreover, I shall trackback where relevant and possible.
7. I shall respect copyright; my own words will be licensed with a Creative Commons license.
8. I shall let the record stand; I shall not delete posts, or parts of them, unless not doing so would violate one of the foregoing principles, and shall give notice that I have done so. If I modify a post, it shall be by adding to it; and I shall mark these additions clearly.
9. I shall reveal material conflicts-of-interest.
10. I shall, as a member of IABC, a trained reporter, a resident of the European Union, and a citizen of the United States of America, remain mindful of the IABC Code of Ethics, the Code of Ethics of the Society of Professional Journalists, and the laws of the European Union and the United States.

It is an interesting framing in that it is cast as a personal statement, which is intended to be read the context of the codes of professional organizations of which he is a member. Tellingly, Jenkins forefronts advocacy as a key indicator of his practice.

It is a fairly robust statement of intent and a powerful weapon for anyone to seize if they believed Jenkins had not lived up to his high standards – particularly from someone who can be forthright, even combative, in his writing. There is certainly no need for most bloggers to go as far as drawing up their own code, but a wise blogger, especially one with PR connections, would do well to include a clear statement of who s/he is and who s/he works for; setting out criteria for comment and so on is also advisable.

The CIPR's Social Media Guidelines revised in 2009 (http://www.cipr.co.uk/socialmedia/) offer a useful starting point, not least in that they provide a common ground. Correctly, the guidelines are designed to explore the key issues set out in the CIPR's own Code of Conduct, which is founded on three core principles of integrity, competence and confidentiality.

# EXAMPLES OF PRACTICE

It is important to remember that as social media spread so will their usage by an organization's own employees. It is not sufficient to simply set out guidelines for official blogs; a responsible organization has an obligation to show the boundaries of acceptable usage in a wider context.

The guidance issued by Sun Microsoft Communities is quite informal, and makes sensible points:[2]

- **Don't tell secrets**. Common sense at work here; it's perfectly OK to talk about your work and have a dialog with the community, but it's not OK to publish the recipe for one of our secret sauces. There's an official policy on protecting Sun's proprietary and confidential information, but there are still going to be judgment calls.
    If the judgment call is tough – on secrets or one of the other issues discussed here – it's never a bad idea to get management sign-off before you publish.
- **Think about consequences**. The worst thing that can happen is that a Sun sales pro is in a meeting with a hot prospect, and someone on the customer's side pulls out a print-out of your blog and says 'This person at Sun says that product sucks.'
    In general, 'XXX sucks' is not only risky but unsubtle. Saying 'Netbeans needs to have an easier learning curve for the first-time user' is fine; saying 'Visual Development Environments for Java sucks' is just amateurish.

Once again, it's all about judgment: using your weblog to trash or embarrass the company, our customers, or your co-workers, is not only dangerous but stupid.

- **Disclaimers**. Many bloggers put a disclaimer on their front page saying who they work for, but that they're not speaking officially. This is good practice, but don't count on it to avoid trouble; it may not have much legal effect.

Although actions motivated simply by the fear of getting caught are not intrinsically moral, it is inescapable that the transparency and porosity inherent in the internet-mediated environment will force a lot of people to think a lot more clearly about the ethical implications their actions. Public relations has a duty to address such issues, and by doing so may well not only improve public perception of its activities but also develop practices that allow it to operate in a more effective manner.

In the online world, boundaries are difficult to draw and harder still to enforce. The territory is defined by porosity, by weak forces and paper-thin walls. Bloggers or social network commentators don't have to be using official channels to link what they may feel is their own private behaviour with that of their employer in ways that can seriously impact on reputation. We live in an era when Google is the first reference tool most of us reach for, and the pieces of the Google jigsaw can fit together all too easily for those who may have conflicting personal and professional norms and standards. Quite simply, the internet and social media have little respect for personal privacy; a Google image search does not distinguish between work and pleasure – as many people are already finding to their cost.

The CIPR suggests that members might look to guidelines drawn up by the BBC and IBM.

# CASE STUDY: EXAMPLES OF SOCIAL MEDIA GUIDELINES

In the spring of 2005, employees at IBM used a wiki to create a set of guidelines for all 'IBMers' who wanted to blog. These guidelines aimed to provide helpful practical advice – and also to protect both IBM bloggers and IBM itself, as the company sought to embrace the blogosphere.

Since then, many new forms of social media have emerged. So the company turned to IBMers again to re-examine its guidelines and determine what needed to be modified. The effort broadened the scope of the existing guidelines to include all forms of social computing.

At the BBC, staff members are allowed to update their personal blog from a BBC computer at work, under the BBC's Acceptable Use Policy for Internet and E-mail.

Many bloggers, particularly in technical areas, use their personal blogs to discuss their BBC work in ways that benefit the BBC, and add to the 'industry conversation'. Their editorial guidance note is not intended to restrict this, as long as confidential information is not revealed.

The BBC makes the point that blogs or websites that do not identify the blogger as a BBC employee, do not discuss the BBC and are purely about personal matters would normally fall outside this guidance.

Three points in the BBC guidelines stand out:

- If you already have a personal blog or website which indicates in any way that you work at the BBC, you should tell your manager.
- If you want to start blogging and your blog/website will say that you work for the BBC, you should tell your manager.
- If your blog makes it clear that you work for the BBC, it should include a simple and visible disclaimer such as 'these are my personal views and not those of the BBC'.

Both companies have made these policies available to the public on their websites.

---

### IN BRIEF

- Public relations practitioners who engage with the social media constructs of 'ordinary' people must consider carefully whether they are in fact invading what those people believe to be private space.
- A blog audience is hard to define.
- There is a need for guidelines.
- The CIPR Social Media Guidelines offer a useful starting point.
- In the online world, boundaries are difficult to draw and harder still to enforce.

## Notes

1. Jenkins, A (2005) http://allanjenkins.typepad.com (accessed 2007)
2. Sun Guidelines on Public Discourse, http://www.sun.com/communities/guidelines.jsp (accessed on 23 October 2008)

# 25

# Monitoring, measurement and evaluation

Repeatedly we have touched on monitoring and evaluation.

The assertion that PR must adapt and evolve holds true across the range of framings of what PR might be – it is as valid for those who see themselves as working in media relations as it is for those who see themselves as information or marketing communicators, reputation or issues managers, or more broadly concerned with relationship management.

It is not necessary for practitioners to be active participants in online practice but they need to be aware of what is happening online. The truth is that what is happening online will influence the practice of PR. People use the internet in ways that affect all forms of practice, as do organizations. Not knowing what is happening online is not very sensible.

Throughout this book we have put forward incontrovertible evidence that the advent of an internet society has brought new challenges for the practice of public relations. There can be few areas in which it is not now necessary to include an appreciation of networked publics, and of the forces of aggregation, transparency, porosity, agency, reach and, in terms of content, richness.

As in all PR, there is a need to monitor the effects of PR interventions; there is a need to be able to measure and weigh such interventions, and there is a need to be able to evaluate effects. As the internet mediates more of what organizations do, the role of monitoring, measurement and evaluation takes on a much more interesting role.

There are those people who are known by the organization and who interact, and in addition there is a large group of people and organizations 'out there' with whom the organization has a tenuous or even unknown relationship. Monitoring these publics is not easy.

Monitoring the combined range of relationships through all the platforms and channels and in all contexts is not possible. To begin with there are some channels that are just not available to most organizations to monitor. Most SMS, instant messaging, VoIP telephony and much e-mail hosted on third-party servers are all but invisible. This tells us that, if we can't monitor it directly, we need to monitor it indirectly and this is what happens for the vast majority of organizations and activities.

If we accept that markets are conversations, that successful organizations cannot perform effectively unless they enter into dialogue with a range of stakeholders, then it follows inexorably that organizations must be aware of and engage with as nearly a full range of communication channels and platforms as possible.[1] This doesn't mean all organizations must utilize all channels (far from it), but it is vital that they are sufficiently aware of these channels and platforms and that they identify which are most appropriate for communication with their particular stakeholders.

Importantly, it seems common sense to be aware of and actively engaged with identifying those channels publics choose to use. Only a small proportion of organizations can afford to be selective about who they listen to. For example, some sceptics have argued that poor spelling and grammar diminish the impact of many blogs. Yes, blogs that are badly written, ill informed or simply boring can all be irritating – but that doesn't mean they should be dismissed or ignored. If we were launching a new product and discovered that sales were poor, we would want to know why. Perhaps there was a design flaw and this had been pointed out by dissatisfied customers who had written to inform us about a simple fix that would rectify the problem. Imagine a manager going to the communications department and noticing a pile of mailbags, all containing such letters. Why, the manager might ask, have we not responded to these letters? 'Oh, we don't bother with letters that contain spelling mistakes, or are delivered in poor hand writing...'

## CASE STUDY: RESPONDING FAST TO SOCIAL MEDIA COMMENT

In September 2008, Google launched a new web browser called Chrome. Within 12 hours there was a hullabaloo about the terms and conditions for its use among bloggers and, eventually the press.

Google was watching for comments and responded in just 24 hours from launch to head off further criticism. It did so on the company's official blog with this comment:

> Whenever we release a product in beta as we just did with Google Chrome, we can always count on our users to come up with ways to improve it. This week's example: several eagle-eyed users and bloggers have expressed concern that Section 11 of Google Chrome's terms of service attempts to give us rights to any user-generated content 'submitted, posted or displayed on or through' the browser.
>
> You'll notice if you look at our other products that many of them are governed by Section 11 of our Universal Terms of Service. This section is included because, under copyright law, Google needs what's called a 'license' to display or transmit content. So to show a blog, we ask the user to give us a license to the blog's content. (The same goes for any other service where users can create content.) But in all these cases, the license is limited to providing the service. In Gmail, for example, the terms specifically disclaim our ownership right to Gmail content.
>
> So for Google Chrome, only the first sentence of Section 11 should have applied. We're sorry we overlooked this, but we've fixed it now, and you can read the updated Google Chrome terms of service. If you're into the fine print, here's the revised text of Section 11:
>
> 11.   Content license from you
>    11.1   You retain copyright and any other rights you already hold in Content which you submit, post or display on or through, the Services.
>
> And that's all. Period. End of section.
>
> It will take a little time to propagate this change through the 40+ languages in which Google Chrome is available, and to remove the language in the download versions. But rest assured that we're working quickly to fix this. The new terms will of course be retroactive, and will cover everyone who has downloaded Google Chrome since it was launched.

This example points towards one of the most fundamental lessons of our book: the internet and associated technologies may offer useful channels for promotion and publicity but their real importance lies increasingly with their ability to allow organizations to hear what is being said about them. More than ever before, monitoring and evaluation are moving to the heart of public relations activity.

# CAN WE EVALUATE SOCIAL MEDIA DISCOURSE?

For many decades the PR industry has attempted to monitor, measure, evaluate and report on its activities in ways that allow a range of management interests to understand the contribution public relations makes to the organization. In all too many cases, absurd assumptions have been woven into such analysis. For instance it has been commonplace for evaluations to make comparisons between advertising and editorial in the printed media. In the digital space, page views (doubtless much obscured by robot visits) have been used alongside crude tallies of visitor numbers to assess interest in a topic. Visits to websites do have a value, but vary widely in cost and value as we discuss below.

However, there are very good indicators that can indeed measure the public relations footprint of an organization. For example, there are the comments that come through monitoring a range of media from the, relatively few but motivated, contributors to the global conversation in social media. To ignore blogs, videos and social network contribution is not sensible for any organization and not a few individuals.

---

**GOOD HOUSEKEEPING**

There are some things that the practitioner should have available as alerts. When something out of the ordinary happens, the practitioner and client will know immediately. The alerts include:

- Web downtime or slow response – this can be technical but mostly it means the site has suddenly become popular or is under attack.
- Big changes in visitor numbers and pages viewed – this can mean a campaign is working well or that the site is being spidered, which can be a security risk if a visitor is downloading all your customer contacts!
- Website pages that are not loading – this may mean that a page has been orphaned, has a technical fault or a navigation glitch.
- Fast growth or decline in inbound links – this can mean a successful promotion or an issue is erupting.
- Editing of your Wikipedia entry – this could be a wonderful addition or some other view of truth.
- Change of details in directories (Yell, listings on media sites, online directory listings, supplier/customer online lists about your organization, its products, services, prices, etc) and official website references (eg Companies House, Stock Exchange, Charities Commission).
- Changes to your website registration information – this may be good housekeeping or someone attempting to use your site URL.

---

> The practitioner can add to this list such that a combination of automated alerting software and RSS page alerts will flag up these changes quickly. They can be dealt with as they occur and do not need a lot of management.

# MONITORING TRENDS

Trend monitoring is very useful. It provides an insight into the effects the company is having online and the effects of third parties on the organization. Best of all, it will show aberrant behaviours that can be investigated and acted on as needed. In addition, practitioners will find it helpful to be up to date with industry and sector research.

---

### TRENDS THAT PR SHOULD KNOW ABOUT

- Website visitor numbers, dwell times, pages viewed.
- Website referrals – where the traffic is coming from.
- Number of pages indexed by search engines, where from, type of organization.
- Links into the site/s.
- Number of searches for the site.
- Demographics of the people searching for the site (from services such as Microsoft Labs).
- Number of blogs referring to the organization (from services like Technoratti, Google Blog Search, MySpace, etc).
- Numbers of media sites referencing the organization.
- Internet research findings from respected organizations (Office for National Statistics internet trends, Oxford Internet Institute, Hitwise, IMRG, Pew Research Center, Morgan Stanley's Internet Trends, Datamonitor, TNS, etc – it's quite a long list).

---

The dynamic nature of social media means that the 'long tail' of content that remains online is a growing asset (or liability) that will 'never go away' and therefore demands strategic management.

## IDENTIFYING THE SELF-SELECTING PUBLICS AND THEIR INTERESTS

Part of that management is in the development of organizational values that catch the interest of the online community and create new content, new interest and new motivations for that community. Monitoring the online community with an interest in the organization and the values they attribute to it and its products, services, people and values provides insights into the self-selecting social/market segment and self-selected values such as brand values.

Using the tools available for SEO, one can identify keywords associated with an organization, brand or concept (see above). These provide insights into the values that are associated with the organization and its products, services and corporate values. They are important because these are the words that are important to the organization's constituents. They are not invented by the organization; they are part of the perception people have of it.

Using such keywords it is also possible to identify the type of websites that interest these people, where they are located, their age, sex and related interests. Tools such as those available from Microsoft Labs provide the means for identifying the self-selecting communities and their interests.

Monitoring, measuring, evaluating and reporting the growing range of content is important but has to be seen in the round. For an organization that is the subject of, say, 100 third-party blog posts each day, any short-term campaign may be no more than a passing blip among the 36,500 comments that accumulate each year. On the other hand such a small injection of comment may change the tone and content of all subsequent comment. Measuring such effects has to be a constant process not a one-off snapshot.

The sheer size and attention of the online 'audience' is another consideration. There is apparently no way of discovering the extent of both direct and indirect interest. The penumbra of interest from those who view and do not comment potentially extends to anyone online, over a billion people, located at the next computer or 8,000 miles away on a PC, mobile phone or any other internet-enabled platform.

Faced with the sheer volume and complexity of information out there that has the potential to impact on reputation, it would be quite understandable if the practitioner simply threw in the towel, conceding defeat in an unwinnable battle.

But there are a number of strategies that can be deployed by the practitioner. The first is to monitor on a regular basis those social media that landscaping has shown are significant or are growing in significance. There are many resources available, and ensuring that such content is monitored regularly and that there is a clear escalation policy for reporting is helpful. This means that the key media must be read each day. If important, it escalates for a decision using agreed protocols (see Figure 25.1) to manage online events. Otherwise, it is kept for monthly reporting.

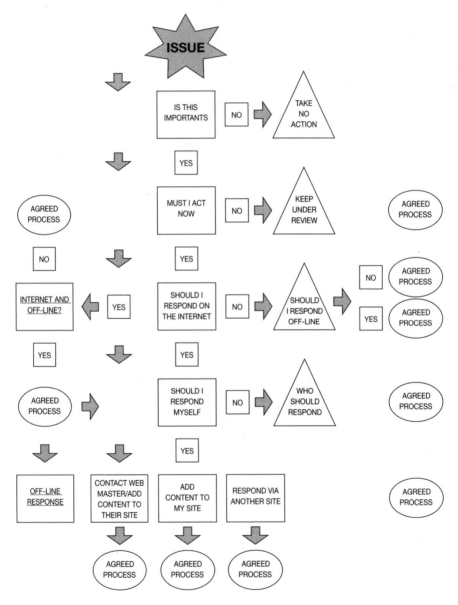

**Figure 25.1** *The Alison Clark Citation Management Matrix developed by Alison Clark for the CIPR/PRCA Internet Commission 1999*

The internet is a network of engaged participants who are actively seeking information. They pull, comment and pass on a lot of their interest (and as social networks evolve, become more proactive). This 'pullability' and proactivity presents a major evaluation opportunity. Just as a news release issued to a magazine that leads to a published story can attract a lot of attention when readers 'pull' the content and pass it around, a blog comment or social network photograph can have the same effect. The important measure is the extent to which an organization is visible through the activities of online communities through which the messages spread. Once people are, behaviourally, stimulated to react or respond to online content generated by the practitioner or the members of the organization, their investment in time and effort begins a process that attracts further attention and interest, and often further involvement. We can seek to measure activity in the first instance. It is the prime measure.

---

### TOOLS FOR MONITORING:

- Google Alerts.
- RSS monitoring using any of the tools available. The key to effective blog monitoring is to add interesting sites until you have about 10. Then look for the next best; if it offers better content, discard one of the others (the network effect will ensure that any important content will come via the 10 in your list).
- Proprietary services. Beware of exaggerated claims. Always evaluate more than three for at least a month.
- Search engines. The specialist search engines are very helpful. They can be used to find information, but more importantly they can help you find the experts 'out there' who make good contributions and who follow and are followed across the online community (instance of a specialist search engine: http://search.twitter.com).

---

We have mentioned that there is a need to maintain landscaping. It is valuable that such monitoring is structured and includes the process for assessment, including risk and opportunity management.

Key considerations for monitoring programs will include a large dose of scepticism. There are lot of vendors who make wonderful claims. There are those who claim to 'monitor the internet'. Well, if neither Google nor the Chinese government can do that, it's a pretty sure bet that no one can.

More realistic are small and incremental steps that will inform the practitioner; monitoring should be by degrees, with a clear escalation policy in place.

Because there are so many forms of monitoring and evaluation, a practitioner might use a closed wiki as a platform to provide these insights to a management team. The advantage is that wikis can include embedded web widgets to show everything from a list of current blog posts to website traffic data, and also include interactive polling. This is a versatile capability that can be extended as necessary or as technologies emerge.

---

## MONITORING METHODOLOGIES

Much information about a company and industry sector comes from online commentators. Many of them are experts and have compelling insights. RSS feeds provide an excellent way to monitor this buzz and give clear early warning of events and activities in a competitive setting.

RSS feeds can be set up for every site on the web and can be keyword constrained, thus providing fast (as in seconds) intelligence about a wide range of online activities (see: http://feedity.com, http://www.dapper.net, http://feed43.com, http://www.feedmarklet.com, http://www.ponyfish.com, and there are many more).

News from publications is available from many sources, including Asomo, Attentio, Brandwatch, CyberAlert, Cymfony, FindAgent, iCrossing, Market Sentinel, Nielsen Online, Onalytica, Radian6, RepuMetrix, Reputica, StrategyEye, Techrigy and Trackur.

There are services that combine monitoring of a range of social media and report in near real time, such as http://alertthingy.com and http://www.twhirl.org.

---

Charlene Li and Josh Bernoff, authors of *Groundswell*, identify people in social media with five characteristics: Creators, Critics, Collectors, Joiners, and Spectators.[2] These are five elements that offer structure to the practitioner's monitoring and evaluation techniques.

Online public relations is one form of PR that has to be monitored and evaluated. The risks in not doing so are far too significant and dangerous to leave to chance. Online public relations is not linear. Stuff happens! This means that practitioners must continually research, landscape, perform situation analysis and re-visit objectives.

One issue that comes up again and again is the 'value' of social media interactions and the value of PR interventions. There are many approaches to value. Attracting the attention of the online community, identifying numbers of involved people, comments and reactions published online are all ways of establishing value. The practitioner may want to know if some article published in a magazine attracts comment on the magazine's website.

Was it bookmarked in Digg or Delicious, Flickr, Facebook or YouTube? Did such interventions add value to the original press release? Was it the inspiration for third-party blog comment (and shouldn't every press relations campaign have such measures embedded in the campaign objectives)? Alternatively, how many visitors is the corporate blog attracting? Is it increasing? How many people have added it to their blogroll, how many comments is it attracting? If such ambitions are part of the online objectives, measuring them shows the value of the PR activity.

The next issue for the practitioner is whether such investment is worthwhile. The long life of online content means that it is an asset and it should, over time, generate a value. Here is a new form of evaluation. Is the asset worth it over time? Return on assets is key in valuing online presence. The cost of developing, maintaining and monitoring the use of assets is part of the capital cost of maintenance of corporate assets. Once this figure is available, identifying return on investment is a lot easier.

# VALUE

It is possible to value websites. They are bought and sold, and in the process we are able to discover how the market values site visitor numbers.

Posts by the blogger Om Malik in gigaom.com and in his CNN articles suggest that acquiring online visitors is expensive. Of course sites vary and the value of visitors will change too. But there are some rules of thumb. In the United States he recalls the acquisition price per unique visitor per month had fallen from an all-time high of $710 (Yahoo's purchase of Broadcast.com) in April 1999 to about 73 cents in November 2001. By 2008, his view was that the asset value was about $10 per visitor; this is confirmed by analysis of sites sold by www.wesellyoursite.com, which suggested an average value of $10.32 per unique visitor per month (though the price ranged from less than a cent to $63). We have little to go on in the United Kingdom because the sale and purchase of websites is not well reported. As a huge generalization, in the United Kingdom the value per visitor at £5 was not unreasonable at the time, and with strong brand building and content that will bring visitors back again and again, site values can increase quite a lot in a short time. Deeper analysis with data from sector sales will offer the practitioner a method for valuing site visits.

In addition to having a view about the value of visits, the ROI of production cost is not too difficult to calculate. A website may cost £X,000 to build and £nnn every month to maintain and host. If it attracts yyy visitors, the return on investment is easy to calculate on a cost-per-visitor basis. The comparison between the cost and value of visitors will reveal the cost of acquisition and ROI.

Valuing of a blogging campaign might include the value of visitors, the secondary value of comments, and the tertiary value of mentions in other social media (the more valuable ones are those that point back to the organization's blog or website). The cost of acquisition, site overheads, monitoring, manpower and management have to be offset against the return on the asset.

Suffice to say that few blogs will show a realistic return unless there is something in excess of 10,000 visitors per month, which will require a significant corporate commitment to be achieved.

---

### IN BRIEF

- All PR practitioners need skills for monitoring online interventions. They affect all forms of practice on- and offline.
- There are some channels that are just not available to most organizations to monitor.
- Be aware of, and actively engaged with, identifying those channels publics choose to use.
- Monitor, on a regular basis, those social media that landscaping has shown are significant or are growing in significance.
- There is a need to monitor so as to be able to react.
- There are some basic monitoring tasks.
- There are some trend measuring tasks.
- Practitioners need to monitor and evaluate self-selecting publics and user-generated brand/organization values.
- It is important to have an effective monitoring, reporting and escalation process ready.
- Small and incremental steps are best to improve monitoring.
- Because there are so many forms of monitoring and evaluation, a practitioner might use a closed wiki as a platform to provide these insights to a management team.
- There are value measures that can be put in place.
- Websites and website visitors have a value.

---

## Notes

1. Locke, C, Searl, D and Weinberger, D (2000) *Cluetrain Manifesto,* Basic Books
2. Li, C and Bernoff, J (2008) *Groundswell: Winning in a world transformed by social technologies,* Harvard Business School Press

# 26

# Influences on policy, corporate speak and bling

The Excellence model developed by James Grunig and various collaborators has provided the underlying paradigm that has dominated much public relations theory for over 20 years.[1] The issue now for those trying to understand the changes being brought about by the internet society is to determine whether the developments outlined in this book are sufficiently dramatic to challenge the Grunig model. Let's try.

We have already seen that for most organizations their web 1.0 presence, the number of page impressions indexed by search engines, runs to many times the number of pages that a website owner might try to influence (Chapter 17). In addition we have shown in this book that the new social media have both more reach and, at an accelerating rate, the capability of attracting users of the internet.

Excellence characterizes the vector of communication as being between an organization and its publics, and is concerned with the balance – the symmetry – of this transaction. The bold claim that emerges from the arguments put forward for 'the new PR' is that the fundamental vector of communication that shapes reputation and an organization's relationship with its stakeholders has flipped through 90 degrees. Now, the truly significant discourse is that which surrounds an organization, product or service, a conversation that is enabled and given form and substance by the interlinked, aggregated messages that emerge from internet mediated social networks.

Yes, this is a bold claim and it is one that is certainly deserving of robust challenge. But what is harder to dispute is that more than ever before it is the actions of an organization that inform reputation, not the partial truths that underlie any promotional activity. Media relations has not gone away, and it is not going to go away, but its role is changing as the long-term vulnerability of 'command and control' models of PR activity becomes increasingly obvious.

# LISTENING TO THOSE VOICES

August 2007 saw a couple of examples that appear to confirm the belief that social media networks are beginning to change the way in which organizations interact with stakeholders.

Within a few days of each other, Cadbury announced that it was going to reintroduce the Wispa chocolate bar for a limited period, and HSBC Bank was forced to rethink its policy on a student overdraft promotion; both decisions appear to have been significantly affected by opinion that was aggregated and articulated through Facebook.

---

The Cadbury example appears quite straightforward. Someone calling himself 'Bass' Dave Brodie created a Facebook group called 'Bring back the Wispa!' and this seemed to strike a chord. Very quickly other similar groups were formed, and a reasonable number of people signed up. The aggregation of views was not unlike an old-fashioned petition, but it is not easy to see how the individual voices could have coalesced into a coherent statement without a very simple platform such as Facebook, nor is it easy to see how Cadbury could have discovered this latent demand – or at least the extent of it – for a product that it presumably had sound marketing and economic grounds for removing from its range. As well as providing a useful weathervane of public opinion, or at least the opinion of an important stakeholder group, the message articulated on Facebook was particularly supportive of the product – lots of people said, apparently spontaneously, how much they liked Wispa, providing a peer endorsement that has much more resonance than a corporate marketing message.

---

It is important not to overemphasize the role of social media in this process. The number of group members remained relatively small, and the real impact in marketing terms was provided when the story broke into traditional media – newspapers and news websites.

The HSBC decision was rather different. Here a number of stakeholders were outraged by the bank's decision to charge graduates 9.9 per cent on their undergraduate overdrafts. They could have written to their bank manager, and the NUS could have mobilized a traditional campaign, but it is hard to see how the protest would have gained the same momentum in such a short time.

---

HSBC had announced that it would impose a charge on graduates of 9.9 per cent on their undergraduate overdrafts to 'help' students reduce their debts more quickly The policy was always reliant on other high street banks following suit – which did not happen.

· Facebook gave the NUS a platform for rapid dissemination to campaign against this policy. It is important not to overlook the role of traditional media in this story – HSBC made its decision to climb down after the story had run in national newspapers and after the NUS had threatened a campaign of flash queues that would have inconvenienced customers well outside the student market. The anti-HSBC message that was being articulated on individual Facebook accounts and being aggregated by social networking was important, but it took on a much greater reputational significance when it began to be carried by mainstream mass media, where it would be more easily seen by a large audience who were not directly connected to existing complainants. Facebook allowed the protest to develop, and at a rapid pace, until it reached the critical mass needed for a traditional media news story.

The bank gave in and withdrew the charges, refunded all interest payments and agreed to hold talks with the NUS about the best way forward. As a bank spokesman said with masterful understatement: 'This has been an exercise in a huge amount of feedback in a short amount of time.'

---

Effective monitoring of the Facebook discourse would have given HSBC the opportunity to at least anticipate an impending problem.

## MISTRUSTING PR MESSAGES

One of the many damaging elements in the HSBC discourse was the observation by many 'ordinary' customers that the bank was engaging in spin, that its decisions were not as they appeared. Without Facebook or a blog, how would other people hear their opinions? Through a media interview or a letter for publication in a newspaper?

The messages being put out by the bank were seen as corporate, and for this reason alone they lacked credibility with the student audience. But, more importantly, there appeared to be a dissonance between the PR message and the reality as experienced by the students – they simply didn't believe that being told to pay more money was actually for their own good.

This is crucial. It is the actions of an organization that shape reputation rather than the image crafted for that organization by communications professionals. That has always been true, but in the developing internet mediated society it is more so than ever before. This shift is being accelerated and brought into sharper focus by the porosity, connectivity and transparency that underpins social media discourse.

The role of the public relations practitioner, when such decisions are being taken, must be to inform those managers who are making the decisions of the likely response of stakeholder groups, and to make an informed assessment of how these groups will respond. This assessment must take into account the changing mechanisms by which stakeholder groups can be mobilized and articulate their views.

# PR COMES OUT OF THE SHADOWS

Earlier in this his book we observed that much good PR is done outside the public gaze, that being the invisible hand is seen as an indication of professionalism. But we have also noted that social media voices need an identity. If they are to be considered as authentic they need to be linked to a particular individual. It may well be the named individual who presents a partial message on behalf of an organization – rather than an anonymous communicator, or information officer who affects value-neutrality.

This is part of the Holy Grail for all practitioners – trust. Online, relationships between members of interest-driven communities are built through the expression of individual values, and these values gain power through the cement of trust. If and when trust between community members exists, the opinions and recommendations exchanged within such groups can be very powerful. It is just like the 'real' world – we form groups based on friendship or professional interest, and the extent to which we allow ourselves to be influenced by the collective opinions of the group is directly related to degree of trust we have in the integrity of our peers.

The 'Lost in showbiz' blog (lostintheshowbiz.blogspot.com/) calls out poor press relations practice and pointed up this e-mail from a reader:

> Call me a cynical old goat, but I just don't believe that anyone can honestly say that they're 'excited' about punting stories about pastel-coloured fridges (especially when those pastel-coloured fridges are a good four or five years past their fashionable 'peak'). Still, you have to admire Publicasity's shamelessness. Or, as a reader has it: Impressive.

The e-mail is published in full (and names are changed to protect the naive):

> From: (name and e-mail address of the account executive)
> Date: 13 August 2008 14:43:50 BST
> Subject: (Client name) – New PR account at (name of consultancy)
> Hello,
> (Our Consultancy) is pleased to inform you that we are now handling the PR account for (the Client), the (a) domestic appliance manufacturer. Obviously we are very excited about working with such an iconic brand, which effortlessly marries style with technology, and will be getting in touch shortly with all the latest news from (the client). Please see below our contact details should you require any product information and/or imagery.
> Speak soon!
> (E-mail sign off)

For a very long time, it has been a habit to 'gild the lily' in making such announcements. Being 'very excited about working with such an iconic brand, which effortlessly...' is just so AbFab. But when a 'cynical old goat' plays it back in public (and to quite an active following – including several *Guardian* journalists who provided more than a few examples), this form of hype loses its lustre, not to mention opportunities for trusted exchanges between journalist, consultancy and client.

If an organization can build this trust it will have a powerful influence on reputation and consequently on performance. The problem is that so many organizations have carelessly squandered online trust and now face an uphill task in rebuilding what they have lost. This task is made all the harder by the seemingly indelible 'long tail' of evidence of past neglect or misdemeanour that is set in amber by internet commentary.

The 'human voice', a person with influence and whose role is transparent, can have a considerable effect. For example Bob Lutz, the CEO of General Motors, used his Fast Lane blog (http://fastlane.gmblogs.com/) to present a very human face for a company that was facing very real problems. His blog voice was perceived as real and to the point, and so enhanced the GM values very quickly. Microsoft and Dell had damaged brands: the software giant was characterized as the 'evil empire', and the PC giant was going to 'hell'. In response, both of these companies made a strategic move. Robert Scoble presented a human face for Microsoft, and became a critic sharing his employer's problems with the online community, while Lionel Menchaca launched the Dell blog, engaged detractors (even in person) and helped to spearhead the revolutionary IdeaStorm (www.dellideastorm. com) site. In the end, many of the problems may or may not be fixed, but the perception has absolutely changed.

The use of a human face that can build and sustain trust is very powerful.

## IN BRIEF

- Now, the truly significant discourse is that which surrounds an organization, product or service, a conversation that is enabled and given form and substance by the interlinked, aggregated messages that emerge from internet-mediated social networks.
- Social media can influence marketing policy.
- Social media can influence management policy.
- Monitoring is significant.
- Message credibility has a major effect.
- More than ever before it is the actions of an organization that shape reputation, rather than the image crafted for that organization by communications professionals.
- Social media voices need an identity. If they are to be considered authentic they need to be linked to a particular individual.
- Online, relationships between members of interest-driven communities are built through the expression of individual values, and these values are consolidated by the cement of trust.
- Establishing trust is made all the harder by the seemingly indelible 'long tail' of evidence of past neglect or misdemeanours that is set in amber by internet commentary.

## Note

1. See, for example, Grunig, J E and Hunt, T (1984) *Managing Public Relations*, Harcourt Brace College Publishers

# 27

# Corporate social responsibility

There is increasing evidence – though by no means a compelling case – that successful organizations can no longer attempt to function outside wider societal frames. The days of markets deciding everything are gone, but the value of corporate social responsibility (CSR) is still being debated. The advent of social media has a range of implications for organizations attempting to position themselves as ethically engaged. One of the dangers of CSR is that it is often seen as at best buying off a guilty conscience, or worse as a publicity stunt. The transparency and scrutiny of social media critiques makes this even more of a challenge.

A discussion paper for Bite Communications develops a new model that combines operations and communications to tackle the threats and opportunities of a changing environment in the social media age.[1] The authors, George Basile and Burghardt Tenderich, begin by suggesting eco-sustainability will become a 'make or break' issue in corporate thinking, and that the way it is practised and preached by a business will determine the fate of small and large corporations alike. Already companies are discovering that the link between eco-sustainability and reputation has new and fundamental implications for how they run their businesses; for them, it is the intersection between companies' efforts of 'marketing green' and actually 'becoming green' in a corporate communications environment that dictates unprecedented levels of transparency.

At the very mention of transparency, readers of this book will know what is to come:

Many corporations are struggling with social media pressure as it relates to their core product offerings, and the additional scrutiny based on eco sustainability issues will serve to increase this pressure to unprecedented levels...

Citizen journalists will examine products and services, scrutinize office buildings and manufacturing plants, check the corporate cafeteria and research internal travel policies. They will dig deep inside the corporate supply chain and partner ecosystem. Many of these Web 2.0 pundits are on the inside of the very businesses that are beginning to address global issues.

Tom Foremski is a highly regarded Silicon Valley blogger. He considered CSR as it applied to employees in the Valley in 2007. To Tom, CSR starts with schools:

In Silicon Valley there is tremendous competition for talent and companies have to offer more than just a salary. Increasingly, companies have to show that they have a higher purpose too, and show that they have a corporate social responsibility.

Companies such as Google and Salesforce.com have established large foundations. And there are many other companies that encourage their employees to engage in community and charity projects. Microsoft's Silicon Valley employees, for example, are the area's largest contributors to the United Way.

As our work life and personal life blurs, companies will have to provide a way for people to express their desire to give back, to be engaged in their communities and local charities. Otherwise they won't be able to attract the talent they need to be successful.

Choosing between two companies offering similar salaries and benefits, people will select the one that also has a visible and vibrant social responsibility role.

And when it comes to Silicon Valley, we should look to our schools, these are the heart of any community.

How can Silicon Valley say to the world 'we are inventing the future' yet our schools are struggling. Our schools are basket cases when they should be showcases.

Within walking distance of any Bay Area school there are tremendous resources, world class talent, world class technologies. Yet all of that seems to matter little in terms of making a difference in the very communities where they are created. It's embarrassing. It has to change.

If you combine the general cynicism faced by corporations with the intense scrutiny that green marketing messages have encountered in the 1990s, you get an idea of the degree of public pressure green companies will experience.

In the words of Jacquelyn Ottman: 'It is not enough to talk green, companies must be green.'[2]

## CASE STUDY: AT BEST SCEPTICISM

Writing in the *Financial Times* in May 2006, David Bowen, website effectiveness consultant for Bowen Craggs & Co, commented on how valuable the web is for CSR. He wrote:

> It is not only politicians who want to be seen as greener than thou. This week Anna Ford, just-retired high profile newsreader from the BBC, has been recruited as a director for J Sainsbury, the UK supermarket chain. Sainsbury's chairman said she would take particular interest in corporate social responsibility. By no coincidence at all, Sainsbury's great rival Tesco announced last week that it would spend £100m on greener energy sources. 'The emphasis on CSR has been stoked by the prospect of another competition inquiry,' this newspaper commented – all of which prompted me to see how the big retailers were presenting themselves as green, friendly and generally fluffy on the web.
>
> The web is even more important than newsreaders in the area of social responsibility. Whether a company is trying to provide data on waste, to explain how friendly it is to the community, or to lay out its policy on child labour, it cannot do so in sound bites – it needs space, and a website has more space than any other channel.
>
> Tesco and Sainsbury both understand this, though having looked at their sites I fear they may also believe CSR is a sub-division of marketing. What surprised me more than this is the variation, and in places lack of interest, I found as I wandered round other giant retailers' websites.

The fact is that there have been many conferences and much talk about CSR and yet its reflection online suggests a nodding acquaintance with the web except when it is a big shop window.

Social media can quickly join up the dots. By 2008, one activist YouTube video attacking Tesco had been viewed over a million times.

Basile and Tenderich conclude that corporations will need to meet the expectations of sustainability watchdogs – and the watchdogs will be everywhere, as evidenced by the constantly growing number of blogs on eco-related issues.

To create the basis for transparency in companies marketing eco sustainable products and services, the corporate functions of communications and operations need to be inter-linked. In most corporations, there has been a limited connection between the operational processes of a company and its communications efforts. Operations on the one side, and marketing communications on the other, have traditionally co-existed peacefully by simply not relating to one another. In a world where eco sustainability takes centre stage, this disconnect no longer represents a viable business strategy.

They suggest, for instance, that if a company that markets organic food does not employ eco-sustainable operational processes, it will risk being deemed hypocritical in the court of public opinion.

> If operations and communications are unsynchronized, companies face the risk of making promises they can't deliver on. These failed promises will be exposed, leading to a vicious cycle that communications alone can't remedy.

## IMPLICATIONS OF SOCIAL MEDIA FOR CSR

Of course, it is possible that Basile and Tenderich are wrong in their critique and that corporate response to climate change will not have a significant impact on organizational success. Equally, it may be true that David Bowen's argument will not evoke more than a few 'cranks' and minority activists to engage with CSR policies. But the argument that the ability of stakeholder groups to impact on performance is considerably enhanced by the reach and influence of social media seems to us to be compelling, even irrefutable. Again, it doesn't matter whether this takes us into territory that is strictly new; what does matter is that relationship managers must find the tools and expertise to cope with these developments. Whereas Cadbury seem to have gained business advantage by monitoring and evaluating the discourse surrounding one of their products, the HSBC experience as reported in various UK newspapers suggests that a business decision was taken without careful regard to its reputational impact. Maybe the version of events that we have presented lacks accuracy or nuance, but it is most certainly the impression we gained from UK media coverage and as such is of reputational significance; that is how media relations has always worked, and is certainly how it works in the internet society.

Just to push the point home, the resources available to the online community are significant. The Business & Human Rights Resource Centre has a list of over 4,000 companies, and each one has a profile. Each profile contains relevant news stories, NGO reports and other sources. It is by no means the only such organization.

---

**IN BRIEF**

- The advent of social media has a range of implications for organizations attempting to position themselves as ethically engaged.
- The transparency and scrutiny of social media critiques makes this even more of a challenge.
- Citizen journalists will examine products and services, scrutinize office buildings and manufacturing plants, check the corporate cafeteria and research internal travel policies. They will dig deep inside the corporate supply chain and partner ecosystem.
- Many of these Web 2.0 pundits are on the inside of the very businesses that are beginning to address global issues.
- Some organizations may also believe CSR is a sub-division of marketing.
- Relationship managers must find the tools and expertise to cope with these developments.

---

## Notes

1. Basile, G and Tenderich, B (2007) Ecological sustainability: the dominant corporate communications issue of the decade, http://www.bitepr.com/services/cleantech/4%20-%20Bite%20Sustainability%20WP%2008-01-07.pdf (accessed August 2007)
2. Ottman, J A (2004) *Green Marketing: Opportunities for innovation*, BookSurge Publishing

# Part 5

# A brief look at the future

# 28

# Humans, public relations and the internet

At its 1995 annual conference, the then Institute of Public Relations was made aware that the internet would be very big for the industry.

E-mail arrived, websites arrived and the influence of the internet grew and grew. The first edition of *Online Public Relations* made it clear that the online interactive nature of communication for individuals and groups would be very significant for PR practice.

We can see this evolution more clearly today from, often personal, experience of chat, instant messaging, Usenet, blogs, MySpace and Facebook, and perhaps Second Life. Every day we see new platforms like games machines, laptops and mobile phones for exchanging information and experiencing things from the virtual world. Interactivity has become mainstream and it has all happened. The result is a changed world that forces PR people to adopt new technologies and adapt to new sociological realities, and that challenges those who wish to understand the new environment to look beyond the social sciences for theoretical insights.

If we want to look ahead, it might be valuable to think about why people are flocking in their millions to websites, instant messenger, social networks and the vast array of platforms and channels available using internet protocols. Perhaps it is time to turn to psychology and new research that looks at what makes humans 'tick', and to consider how such motivations are realized in the online environment. If so, such inquiry demands an understanding of how the human brain evolved and how it develops from infancy

People have a 'need to belong'. Social groups are important.[1] Desire for interpersonal attachments is a fundamental human motivation and is central to the human condition; indeed, humans fade when excluded from their fellows.

Kimble *et al* show that the online context is important, and demonstrate that if the degree of 'context' a medium provides is ignored this can adversely affect the user's perceptions of that medium.[2]

Elizabeth Shove at the Centre for Science Studies, and Alan Warde of the Department of Sociology, Lancaster University, note that social theorists maintain that 'people define themselves through the messages they transmit to others through the goods and practices that they possess and display'.[3] They manipulate and manage appearances and thereby create and sustain a 'self-identity'. An answer to the question: 'What sort of person is s/he?' is now likely to be answered in terms of lifestyle or of visible attachment to a group rather than by personal virtues or characteristics.

This description could fit many social networks like Facebook or Second Life. Shove and Warde note that some social-psychological accounts of consumption explain that people seek new products and new pleasures because they need stimulation; playing new games, trying out new items, exploring new material objects and learning new tastes are ways of averting boredom, a capability evident in the widgets people try in MySpace, Bebo and other online services.

These two academics recall Featherstone, who reflected upon the tendency for the same individual to seek to present him- or herself on different occasions in two or more ways, as bohemian and conventional, as romantic and formal, a not uncommon practice online.[4] At a more material and practical level, as the number of activities in which one might participate increases, so producers widen the range of specialized products targeted at different groups of practitioners. In addition they consider the differentiation of socio-technical systems to which people become attached and that themselves tend to push, and even compel, individuals to consume in particular ways. These human drivers are very evident in the way people use online capabilities.

# A GLIMPSE OF THE FUTURE

These are the straws in the wind that give us a view of the online future. It is a future that is about relationships and the nature of relationships between people, groups and organizations.

Driven by our evolution-modified DNA, we may come to recognize and adopt an internet model that is closer to human drivers.

Each iteration of social media has been richer in content and interactivity, and each has brought more mechanisms for self-expression and our ability to display our likes and dislikes, from favourite films to choice of washing powder, to groups of people who may share similar interests. Internet-mediated social networks are offering people a rich array of facilities and content. Much of this self-expression is replacing many of the benefits humans get from direct, face-to-face relationships. It is a mixture that makes belonging to a group or groups rewarding.

The people who use these media have an agenda described by Professor Stephanie Sanford of the Gates Foundation, who argues that there is a changing landscape in polity that goes beyond the collapse of social capital described by Harvard's Robert Putnam and suggests that previously dom-inant social structures are being replaced by a kind of online substitute.[5]

We humans are a complex blend of private and social selves, and the textured interconnections offered by social media provide a compelling platform on which we can express these multiple personalities.

Mihaly Csikszentmihalyi has examined how we can be completely absorbed in an activity and can 'shut out' other distractions.[6] If you watch a youngster concentrating on a massively multi-player online role-playing game (MMORPG), you can see how absorbing some online activity can be. But such effort is linear. It does not cater for a range of 'selves'.

Facebook is very much the same, as are MySpace, Bebo and other social networks. Both now offer many ways to express a particular self, but not many 'selves' depending on the 'mood' or social frame we are in. As these online facilities evolve to allow for the many 'selves' that each of us already needs to interact effectively in different offline environments such as home, work, pub or the playing field or night club, they will appeal even more than at present.

Way back in the 1990s it was evident that many people online had several different online personalities. Even today, most of us have a number of e-mail addresses, and a Hotmail account serves different purposes from a Gmail or work e-mail account. Our Facebook profile differs from our LinkedIn profile.

So people are involved through their online experience, seek Csikszentmihalyi's engrossing applications and an ability to be the 'self' that matches mood and nature and the current influences on our lives. This desire to seek a place online to satisfy their needs for self-expression is a driver behind this insatiable quest to look for the next social network to be available online to match the moment when it is needed.

Aristotle argued that it was in our interest, given our deeply social nature, to participate in civic life in order to fulfil ourselves. Jefferson followed this through when he wrote the American constitution, and interpreted it as the 'pursuit of happiness'. He believed that small social groups would build a strong country.

There is more modern evidence to support this idea. Robin Dunbar has looked at the nature of social groups across many species, and suggests that there is a correlation between the brain's cortical size and the actual size of primate species.[7]

He believes we are biologically pre-programmed to be personally effective in groups of about 150 people. Small businesses don't seem to need a hierarchical structure until they have 135 employees.

Jennifer Muller suggests that teams can function to monitor individuals more effectively than managers can control them.[8] In companies team size is an issue and when a person may have 150 people in their personal 'tribe', working effectively means working with a small section of this tribal whole, as Muller notes in her article 'Is your team too big? Too small? What's the right number?'.[9] The basic military unit is under 150 too, and has been for thousands of years (a Roman legion's First Cohort, called *Primi Ordines*, consisted of five centuries of 120 men).

Political systems that remove social groups (Communist Russia is an example) eventually crack under the weight of the bureaucracy felt to be needed when dealing with big populations. In fact, social support (looking out for older neighbours and over-the-top teens) is delivered effectively when there are sufficient convergent values in a community – a group of actors within a compass of 150 people held together with values that form a polity – as suggested by J Eric Oliver in his book *Democracy in Suburbia*.[10] He posits that local government is important primarily because it provides an accessible and small-scale arena for the resolution of social and economic conflict.

It would seem that the big state, the big business and the national army all have to obey social rules – and at a personal level conform to the personal 150 rule – in order for the bigger (political, economic, social) institution to thrive. Effective management is of groups of 150 or fewer, not 1,500. If the number is bigger, the notion of 'belonging' breaks down.

This would suggest that online social groups should have a finite size to be effective in developing trust, forming opinion and effectively disseminating interests.

People seek society in different groups, different types of groups and for (sometimes convergent) different purposes and different 'selves'. The portals or structures that provide this will be part of the emerging internet.

In PR this means that, with some exceptions, we should aim to belong to a large number of groups rather than to broadcast in a group with a large number of online members. At this level the cultural, and critically emotional, relationships are high. We have noted elsewhere in this book that, online, mass media thinking has its limitations.

One of the amazing things about people is their ability to extend the capability of the body and brain beyond its biological (physiological) capacity. We can travel further and faster on a bicycle, car or plane because we have extended our physiology with knowledge. We have extended our brain with devices like pocket calculators, digital cameras and computers; that is, we use our brain to make machines do extramural work. We have also extended our memory with access to Wikipedia and the rest of the internet.

We have also limited our physical capabilities because of our civilization. Someone born and raised in London is unlikely to have the skills needed to survive in the Borneo jungle; we have lost skills and knowledge too.

Large brains confer an advantage when responding to variable, un-predictable, and novel ecological demands through enhanced behavioural flexibility, learning, and innovation.[11]

Human have large brains. Better than that, humans like novelty. We are quick to learn causal associations between co-occurring environmental stimuli. Does this resonate with users of Facebook and MySpace trying out and adding new widgets to their accounts? Who has not been distracted when using search engines and diverted to something that looked 'interesting' and novel. Using these online facilities, we pander to our 'large brain' needs.[12]

Our use of the evolving internet, the social internet, is dependent on many services (as Twitter is to Facebook, mobile phone video is to YouTube and adding a hyperlink is to e-mail). It will include achieving even more things to facilitate our physical, intellectual and emotional needs and, above all, our need to join social groups. We will, in the process forgo once common capabilities like typesetting, shorthand and faxing. The internet is and will continue to be a place where we can experiment with novel things and find new ways to achieve gratification. In this sense, we can argue that the progression from Usenet to Twitter and beyond is part of human biology.

As a nerve cell in the human brain is stimulated by new experie nces and exposure to incoming information from the senses, it grows branches called dendrites. With use, you grow branches; without it they are impoverished and you lose them. People can even use parts of the brain to do novel things; we have 'neuro-plasticity', the capacity for changes that occur in the organization of the brain as a result of experience.[13] This means that our brains can change substantially as a result of practice and experience throughout life.[14] Furthermore, a specific variant in humans suggests that the human brain is still undergoing rapid adaptive evolution.[15]

The evolving internet will be more addictive and people will develop their brains to cope. With the new internet we can expect new skills to emerge (even programming a video recorder can be learned!) and we will both learn and evolve to do these things.

Human biology as much as human society seeks to satisfy the need to be sure that the social group can be trusted. We need to be able to trust people. There are dozens of devices that say they offer secure relationships, and for people this means they need to be recognizable. Throughout history, people have recognized people from their looks, voice and mannerisms. But online, it is easy to steal identities. The next evolution of Facebook and MyMelcrum will have eye scanning (biometric iris scanning) built into a security system that allows many 'selves' but only one self.

Finally, there is the question of when will all this happen.

Usenet and IM flourished for five years before the better blog mousetrap came along. MySpace took three years, Twitter a few months. Adoption of new and more 'human DNA'-friendly social networks will accelerate.

Look back five years and the rate of change is fast, but it is the rate of adoption that is more interesting. Usenet was for geeks and sex maniacs. MySpace is for them (still), but mostly for a huge proportion of ordinary and not so geeky young people.

So, who will be using this new internet? As it becomes less complicated it will become more available to more people. And the more its forms complement the drives of human biology, the more pervasive it will become.

The new internet will be closer to human DNA than bits and bytes. It will be more 'human' and the rate of adoption of useful social interaction content will be quick.

In terms of planning how to use the media for a campaign just a few months away, the speed of change may well mean the decision to use specific platforms or channels will be taken late in the day. The media for the 2012 London Olympics will be vastly different to the media familiar in 2008.

## WHAT DOES THIS MEAN FOR PR?

Firstly, we will need to move away from 'mass' and begin to think 'niche'. The concept of 'mass media' is already waning. This means that practitioners will continually need to adopt fresh communication management skills, and be prepared to discard others. Some will be group specific, some interest specific and some community specific. Approaching online communities will require practitioners to demonstrate empathy because they will be 'invading' the societies of our constituency. In addition, the concepts of advertising, long the rich man of communication, will morph too.

When will all this come about? Well, it already has critical mass. Whereas once the power of media ownership lay in the size of circulation, it now rests with linkages within the online community. Where once there was merely e-mail, the channels now include internet telephony and instant messaging, comments in chat and messages in social media sites, SMS texts, videos and voice. Where once people shopped from web pages, they now buy using a mobile phone. While once it was only possible to play tennis using the same grass court, we now use a Nintendo WII to play games online with opponents who are continents away.

The only thing that holds PR back is that it needs to understand these things, see the opportunity and adopt this different way of using PR creativity.

Oh! And if you don't, someone else will.

There is no really good reason that anyone should spend so much time looking at a screen, but most people do, so there has to be a reason.

In looking beyond the usual realms of PR research from social science to anthropology, brain science and psychology, we get a glimpse into the motivations behind this strange behaviour, and in doing so discover that they are very, very powerful. They are drivers from the primitive to modern humanity and there is some cause to believe that these human motivations – cerebral, instinctive and emotional – all find an outlet in using digital capabilities to satisfy deep human motives.

At a superficial level we know by experience that this stuff is not going away, but when we look more deeply we see a future where it becomes integral not just to our habits and convenience, but to satisfying more basic needs and desires.

## Notes

1.  Baumeister, R F and Leary, M R (1995). The need to belong: desire for interpersonal attachments as a fundamental human motivation. *Psychological Bulletin*, **117**, pp 497–529
2.  Kimble, C, Grimshaw, D and Hildreth, P M (1998) The role of contextual clues in the creation of information overload, in *Proceedings of the 3rd UKAIS Conference*, Lincoln University, April 1998, pp 405–12, McGraw-Hill
3.  Shove, E and Warde, A (1999) Reader distributed for the Consumption, Everyday Life and Sustainability Summer School, Lancaster University. http://www.lancs.ac.uk/fass/sociology//esf/inconspicuous.htm (accessed October 2007)
4.  Featherstone, M (1991) *Consumer Culture and Postmodernism*, Sage
5.  Sanford, S (nd) Civic life in the information age: policy, technology and generational change, http://www.compact.org/20th/read/civic_life_in_the_information_age (accessed October 2007); Putnam, R D (2000)

*Bowling Alone: The collapse and revival of American community*, Simon & Schuster
6. Csikszentmihalyi, M (1993) *Flow: The psychology of optimal experience*, Harper Perennial
7. Dunbar, R (1998) *Grooming, Gossip, and the Evolution of Language*, Harvard University Press
8. Her webpage is http://www.wharton.upenn.edu/faculty/mueller.html (accessed October 2007)
9. Muller, J (2006) Is your team too big? Too small? What's the right number? Knowledge@Wharton, 14 June, http://knowledge.wharton.upenn.edu/article.cfm?articleid=1501 (accessed 23 October 2008)
10. Oliver, J E (2001) *Democracy in Suburbia*, Princeton University Press
11. Vrba, E (2007) in F Grine, *The Evolutionary History of the Robust Australopithecines*, Aldine Transaction
12. Turner, D C, Aitken, M R F, Shanks, D R, Sahakian, B J, Robbins, T W, Schwarzbauer C, and Fletcher P C. (2004) The role of the lateral frontal cortex in causal associative learning: exploring preventative and super-learning, *Cerebral Cortex*, August, **14** (8), pp 872–80
13. Palombo Weiss, R (2000) Brain-based learning, *Training & Development*, July, **54** (7), pp 20–24
14. Kolb, B and Wishaw, I Q (2008) *Fundamentals of Human Neuropsychology*, Worth Publishers
15. Mekel-Bobrov, N, Gilbert, S L, Evans, P D, Vallender, E J, Anderson, J R, Hudson, R R, Tishkoff, S A and Lahn B T (2005) Ongoing adaptive evolution of ASPM, a brain size determinant in Homo sapiens, *Science*, **309**, pp 1720–22

# Conclusion

We began this book by saying that the internet changes everything. We are confident that we have made a compelling case that it has to do so.

We have embraced the controversial – and provocative – idea that the internet is driving something that can rightly be called 'the new PR'. We have accepted that social media make it imperative for the discipline of public relations to change, whilst never wavering from our conviction that the essential elements of public relations, which we consider to be *relationship management*, have not changed and will not.

We suggested that online public relations would provide a roadmap for anyone engaging with public relations in the age of social media. Certainly anyone who has got this far will agree that there are endless challenges ahead, and that our response must go way beyond merely developing fresh tactics to also addressing more fundamental strategic questions.

We hope our core argument is proven: that the internet and the rapid growth of social media have at least begun to shift the vector of communication from a vertical organization-to-audience model to a horizontal discourse among networked commentaries that aggregate into reputation. The need for PR to develop messages that can be distributed through mass media channels has not gone away, but it is equally clear that the 'horizontal' vector is becoming ever more important, and that more than ever it will be the actions of an organization that matter rather than the desired messages.

Here is the crucial point: the command-and-control model of PR practice was always something of an illusion, but real enough to fool some of the people some of the time. But social media have blown away the smoke and cast a piercingly perceptive light on the mirrors that created the illusion. Social media are forcing an honesty onto public relations that in fact provides a great opportunity. And at the same time as transparency weaves its magic, organizations are being forced to contend with the limitless interventions of online participants who are creating their own content and have the potential to refract, distort or enhance reputations and relationships.

Let's move directly to the bottom line. *The Guardian*'s media business correspondent Katie Allen wrote a fairly straightforward business story about world's second largest advertising group, WPP.[1] Headlined 'PR industry profits boosted by MySpace phenomenon', her piece credited the popularity of social networking sites like Facebook and MySpace with driving unusually strong growth in public relations business. Although WPP had reported a weaker-than-expected third quarter, it revealed that revenues from PR work were growing strongly. Allen quoted WPP's Sir Martin Sorrell as saying:

> Social networking seems to underline the importance of editorial publicity... Social networking is really recommendation between people about the things that they are interested in and they like... this has stimulated people's attention in terms of the importance of PR.

He said that companies' increasing focus on getting into news stories reflected an appetite among web users for 'ideas and knowledge' from apparently 'independent' sources. Using a PR company to generate more press coverage also helps brands get around social networkers' typical aversion to adverts:

> The people who are going on these sites didn't want to be monetised, they didn't want to be advertised to, so again editorial communication is so powerful, they would rather be communities that can exchange views that are untarnished.

There is a great deal to unpick from Sir Martin's words and some of it has an uncomfortable ring for many PR practitioners. Sir Martin is still talking about using social networking as a vehicle to project messages out, to sidestep gatekeepers; as reported, there was nothing about listening, nothing about conversation. But the important point is that the changes outlined in this book are flashing so brightly in the thinking of a major player, and flashing brightly from the balance sheet.

Public relations must embrace social media. Social media are changing the media landscape in radical ways. Practitioners must explore and experiment with new technologies, new ways of thinking. Whether or not we accept the need for labels like 'the new PR', social media are leading us to something that lies beyond what we have recently considered to be public relations.

The newness is not the point. What matters is that public relations must be considered as a strategic function concerned with relationship management, and that social media are dramatically changing the dynamics of the conversations that shape relationships.

Public relations must move beyond its self-limiting role as the unseen hand that commands and controls messages cleverly targeted at discrete publics; it must take a bold stride out of the shadows to become the eyes and ears of organizations, ensuring that organizational behaviour merits positive consideration in the myriad networked and aggregated conversations that shape an organization's reputation, and hence its ability to create and sustain meaningful and productive relationships.

We opened this book by saying we believe the internet changes everything as fervently as we believe that the internet changes nothing. The fundamental concepts that underpin the public relations function remain unshaken; the ways we achieve our objections, from research through strategy to tactical delivery, have to be rethought from first principles.

It is going to be a challenging journey, but if the challenge is met, the discipline of public relations is set to emerge far stronger than it was before.

## Note

1.  Allen, K (2007) PR industry profits boosted by MySpace phenomenon, *The Guardian*, 19 October.

# Index